YOUR FIRST VEGETABLE GARDEN

starting on the right foot for success

Copyright © 2023 Tony O'Neill (Simplify Gardening)
All rights reserved. No part of this book may be reproduced

Or used in any manner without the prior written permission of the copyright owner, except for the use of brief quotations in a book review.

To request permissions, contact the publisher at publisher@simplifygardening.com
or complete the contact form at simplifygardening.com

Hardcover ISBN 978-1-7397793-4-4
Paperback ISBN 978-1-7397793-5-1
eBook ISBN 978-1-7397793-6-8

First Paperback Edition April 2023

Cover art and layout by SpiffingCovers.com
Images by Tony O'Neill

Publisher Simplify Gardening LTD
publisher@simplifygardening.com
simplifygardening.com

YOUR FIRST VEGETABLE GARDEN

starting on the right foot for success

TONY O'NEILL

Author of *Composting Masterclass: Feed the Soil, Not Your Plants*

DEDICATION

To my dearest wife Tina,

I am filled with gratitude and appreciation as I dedicate this book, 'Your First Vegetable Garden,' to you. Your support and encouragement have been unwavering, and without you by my side, this book would not have been possible.

From the moment we met, you have been my rock, my biggest fan, and my source of strength. Your love and belief in me have allowed me to pursue my passions and follow my dreams, and for that, I am forever grateful.

You have always been my partner in every sense of the word, standing by me through all the ups and downs and cheering me on every step of the way. Your love and support have been invaluable to me, and I am so grateful to have you by my side.

Thank you, babe, for being my everything. I love you more than words can say.

With love and appreciation,

ACKNOWLEDGMENTS

Dear Reader,

I would like to express my deepest gratitude to my beautiful wife Tina for her unwavering support and encouragement throughout the writing of this book. Your love and patience have been a constant source of motivation for me, and I am forever grateful for your partnership.

I am also grateful to my daughters Caitlyn and Amber and my son Wayne for their understanding and kindness as I spent countless hours at my desk working on this project. Your enthusiasm and your willingness to help me test out various techniques have been invaluable.

In addition, I would like to thank my parents Elaine and Edward for their love and support throughout my life. Their guidance and encouragement have played a significant role in my development as a writer, and I am forever grateful for all that they have done for me.

I would also like to extend my heartfelt thanks to the team at Simplify Gardening for their hard work and dedication to this project and managing other aspects of our network. Your expertise and guidance have been invaluable, and I am grateful to have had the opportunity to work with such a talented group of individuals.

I hope that the readers of this book will find value in the information and techniques presented within its pages. It has been a labor of love to research and write, and I am passionate about sharing my knowledge and experience with others. I hope that this book will serve as a helpful guide and resource for those interested in gardening, and that it will inspire and enable readers to pursue their own passions and interests.

I also hope that the readers will simply enjoy reading this book. Whether used as a reference or simply for leisure, I strive to make my writing engaging and enjoyable. I appreciate the time and attention that readers have given to my work, and I hope that it will bring them some enjoyment and fulfillment.

Finally, I would like to thank the readers for your support and encouragement. Whether you have followed along on our website, YouTube channel, or by purchasing my books, your enthusiasm for gardening and your willingness to learn has inspired me to continue sharing my knowledge and love of this wonderful hobby we all enjoy.

Thank you all for your love and support. I couldn't have completed this book without you.

Sincerely, Tony O'Neill

CONTENTS

Introduction 11

Chapter 1
    Why Grow Your Own Vegetables 17

Chapter 2
    Gardening Spaces 29

Chapter 3
    Plant Health 43

Chapter 4
    Weather Considerations 55

Chapter 5
    Preparing the Ground 66

Chapter 6
    Propagation 108

Chapter 7
    Growing Vegetables 117

Chapter 8
    Growing Herbs 232

Chapter 9
    Managing Pests and Diseases 245

Chapter 10
    Monthly tasks 290

Addendum 303

Epilogue 340

INTRODUCTION

The most challenging part of realizing any goal is *the first step*. Congratulations on starting one of the most rewarding projects one could undertake – growing a vegetable garden. After decades of gardening, I can promise you that becoming a gardener has been one of my better decisions – I'm sure it will be for you too.

Appropriately, gardens are often used as a symbolic backdrop to essential encounters and life-changing decisions. In love and betrayal, gardens seem to be an anchor point, a place of reflection, an opportunity to become grounded or to uproot what isn't working. Gardens are endlessly cooperative with the gardener's need for new beginnings, generously responding even if they've been ignored for a while. When taken care of, nurtured, listened to, and loved, your garden will respond in abundance. Nothing quite matches plucking a fresh carrot from the ground, rinsing it under nearby running water, and taking that first bite from the season's harvest! It's a taste of nature's bountiful response to your efforts.

Working with nature, caring for it, knowing and meeting its needs will be amply rewarded – even if the reward is a learning opportunity. For me, my garden reflects my relationship with nature, and it's a healthy relationship of give-and-take, of listening and being sensitive to nature's needs and responding appropriately. Nature has been waiting for you – are you ready?

My name is Tony O'Neill, and I'm passionate about gardening. From early childhood with my grandfather and throughout my life, gardening has been a constant feature, providing endless satisfaction and a sense of wellbeing. If you're familiar with my *Simplify Gardening* website and my YouTube channel, you'll know that I love sharing my discoveries. In writing this book, I want to help vegetable growers flourish, improving the availability of nutritious food at local levels. The book is a companion to my online course of the same name – *Your First Vegetable Garden Course.v*

In writing *Your First Vegetable Garden*, I wanted to produce a guide for both first-time and experienced gardeners. The book is a culmination of years of work, research, and experimentation, and I'm proud to put my name to it. While my website, SimplifyGardening.com, focusses on all things gardening, this book is dedicated to helping gardeners grow vegetables, herbs, and fruits packed with nutrients.

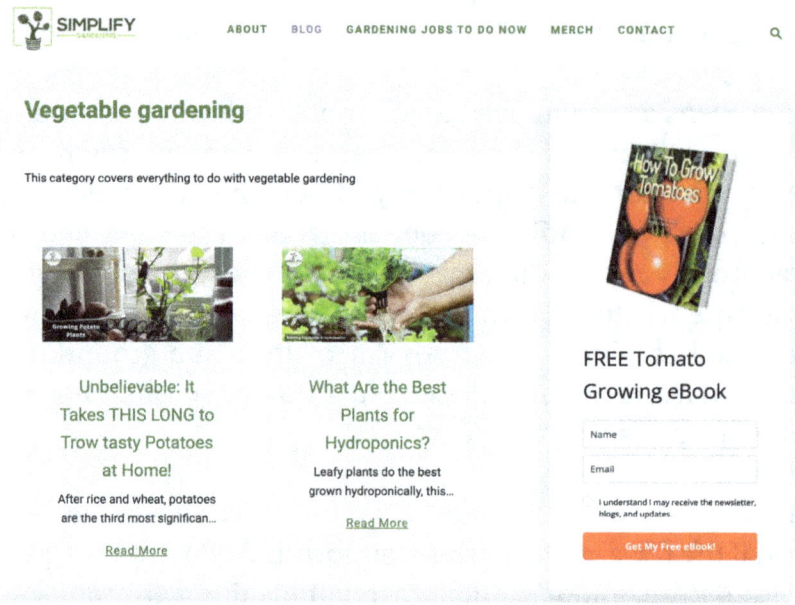

I like to think of gardening as an orchestra with me positioned as the conductor of various players. Your orchestra can be a trio, small ensemble, or a complete, 80-member symphony orchestra – the choice is yours. If you lean into the relationship with soil and all the microorganisms in it, with the different plants and their needs, it becomes addictive. You will want to learn more, try new things, and explore different approaches, not merely for production's sake only, but to strengthen the relationship.

I wish I'd had a similar book to start my gardening journey. The fact is that gardening is ever evolving. Much of the knowledge reflected herein includes recent discoveries as society returns to regenerative gardening. For several decades farming and gardening were about killing pests and using fertilizers to boost growth. In the process, we destroyed much of nature's potential to outperform any pesticide or fertilizer (yes, it's possible). But the tide is rapidly turning, and even large-scale farmers realize that working in harmony with nature is more economical and productive than was initially thought. It's a fascinating world we'll explore together.

Introduction

Chapter 1 – *Why Grow Your Own Vegetables* explores 25 reasons why gardening, in its various forms, is an exceptionally good idea. This book is unapologetically biased towards regenerative practices, and we'll explore the benefits of cooperating with nature in a regenerative process – for improved taste and better plant resilience and performance. Regenerative gardening, or biodynamic gardening as it's also known, is healthier for the soil and plants – and healthier for you.

The great thing about gardening is that it can be practiced in various environments. Even with limited space, you can produce a substantial crop.

Chapter 2 – *Gardening Spaces* explores the spaces where gardening is, or could be, practiced – from herbs in the kitchen to polytunnels and everything in between. We also explore community gardens, setting them up and running them – or merely being part of a community garden. If you're a compulsive gardener, we'll look at all the ways you can get your fix. If you prefer pottering, your explorative spirit can be well satisfied.

It's my wish that everyone, even those with packed schedules, can reap the benefits of gardening – and harvesting is only a tiny part of that benefit. Most of us know what's healthy to do, but ambivalence prevents us from initiating and sustaining the proper habits. Gardening allows different involvement levels, with benefits that far outweigh our efforts. Getting started is always the biggest challenge.

Not over-committing yourself initially will benefit the process of starting your first vegetable garden. Start small and consider doing it with a friend who starts their own garden in the same season. A word of caution – gardening isn't a competitive sport. For me, gardening has been a place of solitude. The gardening friends I have are good friends because they stay in their gardens, and I in mine. Still, they help me with advice, and I reciprocate – we're all continually learning. As a tandem effort, we encourage each other and share discoveries.

In **Chapter 3 – *Plant Health***, we briefly explore plant biology, a broad overview of the needs of different plants, and how to satisfy those needs. As a fundamental building block of healthy plants, we explore photosynthesis processes and sugar levels in plants. We also explore the biodynamic role of these sugars in strengthening symbiotic relationships with soil-borne microorganisms.

Water is an essential ingredient for all of life. In this third chapter, we review the role of water, improving its quality, and how to preserve it without damaging your crop. While water is essential for healthy plants, more gardens are damaged by too much water than vice versa. Plants need air, and when you keep your soils too wet, plants can't breathe. Nature has provided all the solutions; we merely must cooperate.

In **Chapter 4 – *Weather Considerations***, we'll look at how different regional climates impact our gardening efforts. I have created a table that reviews historical weather data (1990–2020) in all 50 state capitols and the most significant cities in the United States of America. While the information focusses on weather in the US, the principles of hardiness zones and frost-free days can be localized globally.

If you live in a semi-arid region, you'll know the difference between day and night temperatures and the challenges these fluctuations present. The book reviews how to navigate weather conditions in four distinct climatic categories: semi-arid, continental, coastal, and humid subtropical. We will also review managing wind, floods, snow, and drought.

In the fifth chapter, we'll review how to produce a harvest packed with nutrients, and it all starts with healthy soil.

Chapter 5 – *Preparing the Ground* looks at how microorganisms benefit gardening and how to become a microorganism farmer by making your own compost. I provide 25 reasons why adding aerobic compost to your soil is essential for gardeners and farmers. Healthy aerobic compost plays a pivotal role in transforming dirt to soil – vibrant with life.

We'll also explore soil structures, soil amendments, and how to test your soil. Depending on the scale of your garden, testing your soil should be about more than mineral content or basicity (pH). Knowing the diversity of the microorganisms in your soil is invaluable to reaching ultimate plant health. Plants with the highest level of health can resist pests and diseases, a product of a healthy soil biome. Nature has made a way for gardens to achieve ultimate health and productivity – without our industrial interference.

The soil food web should be a balanced predator-prey environment of microorganisms, organisms, and small animals. This fifth chapter reviews the role players in the soil food web and their effect on keeping your soil healthy and productive. We also review what can be done to boost specific population groups to meet our plants' needs and control soil and plant pathogens.

Chapter 6 – *Propagation* provides plans and methods to create your garden. From indoor vertical gardens to polytunnel plans, the book contains all the guidance you need to avoid making some of the mistakes I made – like using cedarwood planters. While trees like cedar and black walnut are beautiful, they are poisonous to fungi, and their use to make planters should be avoided.

The chapter also looks at bed types and locations, their respective benefits, and drawbacks. Many of you will have seen my videos on YouTube, showing my successes (and failures) at growing record-breaking vegetables in containers. I gladly share the learning these challenges have afforded me, making them available for you to use.

If you're considering establishing a greenhouse or a polytunnel, I will give you my opinion on which one is better in which situation and how to maintain both. Growing in different structures provides you with an opportunity to mitigate climatic risks, but mistakes can cost you. The book provides you with experience-based knowledge on using different structures to help you avoid some of the pitfalls.

So, you have a growing environment and healthy, weed-free soil, now for the planting.

In **Chapter 7 – *Growing Vegetables***, we review planting and caring for 48 plants – from asparagus to watermelons.

Chapter 8 – *Growing Herbs*, provides guidelines for growing 32 different herbs. For those botanically pedantic folks, please pardon my inclusion of some fruits in the vegetable section, such as tomatoes, cucumbers, and other vine fruits. In total, I've provided growing and caring references for more than a hundred plants.

Chapter 10 – *Managing Pests and Diseases*, reviews the most common causes for failure, though, in gardening, we don't fail; we learn. I cover all the teachers I've met in my almost 40-years of gardening and some I haven't met yet. We also explore ways of avoiding those lessons in the future.

The final chapter, **Chapter 11 – *Monthly tasks***, reviews monthly to-do lists in both warmer and colder climates. Having a monthly gardening to-do list can help you stay on track and plan your time better, and it helps me, so I've included it.

I've provided an addendum at the back of the book to help new gardeners familiarize themselves with uncommon terms. Happy reading, learning, and growing – growing for both you, your family, and your plants.

CHAPTER 1
WHY GROW YOUR OWN VEGETABLES

Growing your own vegetables, herbs, and fruit has several benefits beyond having access to ultra-fresh produce. There are hundreds of studies exploring the advantages of localized food production – below, I have listed the top 20.

Physical Activity

Stress, anxiety, and depression are all reduced by regular physical activity. Still, many of us don't have time to fit it into our already hectic schedules. One of the best things about gardening is that it doesn't require you to hurriedly walk past the gym with your head down, feeling guilty about the money you're spending on a membership that you never use.

Gardening offers you the recommended 150 minutes of moderate exercise per week required for maintaining a healthy lifestyle; this is especially true for those who enjoy gardening for its simple pleasures. Even a leisurely stroll through the garden or watering the plants can burn calories, and the more time you spend tending to your green space, the more you'll be exercising your body. In addition, gardening is a full-body workout that targets all major muscle groups.

Strengthening your upper body and thighs can be achieved by pushing the lawnmower into those hard-to-reach corners, as well as shifting wheelbarrows full of soil or compost. Hands-on activities, such as gardening, can help prevent arthritis and other debilitating conditions later in life by keeping your joints supple and lubricated (as well as strengthening your back). Gardening is a physical activity, and pulling weeds, planting, and digging can burn up to 400 calories per hour. Gardening is also an excellent mental exercise and helps keep your mind sharp.

You can benefit from regular bursts of garden exercise, which will raise and increase your cardiovascular rate without the need for jogging or pedalling on an exercise bike. Taking a walk around the garden in gardening boots can help older people maintain their sense of equilibrium and balance, significantly reducing the risk of falls in other areas of the home or in public.

The best part is that gardening offers you a valid reason to invest in garden furniture and a comfortable space to take a break from work and relax. You'll be able to enjoy the tranquility of your garden while you survey your handy work, taking a break with a fresh lemonade – maybe with lemons from the garden you cultivated.

Nutritional Advantage

Homegrown vegetables are packed with vitamins, minerals, and antioxidants. They are not only tastier but also healthier to eat in their most natural state. Since most supermarket vegetables are picked before they are fully mature, they lack the nutrients we imagine vegetables contain. Distributed produce may sit on the shelf or in storage for an extended time before reaching the supermarket shelves, losing nutritional value along the way.

The fact is that plants start dying the moment they're taken off life-support. While in the soil, a carrot can absorb moisture and nutrients to support its life – pluck it from the ground, and it starts losing moisture and nutrients from that moment. The same applies to all herbs, vegetables, and fruit.

Boosting our immunity requires regularly consuming an abundance of immune-boosting vitamins and minerals like vitamins C and E, iron, and zinc, as well as foods rich in B vitamins. Some examples include:

- Vitamin C – citrus fruits, dark leafy greens such as spinach and kale, bell peppers, Brussel sprouts, and strawberries
- Vitamin E – almonds, peanuts, spinach, broccoli, and avocado
- Vitamin B6 – chickpeas and potatoes
- Iron – Beans, peas, dark green vegetables, raisins, and legumes
- Zinc – Beans, peas, wholegrain cereals

Localized Production

In 2020, food spending by US consumers, businesses, and government entities totaled $1.69 trillion, down from 1.79 trillion in 2019, partly due to the COVID-19 recession that disrupted typical food consumption. Food-at-home spending (food purchased from supermarkets, convenience stores, warehouse club stores, supercenters, and other retailers) increased from $808.0 billion in 2019 to $876.8 billion in 2020, while food-away-from-home spending (food purchased from restaurants, fast-food places, schools, and other away-from-home eating places) decreased from $978.2 billion in 2019 to $813.4 billion in 2020. This resulted in food-at-home spending accounting for 51.9 percent of total food expenditures; the first year, it accounted for more than half of food spending since 2008, during the Great Recession.[1]

Sustainable diets are predicated on the idea that food is produced, processed, and distributed as close to where it is consumed as possible. Supporting local farming and economic viability and reducing greenhouse gas emissions are significant benefits of this approach.

Food Miles

The term 'food miles' refers to the distance food travels from where it is grown to where it is consumed. In other words, the distance food travels from farm to plate. Recent studies have shown that this distance has increased steadily over the last 50 years. Studies estimate that processed food in the United States travels over 1,300 miles, and fresh produce travels over 1,500 miles before being consumed.[2]

---

1 https://www.ers.usda.gov/data-products/chart-gallery/gallery/chart-detail/?chartId=58364
2 https://attra.ncat.org/wp-content/uploads/2019/05/foodmiles.pdf

While studies vary, a typical estimate is that the food industry accounts for 10% of all fossil fuel use in the United States. Of all the energy consumed by the food system, only about 20% goes towards production; the remaining 80% is associated with processing, transport, refrigeration, and preparation – both energy and cost. Growing your own food reduces that impact by 80%.

Cortisol Inhibitor

Cortisol is a hormone produced by the body in times of stress, and its function is to provide you with the resources to deal with a crisis – like when faced with a bear. Cortisol in the bloodstream causes your pupils to dilate, air passages to open, and heart rate to increase – all in preparation to fight, flee, or freeze. Continued exposure to cortisol, caused by living in a stressful environment, can badly affect your health. According to health officials, cortisol is public enemy #1 for mental health concerns, indicating the risks it poses.

When we spend time gardening, the active distraction of connecting with nature can measurably reduce cortisol levels. Focussed activity that's not related to the source of anxiety, mindfulness, and stress reduction all help reduce cortisol levels and benefit physical and mental health enormously. Extended exposure to cortisol in the bloodstream can alter your DNA – gardening is a proven antidote. The mental health benefits of gardening cannot be overemphasized. It is the type of activity that can change the chemistry in your body, improving your health directly.

Vitamin D Exposure

There are numerous health advantages to spending time outside, including the opportunity to soak up the sun's rays (remember to apply a UV-blocker and wear a hat). The benefit stems from the vitamin D the sun helps generate, which is good for us in so many ways! What better way to learn about vitamin D than to look at your cat or dog and see how happy they are when they are basking in the rays of the sunshine?

However, despite the name, vitamin D is not an external vitamin that must be ingested as a supplement. When the sun's rays bounce off our skin, our bodies produce vitamin D as a chemical reaction. The health benefits this reaction provides are numerous.

Vitamin D helps produce calcium, an essential mineral to keep bones and teeth strong and healthy. Vitamin D also boosts the immune system, helps regulate the flow of insulin throughout the body, drastically reduces the risk of developing a condition like diabetes, maintains the health of the heart and lungs, and even reduces the risk of cancer. One of the essential benefits of increasing your direct exposure to the light of day is its ability to alleviate symptoms of stress, anxiety, and depression.

Scientists describe vitamin D deficiency as an epidemic in countries in the North. Many of these countries now have *Sunlight Clinics* to make extended (artificial) daylight available to people living in short-day winter areas. Gardeners are fortunate to have free access to a natural source of light – the sun. Spending time in the garden, tending to your flowerbeds, or relaxing on a bench under the sun can significantly contribute to your wellbeing.

Bacteria Exposure

Our awareness of the risks of viruses has been piqued since the onset of COVID. In the process, antibacterial sales have rocketed. While good hygiene is essential, our ability to produce antibodies to common pathogens is only possible if exposed to some risks. Antibodies form in defense of our health, but only if activated by bacteria and fungi. Trying to create a sterile world creates more risks than benefits – the only organisms that develop resistance to the antibacterial used are the harmful ones.

There are, of course, a few diseases and conditions that can be contracted while spending time outdoors. Still, these can easily be avoided with education and due diligence. Getting your hands dirty is actually a good thing, despite what you may have been taught. It is harder for bacteria to invade your body and make you sick if your body is allowed to build defenses. Effective defenses require some exposure to the bacteria – it sounds wrong, but it's a scientific fact. If we insulate ourselves, we are more vulnerable – more exposure equals an increased potential for resilience.

If your immunity system is depleted, it's strongly advised that you seek professional medical advice before you start gardening. If your body is already

fighting invading viruses or diseases, adding additional stress to the system is ill-advised.

Personal Creativity

Creativity at any level is a proven stress-buster, and it takes a mere 45 minutes to reduce your cortisol levels. Of all the creative exercises, those done outdoors offer the most significant benefits – think of a Zen garden. Repetitive motions, like raking or digging, increase focus on the present and interrupt an overactive awareness of the past and the future. Everything doesn't have to be perfect – instead, strive for simplicity and inner contentment in your gardening.

You can't get any more creative than creating your own private oasis and private garden based on your preferences. Gardening provides a chance to work on something that will fill your heart with joy as you watch it maturing and producing a harvest.

Few things are more satisfying than taking an idea and making it a reality in your backyard, creating an oasis of tranquility and production – and you needn't be an expert. Merely add action to your dreams to make them a reality.

Executive Function

Executive function is a mental skillset that includes mental agility, working memory, and self-control. We use these skills every day to learn, work, and manage daily life. Difficulties with executive function can make it hard to focus, follow directions, or regulate our emotions. Developing executive function is a precursor to a more fulfilling life. People with high executive function can:

- Plan, prioritize, and organize
- Remain focussed amidst distractions
- Complete projects they start
- Understand and accept varied opinions on a topic
- Know what they believe and why they believe it
- Regulate their emotions
- Keep track of their progress over time – self-manage

We all occasionally fail at managing our lives effectively. When there are added factors such as complicated relationships, or perceived threats, keeping all the plates spinning can be challenging. Gardening helps in that it is a tactile, forgiving, and tranquil activity. Planning a garden, planting seedlings, and caring for them during their limited life, is a fantastic way of developing executive function. For me, gardening is a space where I can shut the noise out and focus on the task at hand. That skill is transferable to other situations in my professional life as a fireman.

Mindfulness

Mindfulness is the practice of being present in the *now* – a conscious decision to embrace the moment. The practice of mindfulness is becoming increasingly popular as a tool to still our racing minds. Mindfulness is a proactive way to keep our overactive minds from getting in the way of our enjoyment of the small moments of happiness. There is no better place for this than in a garden where you can stop and smell the roses – and enjoy the moment.

The underlying principle of mindfulness is being present in the here and now. While working in your garden, feel the breeze on your skin, see the bee moving from flower to flower, appreciate the life-space you've made possible. Breathe in and breathe out, focussing on the air entering and leaving your body. It's not an exercise of ignoring reality but rather a shift in focus to the present realities. If your mind wanders to thoughts of yesterday's mistakes or tomorrow's challenges, gently refocus on your breathing, the smell of garden air entering your body, and the tension leaving your body.

Sitting still and doing nothing isn't an option for some people. However, you can still cultivate a sense of mindfulness in the garden while engaging in physical activities. Planting, weeding, and mowing the lawn are all excellent opportunities to practice living in the moment. In the garden, you'll likely never run out of things to do. Use your gardening time to heighten your awareness of your senses – your hand on the spade, your feet in the soil, the different smells and textures.

Our minds are ever busy but have limited bandwidth. Suppose we choose to focus on our senses. In that case, our minds can be trained to think thoughts other than the tired reruns of self-lambasting reproaches and fearful imaginings. Give yourself a break – feel the textures, image your olfactory glands respond to the smells, experience the air entering your lungs. I know we're addicted to the drama, but just for a moment, change the channel – just another example of how a well-tended and cherished garden can positively impact your mental health.

Being Grounded

At the risk of introducing too many alternatives to pharma-promoted remedies, please can I add one more – grounding, also known as earthing. Grounding means being in contact with the earth to support the specific functions of the organs in your body.[3] According to Laura Koniver (M.D.), grounding supports the body's organs at a cellular level. Dr. James Oschman, a biophysicist in energy medicine, believes a lack of "direct physical contact of the human body with the earth's surface" is associated with the rise of modern diseases.

A reduction in stress, muscle tension, and hormonal imbalances are just a few of the benefits of grounding on the body's ability to function better. According to Oschman, our separation from the soil has caused physical damage to our bodies.

According to some earthing experts, health benefits can reportedly be seen in as little as half an hour per day. Even though many people remain skeptical of earthing's purported benefits, I feel a lot healthier when I've spent some time in the garden in contact with Mother Earth. In my mind, it makes perfect sense, we're electrically

---

3   https://www.youtube.com/watch?v=44ddtR0XDVU

charged beings, and electrical units are legally required to have an earth-leakage system. Why would it be different for people?

The studies are conclusive – getting your body in contact with the earth has real benefits for your health. A healthy body has other spin-offs, such as improved libido, weight loss, and better resilience. Finding half an hour a day to spend in your garden is easy, fun, and healthy – especially if you can spend it in contact with the soil.

Youth Involvement

It's encouraging to see that an increasing number of young people are adopting farming, gardening, and even compost production as an occupation. An interest in gardening bodes well for our planet, especially for a generation that will face challenges that we couldn't even imagine. In my opinion, the increased use of artificial intelligence will result in a growing need for people to express their connection and unity with all that is natural.

The urgency is real. The USDA agricultural Survey 2017[4] shows that more than a third of farmers are older than retirement age, and only 8% are under 35 years old. Less than half of the 3.4 million producers have farming as their primary occupation. The average farmer's age in the United States was 57.5 in 2017.

---

4   https://www.nass.usda.gov/Publications/Highlights/2019/2017Census_Farm_Producers.pdf

- Age <35   8%
- Age 35-64   58%
- Age 65+   34%

Getting young people involved at home or in community gardens or Community Supported Agriculture[5] is necessary for their health and the future of a healthy community. According to biologist E.O. Wilson, we're hardwired with a biological propensity to feel better in the presence of natural systems. Getting youngsters to establish a garden may trigger a lifelong interest – like it did for me.

Positive Modelling

My grandfather was an avid gardener, and some of the best years of my life were spent with him in the garden, where he mentored me. He played a crucial role in my continued gardening, establishing my *Simplify Gardening* YouTube channel and all the platforms I use to promote *Simplify Gardening*.

Involving others, children, or neighbors in gardening can trigger a response. You may choose to focus on vegetables and a neighbor on herbs or fruit. That way, you can barter or swap your handiwork with them. Maybe donating a pack of seedlings can get the process going.

Financial Benefits

As seen earlier, 80% of store-bought produce costs are not directly related to farming. If you propagate your own seeds, your time and other input are the only costs. Add your own aerobic compost manufacturing to that, and you could cut the costs down even further.

Skill Development

There are three essential elements to a happy, productive life: Attachment, self-regulation, and competencies. I used the work with disadvantaged youths, helping them develop these three facets of being human. Those who adopted and developed

---

[5] https://www.nal.usda.gov/legacy/afsic/community-supported-agriculture

the skills improved their chances of an ever-improving future. Sadly, in the absence of a desire to change, everything keeps going as it always has.

Attachment is a function of predictability, and routines add predictability. Having a daily, weekly, monthly, and annual routine significantly improves our sense of order and control. ***Self-regulation*** is aided when we understand that our emotions are signposts of what we like, what threatens us, and our values. Emotions should be triggers to thought processes, not unconsidered actions. Gardening can have mishaps – some we cause, some are out of our control. While we could vent and dig it all up, it's healthier to take the failure as a learning opportunity. ***Competence*** is a product of sufficient learning opportunities – gardening offers plenty of these.

Improve flavor and nutrition in edible plants, fruits, and seeds for animals and humans

Synthetic fertilizers often lack macro and micronutrients found in compost, and these soilborne nutrients increase the nutritional value of the produce. Composting enriches the soil with nutrients, reducing the need for pesticides and fertilizers. Pesticides and fertilizers require fossil fuels for their production, and some are potentially harmful to your health.

Comparative studies of homegrown organic crops show they have a significantly higher presence of antioxidants. These include flavones (+26%), stilbenes (+28%), flavanols (+50%), phenolic acid (+19%), flavanones (+69%), and anthocyanins (+51%).

Concentrate and retain growth forces essential to growth and health

Soil health is critical to preserving (and remedying) our waterways. Increased water retention and reduced runoff are two benefits of composting. Effective microorganisms have demonstrable effectiveness at remediating polluted water sources.

Increase soil gas and water holding capacity

Microorganisms produce soil aggregates – clusters of soil particles with microscopic air and moisture channels that benefit soil structure and reduce erosion. The tiny channels and pores increase the soil's capacity to retain air, moisture, and nutrients.

Reduce odor, fly, and other vector problems

Uncontrolled decomposition conditions include the presence of egg-laying flies, anaerobic conditions, foul odors, and seepage. Controlled aerobic composting with sufficient oxygenation, controlled humidity, and effective pile structure and turning eliminates the above conditions.

To improve environmental hygiene

Rotting plants and food waste attracts rodents and flies and can smell like rotting eggs (hydrogen sulfide), vinegar, or rancid butter (butyric acid). Composting food scraps, garden cuttings, and lawn clippings is an effective way to manage hygiene risks. Processes like Bokashi, a fermentation process, help households manage kitchen waste effectively and hygienically.

Limits wastage of valuable resources

Reusing freely available resources such as leaves, weeds, and grass trimmings to produce compost, a substance with known benefits, makes perfect sense. Sending these resources to landfills creates unmanaged anaerobic conditions that pour methane and hydrogen sulfides into the atmosphere. Not only does dumping these resources have no benefit, but it also causes environmental harm.

CHAPTER 2
GARDENING SPACES

Before grabbing gardening gloves and planting seeds, consider the types of vegetable gardens that will work best for your lifestyle. Consider your family size, the crops you want to cultivate, the soil's health, and how much time and money you have to devote to a vegetable garden.

You may establish a conventional in-ground vegetable garden if you have a sunny backyard with plenty of room and decent soil. If your soil is deficient, you might want to try growing on raised beds. Front yards are frequently overlooked – underutilized regions that may offer food if placed in an open community. Many vegetable plants are visually appealing. If your landscape is already established and you don't have space for a typical vegetable garden, interplanting vegetables in your decorative beds is a terrific alternative. Interplanting is also a simple initial step if you are worried about allocating new space for a vegetable garden.

Many veggies grow well in containers, and container gardening is perfect for people who have little outside space. Vegetables cannot thrive indoors without supplementary light, although hydroponically cultivating plants indoors is a developing trend. Hydroponics allows the gardener to manage temperature, light, and nutrients while avoiding disease pressures that would otherwise be present in plants cultivated outside, and it can need significant initial investment. Therefore, it may not be the greatest option for someone new to plant cultivation.

These approaches aren't necessarily mutually exclusive. Cucumbers and maize, for example, might be grown in a standard in-ground garden bed in the backyard, while carrots and broccoli are grown in raised beds that are suitable for your front yard. At the same time, you could interplant kale and Swiss chard in a perennial border, grow herbs in pots on your patio, and grow microgreens hydroponically indoors.

Selecting a Suitable Garden Site

The most crucial aspect to consider when choosing a garden location is sunshine. The garden should be exposed to a minimum of 6 hours of direct sunshine – longer is better. Avoid creating beds in the shade of buildings or trees or where roots from trees or bushes compete for nutrients. Some veggies are more tolerant of shade than others, such as edible stems and leaves (the cabbage family) and edible roots. Flowers and fruit-bearing plants generally require more light – eggplants, melons, peppers, tomatoes, etcetera.

It is also critical to have good soil drainage. Examine your yard after rain – areas where water pools have poor drainage and would not be suitable for a garden without extensive rehabilitation. A garden near the house or a pattern of foot movement across the yard allows for simple access to garden operations and regular inspections. When deciding where to put your garden, consider the ease of access to quality water sources. Having access to a water-point or irrigation system eliminates the need to transport water during the dry months.

Another critical factor to consider is enough airflow. Avoid putting the garden in a low-lying area, such as at the bottom of a slope. These locations are slow to warm in the spring, and frost accumulates more easily because cold air gathers at the lowest point and cannot drain away. Vegetable gardens on higher ground are less likely to be affected by mild freezes, allowing for an earlier start in the spring and a more prolonged harvest in the fall. If you don't have access to land, look into community garden or allotment options.

Garden Types

There is a garden type, or a mix of kinds, to meet the demands of every gardener. Gardens can be planted in the ground, on raised beds, or in containers. Several approaches can also be utilized to maintain the garden. Plants can be set out in typical rows of densely packed plants or vertical spaces. Examine the following categories and procedures and choose the best strategies for your specific circumstance.

In-Ground Gardens

In-ground gardens are less costly, water retention may be better, and the roots remain cooler in the heat. While water drains more slowly from in-ground beds, it might be difficult to feed water solely to planting beds and not neighboring regions. In general, an in-ground garden takes up more room than a raised bed or container garden. Traffic pathways must be carefully designed to reduce the compaction of planting areas, and weeds from neighboring walkways might be difficult to control.

Raised Bed Gardens

Raised beds are garden areas that are elevated 6 to 8 inches above the general ground level. They are linked to the native soil underneath them and may or may not have built sides. They can be created of simply piled-high earth with a flattened top, or they can be framed with logs or boulders, built with wooden boards, or straw bales. Raised beds with just enough width to reach the middle are great for producing veggies. Defined beds make a garden more appealing and minimize cross-contamination caused by foot traffic, compacting the soil. Above ground beds generally drain better and can warm up faster.

Raised beds come in various shapes and sizes, and the soil used inside the beds may be reused. Use dirt from surrounding walkways, mixed with existing soil and organic matter, for shallow beds with no support. Soil can be stacked and compacted to create a raised bed less than 6 inches tall. To avoid soil erosion, slightly slope the bed's sides.

You may need more soil if you're building a taller raised bed or one in a framed box. If your soil is of excellent quality loam, you may screen it into the raised bed and mix it with 50% compost. Raised garden soil mixtures can also be purchased bagged from a nursery. Alternatively, dirt can be purchased by the cubic yard from a landscaping business. Consider that 1 cubic yard of dirt equals 27 cubic feet when calculating how many cubic yards you require.

To calculate the number of cubic feet required in a raised bed, multiply the length by the breadth and depth of your raised bed (convert all measurements to feet). If your bed is 6 feet broad, 10 feet long, and 12 inches deep, the dimensions are: 6 feet × 10 feet × 1 foot = 60 cubic feet (or 2.22 cubic yards (60 divided by 27))

Make sure to inquire about the blend's components. Topsoil, compost, and a soilless mix, such as vermiculite, make up a high-quality combination. Are the materials natural? What is the origin? Does the mix include manure of animals fed on treated grass? Is the compost cured, damp, and less than six months old? Is the topsoil guaranteed to be free of contaminants, weeds, insect pests, illnesses, and harmful nematodes? Buying a raised bed mix isn't enough to keep a garden going for the long haul. After each growing season, raised beds must be treated with a 4-inch layer of organic material to maintain high nutrient levels.

If the sides are made of wood, avoid cedar and walnut as both will negatively impact your soil's microorganism populations. While these woods are more rot-resistant, they will negatively affect your crops. Do not use treated pine either – such as wood from pallets. Wrapping your lumber in weed cloth can extend its life by up to ten years, and untreated wood ought to last six years.

Container gardens

Growing edibles in containers is a common food production method for the household. Many vegetables can be planted in deep enough pots to sustain their roots. Container size is connected to gardening ease and success – the larger the container, the better. The following plants grow well in containers:

Vegetable	Spacing	Minimum Container Depth
Beans	2 to 3 inches	8 inches
Beets	2 to 3 inches	8 inches
Bok choi	6 inches	20 inches
Collards	12 inches	12 inches
Cucumbers	Single plant	8 inches
Eggplant	Single plant	12 inches
Green garlic	4 inches	6 inches
Kale	6 inches	8 inches
Lettuce	4 to 5 inches	8 inches
Mustard greens	6 inches	6 inches
Peas	2 to 3 inches	12 inches
Peppers	Single plant	16 inches
Potatoes	5 to 6 inches	18 inches

Radishes	2 to 3 inches	4 inches
Scallions	2 to 3 inches	6 inches
Spinach	2 to 3 inches	4 inches
Squash	Single plant	18 inches
Swiss chard	4 to 5 inches	8 inches
Tomatoes	Single plant	18 inches

These plants flourish in containers, and it's a great option for persons who have limited space, soil issues, or a lot of animal pressure. Containers can be installed on a rooftop, balcony, patio, deck, entranceway, or pathway. Containers should be positioned in areas that promote crop development. For example, if producing tomatoes, a container may be relocated to a sunny place, a partly shady area for growing lettuce, or a sheltered microclimate during the winter for growing year-round kale. Edible container gardening provides more flexibility than traditional gardening and is ideal for children, renters, beginner gardeners, those with physical disabilities, or seasoned gardeners looking to downsize. There is no digging or tilling in container gardening, and crops are essentially weed-free. Container gardening may also keep aggressive herbs, such as mint, from taking over typical garden settings. Container-grown vegetables require more attention than plants cultivated in regular garden beds in the ground.

Container Selection

Plants can be cultivated in pots that have been purchased, constructed, or repurposed. Container material, size, color, and drainage are four critical factors to consider. You safeguard the plant from stress caused by the container drying out too rapidly, limiting root growth or roots sitting in water, and developing root rot by selecting the correct container.

Container materials are classified into the following categories:

- **Nonporous**: plastic, glazed, or metal
- **Semi-porous**: wood, pressed paper fiber
- **Porous**: terracotta, clay, unglazed ceramic

Choose containers for their size, aesthetics, weight, color, and drainage properties. Porous and semi-porous pots lose moisture faster and must be watered more often than nonporous containers. As a result, porous and semi-porous pots are ideal for growing plants that do not require a lot of water or cannot endure wet feet.

Unglazed ceramic pots should not be used for plants left outside throughout the winter while container gardening outside. These pots absorb water, which causes the pot to freeze and fracture. The temperature of the growth media in outdoor pots can vary by up to 30°F between day and night. This problem might be aggravated when metal pots and tiny containers are placed in the sun. Wooden and plastic containers can be left outside all year.

Cedar and redwood are inherently decay resistant and may endure for up to ten years without staining or painting, but cedar pots must be lined as they are toxic to microorganisms. When overwintering plants, heavy-duty plastic containers are the most lightweight of all containers, maintain moisture efficiently, and can be quickly relocated near a protective wall. Nonetheless, when exposed to direct sunlight for an extended amount of time, their hues might fade. Before use, all containers should be washed with soapy water and disinfected with a non-bleach home disinfectant agent. Appropriate treatment could be EM1.

When it comes to container gardening, we generally choose containers based on their visual appeal rather than their horticultural utility. The weight of the pot, on the other hand, should be addressed for top-heavy plants that will be exposed to wind or are moved about regularly to provide the correct internal habitats. Furthermore, the porosity of the pot is significant. If a person has a habit of overwatering their container plants, a porous container should be utilized. Container gardeners who submerge their plants should use nonporous containers that aid in retaining moisture in the potting mix.

Dark-colored pots absorb more heat than light-colored containers, causing the planting medium to dry faster and the temperature of the potting mix to rise. In the winter, this temperature difference might be beneficial for planting outside. However, in the summer, the increasing heat can scorch delicate roots. The bottom line – avoid exposing dark containers to direct sunlight.

All containers must have drainage holes to avoid plant roots from standing in water and causing root rot. Use bottle caps to lift containers off a firm surface (paved patio) or drill drainage holes 4 inches from the bottom on the sides. Herbs should be double-potted (a smaller pot in a larger pot) if they are to be displayed in an attractive pot with no drainage holes. Using pebbles at the bottom of the pot or container is not advised. Contrary to popular belief, they serve no purpose and create more risks than benefits.

For two reasons, the size of a container should correspond to the plant's growth requirements. For starters, reduced root development leads to lower plant growth. Root limitation is a type of physical stress on the plant that causes a significant reduction in root and shoot development. Consider the container's depth as well as its entire volume (see the Table above). On the other hand, larger containers do not dry up as rapidly and require less regular watering. Annual plants and vegetables with shallow roots, such as lettuce, radishes, and scallions, require a potting mix depth of 6 to 8 inches. Though commonly not advised for containers, carrots grow best with a potting mix depth of 10 to 12 inches. Most herbs may be grown in pots with diameters ranging from 4 to 6 inches. Some plants with a big taproot, on the other hand, require a 12-inch-deep pot. Perennial plants and fruits require big pots for proper root development. Interior plants thrive in pots one size larger than their root system. A container that is 1 inch to 2 inches wider than the present root ball works well for tiny pots, 8 inches in diameter or smaller. For big pots with a diameter of 10 inches or more, a width of 2 to 3 inches broader than the plant's root ball is appropriate.

Gardening Techniques

Most of the yields specified in this book refer to 10-foot rows. More intensive gardening will have more abundant plants but necessarily greater yields. The popular *square-foot garden* is a form of intensive gardening, and another method of maximizing yields is to plant a vertical garden. Let's review each of these separately.

Row Gardening

Many gardeners still use row planting for in-ground and raised beds out of habit. A classic row garden is appropriate if space is not an issue, and row gardens allow using a tiller for gardening tasks. A denser planting regime eliminates weeds, and complementing crops is good practice.

Make them straight to help with cultivation, weed control, and harvesting if you're using garden rows. The entire garden – both the rows and the pathways – is modified in conventional beds with rows. Drive a stake into the ground at either end of the row and stretch a tight rope across it to produce a straight row. Rows are generally in a north-south direction to optimize sun exposure.

Intensive Gardening

An intensively planted garden aims to get as much food as possible from a small space. As cities have become more populated and yards have become smaller, intensive gardening has been popular. Many house settings are too small for a classic row garden; therefore, intensive gardening has become the most viable option. Intensive gardens improve yield by optimizing area utilization and succession planting, but they require careful design. Although intensive gardens are commonly seen on raised beds, they can also be found in-ground or in big containers.

"Square Foot Gardening" is a style of intense planting popularized by Mel Bartholomew in his 1981 book *Square Foot Gardening*. The French were already using these intense gardening techniques in the late 1800s, but Bartholomew popularized the concept. In a raised bed, vegetables are grown in squares of 12 inches each. Beds are made to be no wider than 4 feet across to be managed from the outside. The gardener never steps on the soil where the veggies grow; therefore, the earth is never compacted or cross-contaminated. Gardeners may arrange their square-foot beds in various configurations, utilizing the entire available area.

Beds are delineated in 1-foot squares with a wood lattice, thread, plastic, or reclaimed window blind slat. This helps delineate planting areas and makes following planting density guidelines simple. Many veggies may be cultivated inside each square, and the final size of the veggies growing within that square determines the spacing.

Large plants, such as broccoli or tomatoes, may need numerous squares for each plant to reach maximum growth. Smaller plants (such as beets) can have up to 16 plants per square, whereas smaller plants (such as carrots) can have up to 32 plants per square. Unlike typical row gardens, where there is usually as much vacant space as plant-occupied area, a square-foot garden has no wasted space. Fertilization, irrigation, and control activities are centered on the planting beds in intensive gardening.

Interplanting, or growing two or more vegetables in the same location simultaneously, is another way of intensive gardening. Indigenous Americans have used this method for thousands of years, but it is just now gaining popularity in the United States again. The advantages include higher productivity and a reduction in weeds. Proper planning is required to achieve high crop output and enhanced crop quality. Growing flowers among vegetable plants is another form of interplanting, attracting pollinators and insect predators that may discourage pests while providing color to a vegetable garden.

For each plant combination, the following criteria must be considered:

- Plants' light, nutritional, and moisture needs. Using plants with similar cultural needs promotes the health of all crops.
- The length and pattern of development. Is the veggie tall or short, underground, or aboveground?
- Allelopathy refers to the possibility of one crop having a detrimental impact on another. Toxins produced by some plants, such as sunflowers, inhibit the development of other crops.
- The time it takes to mature. vBy varying maturity dates, you may lengthen harvesting time.

Planting long-season, slow-maturing plants with short-season, quick-maturing plants is one possibility. Peppers and radishes are one example of this pairing, and the radishes are plucked before the peppers overwhelm them. Planting tiny plants near larger plants, such as radishes at the foot of beans or broccoli, is another example of mixing growth patterns. Shade-tolerant plants, such as lettuce, spinach, and celery, can be grown in the shade of taller crops, such as beans or squash.

Alternating rows can do interplanting within a bed (planting a row of peppers next to a row of onions), combining plants (leeks and parsley), dispersing different species across the bed, or putting edibles amid ornamentals. Planting Swiss chard between azalea bushes, for example, or carrots along a pathway between perennial beds.

Intensive Planting Distances

Produce	Plant Separation (Inches)	Produce	Plant Separation (Inches)
Artichokes (globe)	48 to 60	**Kohlrabi**	4
Asparagus	15	**Leek**	3-4
Bean, bush	2-3	**Lettuce, head**	10
Bean, lima	4-6	**Lettuce, leaf**	4-6
Bean, pole	6-12	**Mustard**	4-6
Beets	2-3	**Okra**	12-18
Broccoli	18-24	**Onion**	2-4
Brussels sprouts	14-18	**Parsley**	12
Cabbage	9-12	**Parsnips**	12
Cantaloupes	48	**Pea**	1-3
Carrot	2-3	**Pepper**	9-12
Cauliflower	15-18	**Potato**	10-12
Celery	24	**Potatoes (sweet)**	24
Chard, Swiss	4-6	**Pumpkin**	24-36
Chinese cabbage	24	**Radish**	1-2
Chives	12	**Rhubarb**	48
Collards	12-15	**Rutabagas**	12
Corn, sweet	12	**Southern pea**	3-4
Cucumber	12	**Spinach**	4-6

Dill	24	Squash, summer	18–24
Eggplant	18–24	Squash, winter	24–36
Endive	8–12	Tomato	18–24
Garlic	12	Turnip	3–4
Kale	6	Watermelons	60

Vertical Gardening

Vertical gardening involves trellises, poles, tiered beds, and strings to support growing plants. This strategy is ideal for gardeners with limited gardening space or arable land. Tomatoes, cucumbers, melons, pole beans, and other vining plants are ideal for vertical planting. Some plants weave themselves onto the framework, while others require tying.

Vertical plants throw a shadow, so put them on the north side of a garden bed to avoid shadowing and grow shade-tolerant crops nearby. Vertically grown plants take up considerably less space, and while the yield per plant is lower, the yield per square foot is significantly higher.

Vertically growing plants are more exposed to the elements, causing them to dry out faster – remember to compensate for the loss by watering more regularly. This rapid drying is beneficial to plants that are prone to fungal infections. Raised beds tiered beds are typically used in vertical gardening.

Optimizing Available Garden Space

A diagram can help you plan your garden once you've decided on the size and style of garden that will best fit your needs. When drawing a garden diagram, there are various factors to consider.

- To correctly design the dimensions of the garden bed and plants, use graph paper or a scale.
- Draw a north arrow and record the sun's position throughout the day.
- Make a note of where you can get water and where you can compost.
- For each variety of vegetables, choose a distinct color or form.

- Review each crop's planting dates to help you plan for succession throughout the growing season. Ideally, after harvesting one crop, another crop is ready to be planted in its place.
- Plant from north to south to make the most of the available sunshine.
- To prevent shadowing shorter plants, group tall crops (corn, okra, sunflowers) and trellised vines (peas, beans, squash) together on the north side of the garden. Crops such as leafy greens are a good stopgap for shady spots against a perimeter wall or in the vicinity of a tree (not under).
- Leave walkways so that you can access the plants or beds from all sides.
- Display the plant's mature size to ensure appropriate space is allocated.

For those with the space, an area of 625 square feet should be sufficient for a family of four to meet most of their produce needs throughout the growing season. Begin small and gradually grow your garden as time and interest allow. Start with a small area; it's easy to become overwhelmed by the weeds and labor of starting a new garden. It is simple to expand once you get started.

CHAPTER 3
PLANT HEALTH

We're all part of a complex symphony of life, and none of it depends on humans' presence. It all fits together from the smallest microorganisms to the largest mammals, each playing a leading role. Without plants, life on Earth would not be possible. They supply nourishment to all animal life, either directly or indirectly. Their roots hold the earth and prevent erosion, while their leaves produce oxygen. Their branches shade and chill the ground, and their unique forms, colors, textures, and aromas provide beauty to our surroundings. Botany is the study of plants as a science. This chapter covers vegetable plant classification, structural and reproductive components, development processes, and environmental influences. The aim is to help you understand how plants grow, their needs, and proper management approaches to navigate challenges.

Four fields of study are of interest, though the scope of this book will restrict us to the fundamentals of each field:

1. *Taxonomy* – how plants are classified, grouped, and named
2. *Anatomy and Morphology* – plant structures and adaptations
3. *Physiology* – internal functioning and development
4. *Ecology* – their interaction with their environment

Plant Taxonomy

There are more than 350,000 different types of plants on Earth, with this number continuously changing as new species are discovered, and others become extinct. There is an international system by which plants are classified based on characteristics, natural habitat, and reproduction forms. These are grouped in a hierarchal structure, with each tier subdivided in further groupings as follows:

- Kingdom
- Phylum
- Class
- Order
- Family

- Genus
- Species
- Variety, or cultivar

An example would be the Brassicaceae Family, in which there are approximately 338 genera and 3,700 species. One of those 338 genera is the genus Brassica, in which we have:

- Broccoli *(Brassica oleracea var. italica)*
- Brussels sprouts *(Brassica oleracea var. gemmifera)*
- Cabbage *(Brassica oleracea var. capitata)*
- Cauliflower *(Brassica oleracea var. botrytis)*
- Kale *(Brassica oleracea var. acephala)*
- Kohlrabi *(Brassica oleracea var. gongylodes)*
- Rutabaga *(Brassica napus var. napobrassica)*
- Turnips *(Brassica rapa)*

Other genera and variants in the Brassicaceae family are:

- Horseradish (*Armoracia rusticana*)
- Radish *(Raphanus sativus)*

Plant Anatomy and Morphology

Plants are distinctly divided into two main parts – roots and shoots, the one visible and the other generally below the surface of the pedosphere. What happens above the ground affects what happens below and vice versa.

Roots

Roots usually grow from the bottom of a plant or cutting. Roots' primary roles are to absorb nutrients and water, anchor the plant in the soil (or other growth media), give physical support for the stem, and act as food storage organs. Roots are used as a propagation technique in some plants,

either naturally or through human intervention. Roots interact with microorganisms, forming symbiotic partnerships for mutual benefit. Root structure and growth patterns significantly impact a plant's size and vigor, propagation mode, adaptability to certain soil types, and response to cultural techniques and irrigation. Certain vegetable crop roots are also essential food sources.

Root growth influencing factors include:

- Roots thrive in soil that has a good mix of moisture and air.
- Soil richness and pH determine the pace and depth of root development.
- A lack of oxygen in the soil restricts growth, reducing total water and nutrient absorption.
- Root development is hampered by soil compaction.

Stems

Stems are the structures that hold buds, flowers, and leaves in place. The vascular tissue system, which comprises the xylem, phloem, and, in most plants, the vascular cambium, is the most important internal component of a stem. The plant's vascular tissue system carries food, water, and nutrients while providing support. Water and minerals are transported by the conducting elements in the xylem, whereas the conducting elements in the phloem transport food. Hormones can be carried by both xylem and phloem.

Buds

A bud is an immature branch from which new leaves or flower components emerge. Temperate zone tree and shrub buds generally grow a protective outer coat of tiny, leathery bud scales. Annuals and herbaceous perennials have bare buds with outer leaves that are green and succulent. Buds are named based on where they appear on the stem surface. Terminal buds grow at the very tip of a stem, and lateral buds form on the stem's sides. Axillary buds are lateral buds that grow in the axil of a leaf (the narrow angle between the plant's stem and the leaf attachment).

In rare cases, more than one bud forms. Adventitious buds appear in locations other than the terminal or axillary positions. Adventitious buds can form from the internode of a stem, the edge of a leaf blade, callus tissue at the cut end of a stem or root, or laterally – from the roots of a plant. A leaf bud is a small stalk with immature leaves, and these buds grow into green stalks. Leaf buds are frequently more pointed and plump than flower buds. A flower bud comprises a short stalk and embryonic floral components.

Leaves

The fundamental purpose of most leaves is to collect sunlight to produce plant sugars through a process known as photosynthesis (more on this in the next section – **Plant Physiology**). Each leaf grows into a flattened surface with a big area for effective light energy absorption. A stem-like extension called a petiole supports the leaf away from the stem. At the node, the petiole's base connects to the stem.

Flowers

Flowers are appreciated for their beauty and perfume, yet their main function is sexual reproduction. Wind pollinated plants, such as grasses and pines, have no need to attract an insect or animal, so they invest minimal energy on aesthetics and instead generate vast amounts of pollen for the wind to disseminate. On the other hand, other plants have evolved fragrant, pale, night-blooming blooms to attract pollinating moths.

Most fragrant, showy flowers with landing platforms (or nectaries) have developed to attract insect pollinators in order to secure the plant's reproductive success and survival. Insects can tell how to approach and where to land by the markings on the petals. Flowers fertilized by bees reflect ultraviolet light, which humans cannot see. Flowers that look and smell like females of an insect species fool certain male insects into sharing pollen. Bees, butterflies, moths, and other insects are drawn to fragrant flowers. Flowers with unpleasant scents attract flies, beetles, and other insects. Flowers are also pollinated by other creatures such as birds and bats. Some flowers contain nectaries at the ends of lengthy tubes that correspond to the body sections of the pollinators.

Fruit

Fruits are essential for human sustenance and frequently take center stage in a garden. A fruit is an ovary that has matured and contains one or more seeds, and the fruit protects the seed until it is mature enough to disperse. Because many fruits are appealing to animals, a fruit's seed can be eaten, transit through a digestive tract, and end up far away from the parent plant, distributing genes and assuring the plant's long-term survival. Some fruits, such as dandelion fluff and maple winged samara, rely on wind to disseminate their seeds.

Seeds

A flower's final result might be seeds. A seed is comprised of three parts:

- An embryonic plant (miniature plant) that remains dormant.
- The endosperm is a food supply for the embryo that is stored in the form of proteins, carbs, or lipids.
- A seed coat or covering surrounds the seed and protects the embryo from illnesses, insects, and moisture until germination.

When the right temperature, moisture, oxygen, and light conditions are fulfilled, germination occurs. The radicle is the first portion of the seed to develop as water is taken in through the seed coat. The radicle will grow into the primary root, from which root hairs and lateral roots will shoot. The hypocotyl develops into the stem in due course.

Plant Physiology

Photosynthesis, respiration, and transpiration make a plant's growth and development possible. Like all living organisms, including you and I, wellbeing is an environmental factor – our environment's influence and interaction with us. For plants, elements such as weather conditions, temperature levels, day length, soil conditions, and systemic threats contribute to their health. Studies have shown that a healthy plant is pest and disease resistant – a combined product of healthy photosynthesis, optimal hydration, and soil that consists of a healthy biota.

Photosynthesis

Plants, unlike mammals, can produce food for themselves internally. Plants make simple carbohydrates by using energy from sunlight, carbon dioxide from the air, and water from the soil in a process known as photosynthesis. Different mechanisms convert these carbohydrates (such as glucose) to complex sugars that may be delivered to the stems, roots, flowers, and growing tissues for immediate use. These sugars can also be stored as starch or utilized to construct more complex compounds such as oils, pigments, proteins, and cell walls.

The chemical equation for photosynthesis, which means 'to bring together with light,' is as follows:

6 molecules of Carbon dioxide + 12 Water + Light → (produces) 1 Glucose + 6 Oxygen + 6 Water

$6CO_2 + 12H_2O \rightarrow$ *light captured by chlorophyll* $\rightarrow C_6H_{12}O_6 + 6O_2 + 6H_2O$

This equation shows that chlorophyll, a green pigment found in chloroplasts, is an essential component of photosynthesis. Although any green plant tissue may catch light energy and perform photosynthesis, leaves are normally the site of most food production due to their specific architecture. Their interior tissues are made up of cells with many chloroplasts arranged to allow the simple circulation of air and water. The stomata of a leaf enable carbon dioxide (CO_2) to diffuse into the leaf, and the CO_2 is utilized to create carbohydrates.

Respiration

Photosynthesis produces carbohydrates, which are turned into energy for cellular activities via a chemical process known as respiration. It is comparable to burning wood or coal to generate heat, but it is a more gradual and regulated release of energy. Respiration produces adenosine triphosphate (ATP), a chemical needed in various metabolic pathways in plant cells to carry out the cellular function. ATP is frequently referred to as the 'life energy currency.' This equation illustrates cell respiration the simplest way:

Sugar + Oxygen → Carbon Dioxide + Water + ATP

$C_6H_{12}O_6 + 6O_2 \rightarrow 6CO_2 + 6H_2O + ATP$ (energy)

Respiration happens in all living things and all cells. At the cellular level, carbon dioxide is released, and oxygen is taken in. Blood in animals transports carbon dioxide and oxygen to and from the atmosphere via the lungs or gills. Carbon dioxide and oxygen are diffused into the open areas within the leaf by plants, and exchange happens via the stomata. Flowers, fruits, and vegetables continue to breathe even after being picked. As a result, cooling and humidity control can reduce respiration and extend product shelf life.

Transpiration

Plants have vascular tissue called xylem that transfers water from the terminals of roots to the tips of shoots. This water produces a continuous column in the plant, which aids in the plant's erectness and firmness (turgidity). The hardness of the cell is referred to as turgor pressure. In the transpiration process, water is lost, typically through its stomata, requiring additional water to be drawn up the xylem. Transpiration accounts for approximately 90% of the water taken up by a plant. The remaining 10% of water is utilized in chemical processes and plant tissues. Transpiration is required for:

- Mineral transport from the soil to the plant
- Evaporation cools the plant
- Transports plant compounds, sugars, and plant hormones
- Maintaining the pressure that prevents wilting (turgor pressure)

The rate of transpiration is affected by several environmental conditions. An increase in light, temperature, wind, or a combination of these elements, enhances transpiration. As humidity increases, on the other hand, transpiration is reduced.

When the rate of water loss by transpiration exceeds the water absorption rate, the leaves of many plants begin to wilt. Leaves and herbaceous stems become limp or flaccid as the water level in plant cells decreases. During drought or high-temperature stress, the stomata normally shut, limiting additional water loss. Wilting helps to minimize transpiration losses by decreasing the damaged leaf surface. When the plant absorbs enough water, the cells expand and return to their pre-stress size, becoming turgid (having a high turgor pressure).

When stomata shut down owing to a lack of water, the rate of photosynthesis falls. Not only is there less water available for metabolic activities, but carbon dioxide from the environment cannot permeate into the leaf tissue. Cell shrinkage has a substantial impact on other vital metabolic processes as well. As a result, momentary withering might be detrimental to the plant. Plant development can be greatly reduced by frequent wilting and sluggish recovery under dry soil conditions. This phenomenon explains why plants shrink when there is a water deficit. Most crops never attain their full potential during droughts.

Plant Ecology

To grow and reproduce, plants must balance their core life activities of photosynthesis, respiration, and transpiration. Light, temperature, humidity, water, carbon dioxide, and oxygen levels can all impact how plants accomplish key biological tasks. Understanding how these environmental elements impact plants enable us to improve yields, prevent risks and provide better plant management.

This section will go through how the following environmental elements can have an impact on plants:

- Light
- Temperature
- Water
- Oxygen
- Carbon dioxide
- Soil microorganisms

Light

Three major factors are essential for effective photosynthesis: quality, duration, and amount. Duration is the exposure time, and light amount refers to the intensity or concentration of sunshine, which fluctuates depending on the season. Summer has the most powerful light, and winter has the least.

The colors or wavelengths of light that reach the plant surface are light quality. A prism separates sunlight into red, orange, yellow, green, blue, indigo, and violet. Either end of the spectrum, red and violate, have the greatest impact on photosynthesis. Plants primarily reflect green light, resulting in the green hue we see and associate with them. Blue light is largely responsible for fostering vegetative development. Infrared and ultraviolet (UV) are the non-visible waves on either side of the visible spectrum.

Fluorescent and incandescent plant lights, sometimes known as 'grow' lights, use a combination of red and blue wavelengths to mimic sunshine as nearly as possible. Fluorescent light, particularly cool-white tubes, can be employed to promote foliage development. This type of light is ideal for germinating seeds. Incandescent light has a high red-orange wavelength range yet creates a lot of heat.

Temperature

Temperature influences flowering and fruit set, photosynthesis and respiration, water usage, and dormancy in plants. Thermoperiodism is the term used to explain the time plants need to be exposed to particular temperatures to promote or inhibit certain developmental phases in their life cycle – as explained below:

- *Flowering and Fruit Set* – Cool-season crops, such as spinach, can blossom prematurely (bolt) rather than grow the necessary leaves if temperatures are high and the day duration is long. Temperature extremes can also result in stunted growth and poor quality. High temperatures, for example, cause bitterness in lettuce and cucumbers. Furthermore, pollen may become ineffective at high temperatures, inhibiting fruit sets. Temperatures that are too low for warm-season crops, such as tomatoes, will, on the other hand, impede fruit set. Temperature adjustment, either alone or in conjunction with day duration, can influence when particular flowers bloom.
- *Photosynthesis and Respiration* – Photosynthesis and respiration rates normally increase as the temperature rises. However, extremely high nighttime temperatures can cause respiration to outpace photosynthesis. When this happens, the plant consumes food quicker than it can generate it. Photosynthesis occurs at its maximum rate for most plants in the temperature range of 65 to 85°F and diminishes when temperatures are higher or lower than this range. As a result, when day temperatures are 10 to 15°F higher than night temperatures, plants have the most effective thermoperiod (day temperature range). This temperature range allows plants to photosynthesize and respire (break down food) during the day but decreases respiration at night when there is no light and the plants cannot manufacture food.
- *Water Use* – Temperature extremes can harm how plants use water. Plants lose water quicker than they can absorb it in hot weather, producing withering and limiting development. Extremely low temperatures can cause the soil to freeze, significantly limiting the passage of water into the plant. Plants continue to transpire (give up water) on a windy, bright winter day and may become dry (dried out). In addition to dehydration, freezing temperatures can promote the development of ice crystals within and between plant cells, which can cause considerable physical damage.
- *Dormancy* – Plant dormancy is affected by temperature. Many plants' buds require a certain number of days below a critical temperature (chilling hours) before they resume growth in the spring. Peaches are an excellent example. Most cultivars require 700 to 1,000 hours of dormancy below 45°F and above 32°F

before breaking dormancy and growing. The period varies depending on the variety. Buds can endure extremely low temperatures when dormant. However, once the rest phase is through, buds become more vulnerable to late cold or frost and are readily injured by these circumstances. While extremely cold temperatures can hurt nonhardy plants, unusually high winter temperatures can trigger premature bud break in some plants and subsequent bud-freezing damage when temperatures drop.

Water

Water has several critical roles in photosynthesis. It keeps a plant's turgor, or the firmness or fullness of plant tissue, stable for starters. Turgor pressure in a cell is comparable to the pressure of an inflated balloon, and plant cells require water pressure, or turgor, to retain form and enable cell development. Second, the solar energy collected by chlorophyll in the plant's leaves splits water into hydrogen and oxygen. Oxygen is emitted into the environment, whereas hydrogen is employed in the production of carbohydrates. Third, water dissolves soil minerals and carries them upward from the roots and throughout the plant, where they serve as raw materials for creating new plant tissues. The soil moisture around a plant should alter – before re-irrigating, the soil should be left to dry before rewetting it.

Oxygen

Plants need oxygen for respiration to generate energy by breaking down the carbohydrates produced during photosynthesis. The aboveground sections of a plant have an abundance of oxygen, but soil oxygen can be a plant growth-limiting factor.

Soils with a healthy soil biota have extensive pore spaces that allow air and water to circulate readily. Soils that are well-aerated offer the oxygen that seeds and roots require to sprout and flourish. Some soils are poorly drained, resulting in little or no pore space for oxygen and anaerobic conditions. Soils that are oversaturated with water or compacted might prevent oxygen from reaching the roots and induce root death. For more information on ensuring optimal soil oxygen levels, see **Chapter 5: Preparing the Ground**.

Carbon Dioxide

Carbon dioxide is an important component of photosynthesis. Carbon dioxide is abundant, and its concentration in the atmosphere is rarely a limiting factor for plant development. During the day, when sunlight is available, and photosynthesis is active, most plants take in carbon dioxide through open stomata. If the plant does not open its stomata throughout the day, carbon dioxide can be a limiting factor. When stomata shut, photosynthesis slows and even halt entirely. If the plant is drought-stressed, the stomata may shut down to reduce water loss throughout the day.

Soil Microorganisms

One of the most neglected elements of ensuring an environment optimal for plant growth is the soil life cycle (or soil biota). Because this is often the missing ingredient to successful vegetable gardening, I have given this factor a chapter of its own (see ***Chapter 5: Preparing the Ground***).

CHAPTER 4
WEATHER CONSIDERATIONS

Global climate changes require gardeners to become more agile in their approach to the craft. We all need to draw alongside nature, forming a symbiotic relationship to help both flourish, even in challenging times. Extended droughts, higher temperatures, colder winters, floods – nature has an appropriate response for them all, but humans need to listen. The Earth's global average surface temperature in 2019 was 1.71°F above the 20th-century average. Nine of the ten warmest years on record have occurred since 2005.

Like any healthy relationship, we need to be attuned to the changing needs of our partners. In the absence of regular rain, our soil needs better water-holding capacities. In floods, our soil needs improved cohesive strengths. While nature is often remembered for its tempestuous display of force, the trick to becoming an effective gardener is to listen for her whispers. We need to be present in the relationship, listening and responding – and nature will do the same; she always does. What are the plants and soil saying, the birds and the bees? Are there earthworms in the soil? Is the color of my plants' foliage changing year-on-year? Are you attentive and finely sensitive to your garden's needs?

A healthy relationship is one where the needs are met with finesse. Is it better to water more, or is it better to add microorganisms, mulch, and organic matter to help address the thirst? Do you rush in, adding nitrogen, insecticides, everything you think your plant needs, or do you approach your garden with love and understanding? Nature loves natural solutions. In managing changing weather patterns, we need to work with nature, implementing subtle adjustments that prevent a pendulum swing from one extreme to the next.

Most people's lives are filled to capacity, so I'm hesitant to add more to your to-do list. However, your relationship with your garden requires some experiential understanding. You need to know what your plant is experiencing – when last it had some unchlorinated water, sunshine, soil biota population, and the pests it is fighting. I have a simple chart to record the rainfall, full sun days, and pest prevalence. It's the only way to recognize patterns and devise appropriate responses.

Hardiness Zones

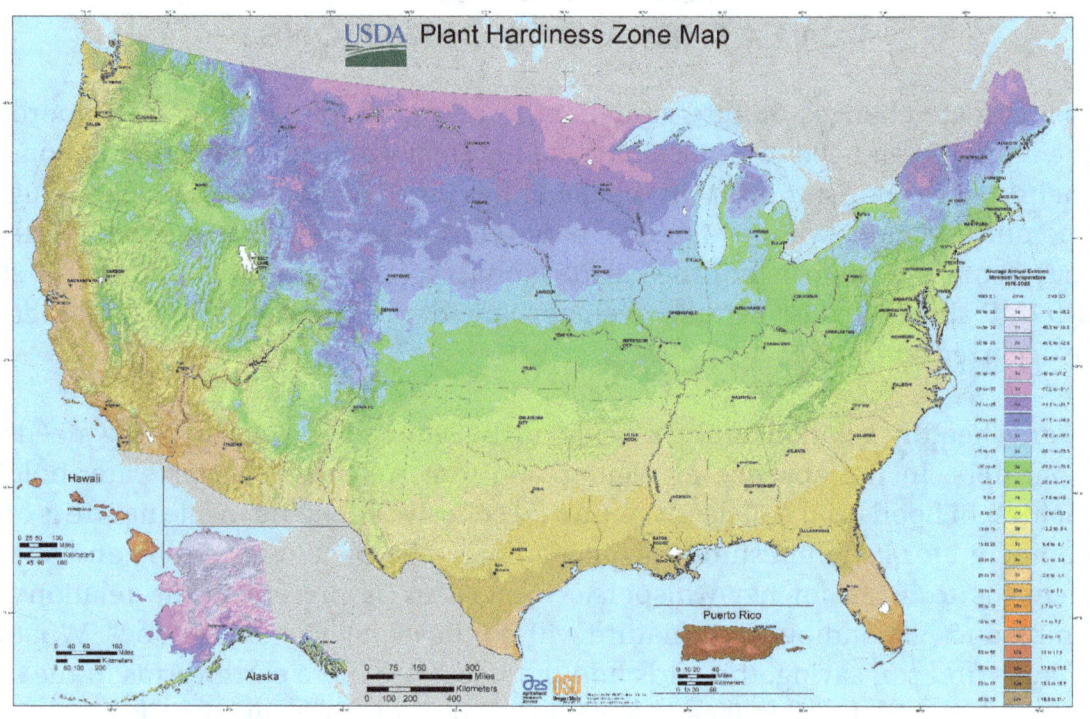

-60 to -55	1a	-51.1 to -48.3		5 to 10	7b	-15 to -12.2
-55 to -50	1b	-48.3 to -45.6		10 to 15	8a	-12.2 to -9.4
-50 to -45	2a	-45.6 to -42.8		15 to 20	8b	-9.4 to -6.7
-45 to -40	2b	-42.8 to -40		20 to 25	9a	-6.7 to -3.9
-40 to -35	3a	-40 to -37.2		25 to 30	9b	-3.9 to -1.1
-35 to -30	3b	-37.2 to -34.4		30 to 35	10a	-1.1 to 1.7
-30 to -25	4a	-34.4 to -31.7		35 to 40	10b	1.7 to 4.4
-25 to -20	4b	-31.7 to -28.9		40 to 45	11a	4.4 to 7.2
-20 to -15	5a	-28.9 to -26.1		45 to 50	11b	7.2 to 10
-15 to -10	5b	-26.1 to -23.3		50 to 55	12a	10 to 12.8
-10 to -5	6a	-23.3 to -20.6		55 to 60	12b	12.8 to 15.6
-5 to 0	6b	-20.6 to -17.8		60 to 65	13a	15.6 to 18.3
0 to 5	7a	-17.8 to -15		65 to 70	13b	18.3 to 21.1

When it comes to determining which plants are most likely to thrive in a given location, the 2012 USDA Plant Hardiness Zone Map (PHZM) is the standard for the United States of America. Each 10°F zone is based on an average annual *minimum* winter temperature.

It is not the lowest temperature that has ever been recorded, nor is it one that is likely to be in the near future, that is used to determine the hardiness zones. Remembering this when choosing plants is essential, especially if you plan to 'push' your hardiness zone by growing plants that are not rated for it.

Small heat islands, such as those created by blacktop and concrete, or cool spots created by small hills and valleys are examples of microclimates, minor variations in climate on a fine scale. The microclimates of individual gardens may also be very localized. Because your yard is sheltered or exposed, it may be warmer or cooler than the rest of the neighborhood. Your garden may also have warmer or cooler areas than the general climate in your area or the rest of your yard, such as an area in front of a south-facing wall or a low spot where cold air settles (because cold air is heavier than warm air). No map of hardiness zones can replace the in-depth knowledge that gardeners gain from working in their own gardens.

As the days grow shorter and the temperature drops in the fall, many plants develop a greater tolerance to cold. As temperatures rise and daylight lengthens in late winter, this hardiness fades away. Even if temperatures don't fall below your zone's average low temperature, an early fall freeze can harm plants. In the same way, unusually warm weather in the middle of the winter, followed by a sudden change to cold weather, can harm plants. The USDA PHZM does not take into account these issues.

All PHZMs are nothing more than a set of guidelines. As a result, they are based on average low temperatures rather than the record-breaking lows. With an extreme cold snap lasting only a few days or even hours in the coldest zone, plants that have thrived for years could be destroyed in a single year if grown in this zone. Keeping that in mind, gardeners should be aware that past weather records do not guarantee future weather variation.

OTHER FACTORS

Cities	Season Length (Days)	Avg. Annual Rainfall	Jul Avg. Max. Temp °F	Jan Avg Min. Temp °F	Rainy Season	Frost-Free Season
Huntsville, AL	217	54.29	91.5	33.1	Dec–Mar	Mar 30–Nov 03
Montgomery, AL	243	51.16	93.7	36.5	Dec–Mar	Mar 12–Nov 11
Juneau, AK	139	66.99	64.0	23.8	Year-round	May 10–Sep 27
Anchorage, AK	139	16.42	66.2	11.0	Aug–Sep	May 07–Sep 24
Phoenix, AZ	209	7.22	106.5	46.0	Aug	Apr 04–Oct 30
Little Rock, AR	237	50.42	91.7	30.9	Oct–May	Mar 19–Nov 12
Sacramento, CA	276	17.97	93.6	38.1	Dec–Mar	Feb 22–Nov 25
Los Angeles, CA	362	11.77	77.2	49.2	Dec–Mar	Jan 14–Dec 30
Denver, CO	147	15.36	90.2	17.6	Apr–Aug	May 09–Oct 04
Hartford, CT	169	47.50	85.2	18.8	Year-round	Apr 25–Oct 11
Bridgeport, CT	208	44.09	83.4	38.4	Year-round	Apr 08–Nov 03
Dover, DE	184	47.61	86.9	27.6	Year-round	Apr 22–Oct 23
Wilmington, DE	203	45.30	86.8	25.6	Year-round	Apr 10–Oct 30
Tallahassee, FL	252	58.81	92.1	44.5	Jun–Aug	Mar 13–Nov 20
Jacksonville, FL	286	51.82	91.2	44.7	Jun–Oct	Feb 12–Dec 04
Atlanta, GA	238	48.13	90.0	33.5	Year-round	Mar 20–Nov 14
Honolulu, HI	365	34.49	88.1	66.8	Nov–Mar	- - -
Boise, ID	158	11.51	92.7	25.5	Nov–May	May 05–Oct 11
Springfield, IL	191	38.04	86.8	19.9	Apr–Jun	Apr 13–Oct 21
Chicago, IL	188	34.42	85.0	19.4	Apr–Oct	Apr 18–Oct 25
Indianapolis, IN	183	43.63	85.2	20.9	Apr–Jul	Apr 19–Oct 20
Des Moines, IA	176	36.55	85.6	13.8	Apr–Aug	Apr 21–Oct 14
Topeka, KS	192	36.53	90.2	20.0	May–Aug	Apr 14–Oct 23
Wichita, KS	197	34.31	92.6	22.5	May–Aug	Apr 11–Oct 25
Frankfort, KY	183	47.34	87.6	25.1	Mar–Jul	Apr 21–Oct 22
Louisville, KY	208	48.34	89.0	27.8	Mar–May	Apr 06–Oct 31
Baton Rouge, LA	273	61.94	91.9	41.6	Year-round	Feb 23–Nov 24
New Orleans, LA	348	64.60	93.9	45.5	Jun–Aug	Jan 18–Dec 27
Augusta, ME	166	41.84	79.9	12.1	Year-round	Apr 27–Oct 11
Portland, ME	152	48.12	79.5	15.6	Year-round	May 05–Oct 05
Annapolis, MD	239	43.99	86.0	29.8	Jun–Oct	Mar 24–Nov 19
Baltimore, MD	200	43.73	90.1	30.0	Jul–Sep	Apr 11–Oct 28
Boston, MA	215	43.59	82.1	23.1	Year-round	Apr 06–Nov 08
Lansing, MI	149	33.33	82.8	17.2	Apr–Oct	May 08–Oct 04
Detroit, MI	183	29.89	83.5	19.8	Apr–Sep	Apr 23–Oct 24
St. Paul, MN	166	29.20	82.6	8.6	May–Aug	Apr 27–Oct 11

City						
Minneapolis, MN	154	31.62	83.4	8.8	May–Aug	May 03–Oct 04
Jackson, MS	262	51.33	92.1	37.5	Year-round	Mar 01–Nov 19
Jefferson City, MO	189	43.60	88.0	21.0	Apr–Sep	Apr 13–Oct 20
Kansas City, MO	206	38.13	90.2	22.2	Apr–Sep	Apr 07–Oct 31
Helena, MT	128	11.40	86.1	13.5	May, Jun	May 16–Sep 22
Billings, MT	149	15.43	86.3	14.4	May, Jun	May 06–Oct 03
Lincoln, NE	163	29.34	89.4	14.4	May, Jun	Apr 25–Oct 07
Omaha, NE	188	31.86	88.1	15.2	May–Aug	Apr 04–Oct 20
Carson City, NV	54	9.34	89.5	24.1	Dec–Mar	Jul 02–Aug 25
Las Vegas, NV	286	4.27	105.7	38.0	Jan–Mar	Feb 15–Nov 29
Concord, NH	128	41.95	83.0	12.9	Year-round	Apr 24–Sep 24
Manchester, NH	176	40.39	84.1	17.1	Year-round	Apr 22–Oct 15
Trenton, NJ	200	45.47	86.0	24.3	Year-round	Apr 09–Oct 27
Newark, NJ	215	46.60	86.9	25.5	Year-round	Apr 04–Nov 06
Santa Fe, NM	161	10.70	88.5	19.9	Jul, Aug	May 04–Oct 13
Albuquerque, NM	194	8.54	91.2	26.4	Jul–Sep	Apr 16–Oct 28
Albany, NY	179	40.68	83.9	18.9	Year-round	Apr 20–Oct 17
New York City, NY	217	49.52	84.9	27.9	Year-round	Apr 08–Nov 11
Raleigh, NC	225	49.36	90.6	31.6	May–Sep	Mar 29–Nov 09
Charlotte, NC	232	43.60	90.3	31.8	Year-round	Mar 24–Nov 12
Bismarck, ND	130	19.50	84.7	2.4	May–Aug	May 14–Sep 21
Fargo, ND	137	23.95	82.1	0.2	May–Aug	May 12–Sep 27
Columbus, OH	180	41.57	85.4	22.0	Year-round	Apr 23–Oct 20
Oklahoma City, OK	216	36.39	93.1	27.0	Apr–Sep	Apr 01–Nov 04
Salem, OR	192	40.08	83.6	35.8	Nov–Jan	Apr 17–Oct 27
Portland, OR	281	44.07	80.3	37.3	Nov–Jan	Feb 19–Nov 30
Harrisburg, PA	194	44.23	86.8	23.0	Year-round	Apr 14–Oct 25
Philadelphia, PA	226	50.69	89.3	27.8	Year-round	Apr 02–Nov 15
Providence, RI	191	47.54	83.6	22.1	Year-round	Apr 14–Oct 24
Columbia, SC	243	48.11	95.6	36.7	Year-round	Mar 16–Nov 15
Charleston, SC	304	44.26	87.5	43.6	Jun–Sep	Feb 15–Dec 18
Pierre, SD	151	20.20	88.3	9.3	May, Jun	May 05–Oct 04
Sioux Falls, SD	161	28.30	84.8	7.4	Apr–Sep	Apr 30–Oct 09
Nashville, TN	211	50.51	90.9	30.1	Year-round	Apr 02–Oct 31
Austin, TX	266	35.57	96.1	37.7	May, Oct	Mar 03–Nov 25
Houston, TX	307	51.84	94.5	43.7	Jun, Oct	Feb 09–Dec 13
Salt Lake City, UT	178	17.72	91.4	27.6	Mar–May	Apr 23–Oct 18
Montpelier, VT	134	41.35	81.5	7.3	Year-round	May 16–Sep 27
Burlington, VT	148	37.53	82.4	12.9	Apr–Oct	May 08–Oct 04

Richmond, VA	205	45.50	89.5	28.8	Year-round	Apr 08–Oct 30
Virginia Beach, VA	244	46.62	87.4	31.6	Jul–Oct	Mar 20–Nov 20
Olympia, WA	155	50.62	77.6	33.2	Nov–Jan	May 06–Oct 09
Seattle, WA	233	36.49	77.3	36.8	Nov–Jan	Mar 22–Nov 12
Charleston, WV	183	46.24	86.0	26.1	Year-round	Apr 21–Oct 22
Madison, WI	149	40.18	82.2	11.1	Apr–Sep	May 07–Oct 03
Milwaukee, WI	175	34.57	81.9	17.2	Apr–Sep	Apr 26–Oct 19
Cheyenne, WY	135	15.41	84.1	18.1	Apr–Jul	May 15–Sep 28

In addition to hardiness zones, many other environmental factors play a role in the success or failure of plants. Wind, soil type, soil moisture, humidity, pollution, snow, and winter sunshine can all significantly impact the survival of plants in the winter. A plant's survival may be influenced by several other factors, including where it is planted, how large it is, and how healthy it is.

Plants need the right amount of light to grow and prosper. For example, during the winter, plants that need partial shade may be damaged by too much sunlight because it could cause rapid temperature changes. Depending on the season, plants may have different needs for soil moisture. Typically hardy plants in your area may be damaged if soil moisture levels fall too low in the late autumn, causing them to go into dormancy.

Plants thrive in a range of hot and cold temperatures just right for them. Some species and varieties have a broad range, while others have specific temperature requirements. Many plants that can tolerate short periods of cold weather may not tolerate cold weather for more extended periods. High relative humidity facilitates low moisture loss from leaves, branches, and buds. Evergreens, in particular, are more susceptible to cold injury when humidity levels are low.

Wind

The Science

Just for interest, let's start with some handy science. Air moves from high-pressure areas to low-pressure areas caused by hot air rising and colder, more dense air rushing to take its place. The difference between the pressure in each area determines the speed with which the air moves, i.e. wind strength. The relative weight of the air causes the pressure differences – warmer air is lighter and colder air has more dense atoms and molecules, so it's heavier.

Differences in atmospheric pressure generate winds. The sun warms the Earth's surface area around the equator more intensely than it does the rest of the globe. This hot air rises to high altitudes, and the dense air from the poles moves over the Earth's surface to replace the risen air. Where the air is hot and rising is referred to as a low-pressure system. High-pressure systems are colder, denser air, and the meeting point of the two systems is known as a front.

The interaction between the two systems is complex. The low pressure rises naturally, and the cold front forms a wedge to lift it, causing different wind and weather patterns. Added to this, we have the centrifugal force exerted on the atmosphere, an effect of the spinning globe. This is known as the Coriolis effect. The Coriolis effect makes draining water and wind systems twist clockwise in the Southern Hemisphere and counterclockwise in the Northern Hemisphere. We have air movement between the equator and the poles, but we have east-west winds because the Earth is spinning.

Typically, prevailing winds blow east-west rather than north-south. The biased leaning indicates the direction of the prevailing winds in your area of trees – years of wind from a given direction cause trees to lean away from the oncoming wind.

Polytunnels versus Wind

Wind plays an essential role in maize farming, where it's responsible for pollination. In other forms of gardening, winds can be a force that can cause significant damage. The skilled gardener knows how to mitigate these risks.

For example, let us consider a 20 x 10-foot polytunnel with a height of 8 feet and a mass of 68 pounds standing with its 20-foot side facing an oncoming wind of 15 miles per hour. To calculate the wind force, use the formula:

$F = A \times P \times C_d$

Where F is the wind force;
A the surface area;
P the wind pressure per square foot, and
C_d is the drag coefficient of the wind on the surface.

- **A** = Area = Length x Height = 20 x 8 feet, equaling 160 square feet.
- **P** is the wind pressure per square foot. This is a product of wind velocity squared multiplied by a constant factor of 0,00256. Thus 15 x 15 x 0.00256 = 0.576 pounds of air pressure per square foot.
- **Cd** has no unit of measure and is a variation between 0.8 to 1.2. For a cylindrical shape with a taut, smooth surface, like our lovely polytunnel, we shall use a conservative drag coefficient of 0.8.

Thus, the wind load caused by the 15-mph wind on our 20 by 8-foot polytunnel is 160 x 0.576 x 0.8 = 73.728 pounds. This is almost 6 pounds more than the weight of the tunnel (68 pounds) and will result (if no countermeasures are taken) in the polytunnel becoming one with the moving air. Wind 1: Polytunnel 0.

Protecting our polytunnel from being blown away by wind will require us to reduce the controllable risk factors:

- Lifting weight
- Size of exposure
- Air pressure
- Drag-coefficient of our surface

Lifting Weight
Because the mass of the polytunnels is a given, the only solution is to increase the amount of force required to lift it off the ground by weighing or anchoring it down. More on this, in some detail, under the topic *Anchoring Your Polytunnel.*

Size of Exposure
The size of the surface directly exposed to the wind is critical. To reduce this, we: a) need to know the general wind direction; b) need to position the polytunnel so that the directly exposed surface is the smallest possible size; c) consider exposing the strongest point of a polytunnel (a braced corner) to the wind's onslaught.

The slant of trees and bushes often betrays the general wind direction. Constant high winds will cause higher plants in the area to demonstrate a biased slant in the direction of the wind, a result of prolonged yielding to wind load and the subsequent growth in that direction.

If possible, position your tunnel with the most potent point facing the wind. This would be the braced corner of the polytunnel. A good approach is to face the back of the tunnel, slightly off-center, to the wind. Your tunnel will be aligned to local trees, and bushes slant from a bird's eye view.

Air Pressure

Though the per square foot air pressure caused by wind is an immutable factor of wind velocity, some steps can be taken to reduce the immediate impact on our polytunnel. Windbreaks are a common way to protect your polytunnel and garden from wind damage.

Strategically grown tree lanes or hedges and a special broad-ribbed netting are standard solutions to reducing the impact of wind directly on your polytunnel.

Drag-coefficient

A loose surface folds and pleats under the force of a wind resulting in increased wind-flow resistance. A tautly wrapped polytunnel will significantly reduce the drag-coefficient factor. Because it is not possible to create a glass finish, it is advised that the combination of tautness and strategic windbreaks be considered.

Summary

There are few countries more aware of the destructive nature of winds. Tornadoes and hurricanes seem to be a growing annual feature in the United States. While the gardener can manage prevailing wind patterns, these forces of nature are primarily unmanageable.

A strategically placed hedge can create a wind-free island. Positioning your beds to run along the prevailing wind lines (east-west) also helps pollinators in their efforts. As the wind blows, they can flow with it from one plant to the next.

Rain

Water

Plants, and any form of living organisms, cannot live without water. Water constitutes between 80 and 90% of the plant cell in plants. The amount of water in different plant parts varies:

- The apical portion of root and shoot   >90%
- The stem, leaves, and fruits   70–90%
- Woods   50–60%
- Matured parts   15–20%
- Freshly harvested grains   15–20%

Water acts as the base material for all metabolic and biochemical activities in plants. Water plays a critical role in the plant's respiration and transpiration systems and is essential for photosynthesis. Without water, there can be no germination, no growth, and fruit. Water serves as a plant nutrient solvent and microorganisms sustainer in the soil. A plant's ability to remain erect (turgidity) is water-dependent – in its absence, the plant wilts.

Water helps to maintain soil temperatures balance salinity and pH. Water is essential for microbial life, and microorganisms, in turn, enhance water efficacy. Water, like microorganisms, helps improve the soil's tilth. The effectiveness of all the gardener's labor is dependent on water.

Soil Moisture

In this book, as in most planting guides, we refer to soil moisture levels as hydric, mesic, and xenic – high moisture habitat, medium moisture habitat, and arid habitat. Each descriptor has ranges within that are hard to pin down, and as far as possible, we will explain these.

Gardening in Semi-arid Areas

Extreme fluctuations between temperatures mark semi-arid regions in the USA. Below is a sample taken in Oregon, and I suspect that similar fluctuations will occur in other semi-arid regions.

Month	Max	Min	Variance
January	40.20	22.10	18.10
February	43.55	22.50	21.05
March	49.65	26.40	23.25
April	55.55	29.65	25.90
May	63.85	35.60	28.25
June	71.85	41.25	30.60
July	81.60	46.60	35.00
August	81.45	45.10	36.35
September	73.95	38.35	35.60
October	61.75	31.60	30.15
November	46.30	26.90	19.40
December	38.50	21.15	17.35

Most plants prefer air temperatures ranging from 50°F to 90°F. At low air temperatures ranging from 32°F to 50°F, growth slows or stops. Cool nighttime temperatures are common in semi-arid environments, resulting in sluggish plant growth/maturity, decreased pollination, and lower yields, particularly for heat-loving crops like tomatoes and peppers. You might wish to buy a max-min thermometer and record your garden's daily temps to understand temperature changes better.

The seasons do not progressively warm up and cool down in the high desert as they do in more temperate locations. During the growth season or dormancy, sudden temperature fluctuations can cause damage to plant tissue (e.g. sapwood, buds, leaves).

CHAPTER 5
PREPARING THE GROUND

Converting Dirt to Soil

There's a growing understanding of microorganisms' role in sustainable, productive, and healthy farming. We're finding harmony between ourselves and all living creatures, allowing nature to become its best self. Your garden can be a space where nature thrives – resistant to pests and diseases, super healthy, and able to produce food loaded with nutrition. Isn't it what we all want for ourselves too?

According to the Global Food Security Index (2021),[6] food prices in the USA increased 12.1% yearly. The trend is expected to continue as input costs increase. Much of those input costs are linked to fuel and fertilizers. But there's a gradual shift to doing things differently, better, more sustainably. Much of the solution lies in cooperating with nature and using soil biology to our advantage. If you are starting a garden, you have an opportunity to do it right from the outset. If you already have a vegetable and herb garden, adopting some new habits will surely improve your gardening experience.

Six soil-related elements are essential for effective traditional gardening:

- Soil structure
- Soil nutrition
- Organic matter
- Soil biology
- Water and oxygen

Soil Structure
The starting point for creating fertile soil is knowing what type of ground you have. Your ground is predominantly one of the following; clay, sand, or silt. A balanced mix of the three is known as loam soil – a good starting point. Suppose you're unsure of that type of soil you have. In that case, you can enter your zip code into the USDA Web Soil Survey portal[7] or select a county – over the page is a sample from the portal for Baldwin, AL.

---

6   https://impact.economist.com/sustainability/project/food-security-index/
7   https://websoilsurvey.sc.egov.usda.gov/App/WebSoilSurvey.aspx

Baldwin County, Alabama

BoC—Bowie fine sandy loam, 5 to 8 percent slopes

Map Unit Setting
National map unit symbol: c0f1
Elevation: 0 to 450 feet
Mean annual precipitation: 40 to 67 inches
Mean annual air temperature: 52 to 77 degrees F
Frost-free period: 217 to 270 days
Farmland classification: Not prime farmland

Map Unit Composition
Bowie, (malbis), and similar soils: 85 percent
Minor components: 5 percent
Estimates are based on observations, descriptions, and transects of the mapunit.

Description of Bowie, (malbis)

Setting
Landform: Hillslopes
Landform position (two-dimensional): Backslope
Landform position (three-dimensional): Side slope
Down-slope shape: Convex
Across-slope shape: Linear
Parent material: Loamy marine deposits derived from sedimentary rock

Typical profile
H1 - 0 to 8 inches: fine sandy loam
H2 - 8 to 33 inches: clay loam
H3 - 33 to 60 inches: sandy clay loam

The USDA should be applauded for making this depth of information so readily available – and gardeners should use it. Let's look at what it means and how the information will impact how you approach your garden.

Mineral Portion of Soil

The inorganic part of the soil consists of deconstructed rock, tiny mineral particles called clay, silt, and sand, each identified by their particle size. Imagine a grain of sand is the size of a baseball; then, comparatively, a particle of silt would be a size of a pea and a particle of clay the size of a pinhead. Depending on the representative ratio of each of these, soil texture could be defined as:

- Clay
- Silty Clay
- Silty Clay Loam
- Clay Loam
- Sandy Clay
- Sandy Clay Loam
- Sandy Loam
- Loam
- Silt Loam
- Silt
- Loamy Sand
- Sand

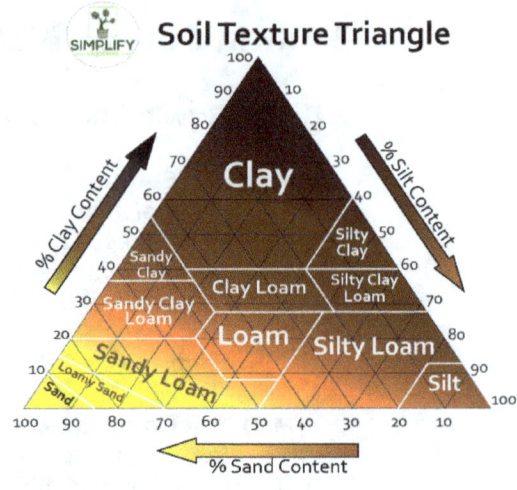

If you wish to test your soil texture, here are four guidelines.

When wet, a sandy soil's texture is gritty, and a ball made of it will crumble easily.

Soil that is both gritty and easy to work is called loamy; it is composed of sand, silt, and clay, and when it is moist, it forms a ball that holds its shape but breaks apart when squeezed.

It's easy to break apart silty soil, and when it dries, it looks like flour. When wet, silty soils are slippery and do not form a ribbon when pinched between the fingers and thumb.

Large, hard clods of clayey soil are formed, and cracks appear on the surface. When wet, clayey soils feel squishy and pliable. A ribbon can be created when the soil is moist by pinching it between the thumb and fingers. A more significant amount of clay is indicated by a longer ribbon that forms before it breaks.

Below are the characteristics of the different base textures:

Characteristic	Clay	Silt	Sand
Looseness	Poor	Fair	Good
Water and Air Space	Poor	Fair	Good
Water Management	Poor drainage	Fair	Poor water retention
Clod-Forming Inclination	Good	Fair	Poor
Workability	Poor	Fair	Poor

Fertility	Fair to Good	Fair	Poor
Cation-Exchange Capacity (CEC)	Good	Poor	Poor

Soil Nutrition

Photosynthesis is one of nature's miracles. Photon cells of different sizes allow some plants to thrive in the shade while others need full sun. Plants, taking up chemical elements in inorganic ion form, use the sun's energy to manufacture their food, combining the chemical elements into many organic compounds. Essentially, photosynthesis is a chemical process in which light energy is captured and mixed with carbon dioxide and water to make sugars used as a chemical energy source. Using the sun's energy, plants can take six carbon dioxide molecules and 12 water molecules and produce carbohydrates, six water, and six oxygen molecules. Amazing!

6 x CO2 (carbon dioxide molecules) add 12 x H2O (water molecules). The photosynthesis cell using sunlight produces C6H12O6 (fructose), 6 x H2O (water molecules), and 6 x O2 (oxygen molecules)

Plants require 17 nutrients to thrive and cannot complete their life cycles if any of these 17 elements are missing. Some of the plant's chemical processes cannot occur without microorganisms' assistance.

Through carbon dioxide and water, plants receive the necessary nutrients and, using light, manufacture their food. Most plants are composed primarily (95%) of these three components – carbon, oxygen, and hydrogen. The remaining 14 elements make up the remaining 5% of the plant's dry matter. A deficiency in one or more of these 14 essential elements may impede the plant's growth ability. The 17 elements are crucial, but others are also ingested by plants, though their purpose is uncertain.

Plants primarily ingest these elements from the soil's solution. According to the amount of nutrients plants need and the extent of deficiency, the 14 mineral nutrients are categorized as primary, secondary, or micronutrients. Deficiencies in primary nutrients are often the first to show up in the soil, as they are used the most. A macronutrient is a term used to describe primary and secondary nutrients. Unlike primary nutrients, secondary nutrients are more rarely deficient in soils. Micronutrients (also known as trace or minor elements) are required in much smaller quantities and are less frequently deficient soil. Nutrients are used in varying amounts, but each one is just as critical to the growth of plants. Below is a list of the 17 essential plant nutrients.

The 17 Essential Plant Nutrients

Sourced from Water
Carbon (C)
Oxygen (O)

Sourced from the Air
Hydrogen (H)
Oxygen (O)

Sourced from the Soil

Primary Nutrients
Nitrogen (N)
Phosphorous (P)
Potassium (K)

Secondary Nutrients
Calcium (Ca)
Magnesium (Mg)
Sulfur (S)

Micronutrients
Boron (B)   Manganese (Mn)
Chrorine (Cl)   Molybdenum (Mo)
Copper (Cu)   Zinc (Zn)
Iron (Fe)   Nickel (N)

Electrically charged ions are the natural form in which all chemical elements, including plant nutrients, exist. Ions are either positively or negatively charged. Ions with a positive charge are called cations (the C reminds me it's charged). Ions with a negative charge are called anions. Plants can only use nutrients in their ionic form. Still, plants can use some nutrients in more than one ionic form simultaneously. Below is a list of some of the most common soil cations and anions.

Cationic Nutrients

- K^+ — Potassium — Primary Nutrient
- NH_4^+ — Ammonium — The Nitrogen part is a Primary Nutrient
- Mg^{+2} — Magnesium — Secondary Nutrient
- Ca^{+2} — Calcium — Secondary Nutrient
- Mn^{+2} — Manganese — Trace Element
- Zn^{+2} — Zinc — Trace element

Anionic Nutrients

- NO_3^- — Nitrate — Primary Element (Nitrogen)
- SO_4^{-2} — Sulfate — Secondary Nutrient (Sulfur)
- $H2PO_4^-$ — Dihydrogen Phosphate — Primary Nutrient (Phosphorous)
- HPO_4^{-2} — Hydrogenphosphate — Primary Nutrient (Phosphorous)
- Cl^- — Chloride — Trace Element (Chlorine)
- BO_3^{-2} — Borate — Trace Element (Boron)
- MoO_3^{-2} — Molybdenum Trioxide — Trace Element (Molybdenum)

Cationic Non-Nutrients
- Na^+ Sodium
- H^+ Hydrogen‡
- Al^{+3} Aluminum

Anionic Non-Nutrients
- OH^- Hydroxyl
- $H2CO_3^-$ Bicarbonate
- $CO3^{-3}$ Carbonate

‡ Plants get their supply of hydrogen from water through photosynthesis. Excess hydrogen ions in soil affect pH, which affects several chemical and biological processes.

Organic Matter and Soil Biology

Knowing how to develop healthy soil, in my opinion, should be a life skill taught at schools. Composting is nature's preferred method of ensuring productive soil – there is nothing better. Creating healthy soil does not require land – it can be done in apartments as well. You can fill your indoor space with pot plants and vertical gardens by using kitchen scraps, cultivated microorganisms, and store-bought ground. Increased indoor vegetation is known to contribute to improved mental and physical health positively.

Creating healthy soil not only benefits plants but benefits the environment holistically. Composting is a meaningful, easy, and effective way of reversing some of the negative impacts we've had on our environment and the planet. If you have healthy soil, your plants will be healthier and more nutritious, and you will be healthier too. My motto – take care of the soil, and it will take care of your plants.

Below is an extract from a review done by David Thomas[8] in 2007. He reflects on the differences in nutritional content between organic and conventional vegetables: mean percent difference for four nutrients in five frequently studied vegetables.

Vegetable	Vitamin C	Iron	Magnesium	Phosphorus
LETTUCE	+17	+17	+29	+14
SPINACH	+52	+25	-13	+14
CARROT	-6	+12	+69	+13
POTATO	+22	+21	+5	0
CABBAGE	+43	+41	+40	+22

[8] THE MINERAL DEPLETION OF FOODS AVAILABLE TO US AS A NATION (1940–2002) – A Review of the 6th Edition of McCance and Widdowson

The situation's urgency is marked by a recent Subcommittee Hearing – The State of Nutrition in America 2021, Subcommittee on Food and Nutrition, Specialty Crops, Organics, and Research.[9] There is a growing concern as the nation spends 1.1 trillion dollars on food, which causes them to spend the same amount on healthcare to mitigate the risks of the foods they eat.

There is ample evidence that growing your food is the best route to better health. The improvement of the nutritional value of food grown without fertilizers, pesticides, and herbicides, i.e. organic food, is a game-changer. Growing vegetables in soil with a healthy soil biota not only improves nutrition but also improves taste as well. Listed below are five reasons why using compost makes a difference,

Soil Composition and the Role of Compost

When it comes to sustaining life on Planet Earth, the soil is the foundation for all of it. This comparatively thin outer layer also serves as a habitat for crucial microorganisms. The primary decomposers in terrestrial ecosystems, soil microbial communities play a vital role in soil nutrient cycling and energy flows. They can be sensitive to and influential in predicting small changes in soil ecosystems. They are the foundation of soil ecological function.

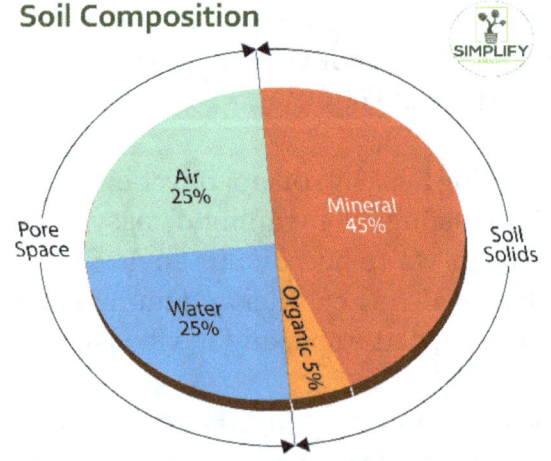

A generalized organic and inorganic mix ratio is 45% minerals, 25% air, 25% water, and 5% organic matter within the top 18 inches. Our consideration of the above ratios is because compost has an almost magical balancing effect for all the above.

Compost aerates clay for improved soil textures, accommodating air and aerobic microorganisms; improves sand's water-holding ability and increases its organic matter; compost manages water and air content for optimal organic activity in silt. Compost is a wonder product that brings soil biology to environments that would otherwise be mostly sterile. Compost's further benefits for mineral soil are the reduction of erosion susceptibility, increased cation-exchange capacity, pH buffering capabilities, and improved soil tilth.

---

9   https://www.agriculture.senate.gov/hearings/the-state-of-nutrition-in-america-2021

Reduced Erosion Susceptibility

Soil is a three-part open system with solids, liquids, and gasses with strong interaction between the parts. Primary soil particles, particularly silt and sand, would be prone to erosion if they were not cemented together in groupings called aggregates. The shape and strength of the aggregates influence pore size and distribution and water and gas holding capacities. However, the binding matter used by bacteria, fungi, and actinomycetes has built-in channels, ensuring continued porosity for air movement and moisture management.

Cation-Exchange Capacity (CEC)

Cation-exchange capacity (CEC) is a fundamental soil property, influencing nutrient availability, soil structure stability, reaction to fertilizers and other ameliorants, and soil pH. It's an indicator of the soil's ability to hold positively charged ions.

Opposites attract, at least it's true in electric and magnetic fields. Like magnets, negatively charged soil particles attract positively charged molecules. These molecules could be water, soil amendments, and nutrients. This attraction due to positive or negative charges is called the cation-exchange capacity (CEC). Suppose the soil's CEC value is low. Few molecules are attracted to the soil particle's surface, and the particles cannot hold on to water and nutrients. The opposite is true – good attraction, good chemistry.

For now, with some writers' creative liberty, we can generalize and throw out the following general guidelines. When you have your soil analyzed (tested), the report will have your CEC value listed. Sand has the lowest (about 10) CEC, and clay has the highest (25). However, adding organic matter will boost the CEC to 100 – the best possible score. The electrical activity in leaf mold, for instance, is so high it can power a small gadget – high CEC.

The high CEC in clay keeps water from draining. Conversely, the low CEC in the sand allows water to run through at a rate of 20 inches per hour. Plants need access to water and nutrition, something that organic matter makes possible by boosting the cation-exchange capacity. It's a multi-level system of boosting microorganisms and CEC to better plant health by adding compost.

Buffersalt Effect – pH Buffering

It doesn't matter if your soil is acidic or alkaline; compost can effectively correct the pH. The microorganisms' ability to influence pH is responsible for this buffering effect. Acidity levels are reliable indicators of soil health. Acidity directly impacts the yields of crops, their suitability, the availability of plant nutrients, and the activity of microorganisms in the soil.

Climate, mineral content, and soil texture are factors that cannot be altered. The soil's pH results from the interactions between parent material, time, relief or topography, climate, and organisms. Minerals in the soil's parent material determine the pH of newly formed soils. Soil mineral weathering is controlled by temperature and rainfall. A process known as soil acidification occurs in warm, wet environments due to the leaching of rainwater into the soil. Due to less intense soil weathering and leaching in dry climates, pH can be neutral to alkaline.

Clay and organic matter-rich soils are better able to withstand changes in pH (buffering capacity) than sandy soils. Although clay content cannot be altered, organic matter content can be changed through management. Low organic matter content in sandy soils results in high water throughput, making them more susceptible to acidification than other soils. The addition of compost to any soil will positively affect the soil's health, including the pH.

Compost and Improved Soil Tilth

Tilth is a term used to describe how the soil structure affects plant growth. Soil with healthy tilth has excellent drainage and water-holding capacity, making it ideal for plant growth and easy for gardeners to work. Also, bulk density, the weight per soil volume, is related to a tilth. Low-density soils have greater porosity and tilth than higher-density ones. Roots will penetrate and grow through well-aerated and evenly distributed large and small pores in soils with ample pore space and even distribution of large and small pores. The larger pores are protected from clogging by loose particles thanks to the high aggregate stability.

Soil tilth is a central soil-health indicator called friability or mellowness. When walked on, mellow soil will crumble and give a little. Soil with a healthy tilth is very easy to cultivate. On the other hand, ground with poor tilth can feel heavy, compacted, or overly sandy. Soil tilth is an essential indicator of soil health.

Gardeners often talk about tilth, friability, and mellowness as hard to define with precision since they are so location specific. However, gardeners (and farmers) agree that working with soil with healthy tilth is a delight that is hard to describe until you work with soil without these characteristics.

Healthy tilth has the following characteristics:

- The soil has suitable aggregates, soil particles (i.e. sand, silt, and clay) held together in a single mass or cluster. Stable soil aggregates are a product of the binding action of compost (humus, soil organic matter, the activity of microorganisms) and the growth of plant roots in the soil. Natural aggregates are called peds. Clods are a product of tillage when underground soil biota activity is disturbed.
- Aggregate stability is the ability of natural aggregates to resist breaking apart. Aggregate destruction is mainly caused by tillage but can also be caused by water action. Soil is said to have poor aggregate stability if individual aggregates readily break apart.
- Soil consistency refers to the ease with which the fingers can crush a lump.

Soil tilth and structure are directly impacted by how you manage your soil. Regular assessment of your soil's health will help you identify whether your current management practices promote or impede the free movement of water and air through the ground. The size of your earthworm population is a good indicator of healthy soil biota. It is important to note that rainfall is the most significant soil compacter. Adding compost to your soil and using it as a mulch is the quickest route to a healthy tilth. Avoid working with soil that is too wet, as this destroys aggregates.

Soil Health

Listed below are the ten most essential indicators of healthy soil. You will notice that compost plays the lead role in all ten vital soil-health building elements. State extension programs, supported by USDA, have standardized soil quality assessments that use the list below as indicators.

Surface Cover

Surface cover plays a vital role in minimizing weeds, preventing soil compaction due to rain, and further strengthening the soil microorganism population. Following a *See-no-Soil* policy is the productive way towards healthier soil. Surface cover can either be a mulch or green compost (legumes as a growing ground cover). The role of compost is evident.

Soil Structure

Soil structure is a factor of aggregates, tilth, and surface penetrability. The absence of hard-to-break clods indicates a healthy soil structure. Health soil forms a ball in your hand that readily breaks when poked. Also, consider the level of crusting on the soil surface – it should not prevent quick water absorption. Compost is essential for improving the quality and capacity of your soil. Better put, microorganisms are essential for sustainable, healthy, nutritious gardening.

Organic Matter

Humus is the color of dark chocolate – not black nor caramel. Soil with a healthy portion of organic matter (at least 5% of the total dry matter weight) is dark brown. The adjustment of your soil to reflect an abundant presence of organic matter may take a couple of seasons but being forewarned allows you to work towards that goal.

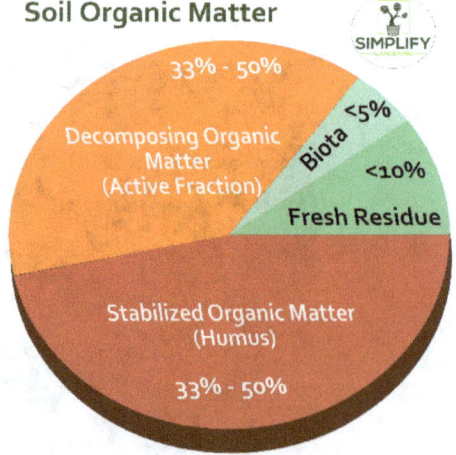

Both agriculturists and archeologists use the Munsell soil color charts as a comparative color guide. Depending on the color of the soil in each area, the land's suitability for various purposes, such as wetlands, the best crops to plant, the viability of wastewater systems, and other uses, can be determined. The charts are adjusted to both dry and wet soil colors.

The percentage of decomposed plant and animal matter is called organic matter, and it is expressed as a percentage of the soil material that is less than 0.08 inches (2mm) wide. As organic matter, such as manure, straw, or plant residue from a previous harvest decompose, it adds organic matter to the soil. When decay is active, organic matter will be in various stages of decomposition, from identifiable plant parts to individual plant fibers to dark chocolate brown humus.

Plant residue is decomposed by soil organisms and recycled in various ways that benefit the soil. Microbial activity accounts for the vast majority of soil decomposition, and soil microorganisms like bacteria and fungi benefit from breaking down the organic residue by larger soil organisms. Plant residue decomposition is a good indicator of the health of the soil's microbial community. The absence of a visible residue indicates that low residues were produced and returned to the earth. But an excessive amount of residue means soil organisms cannot break down the material. The more significant parts of the decomposition process are preferred because they contribute to the soil's tilth and structure. In contrast, soil microorganisms feed on smaller pieces.

Organic matter is essential to soil quality because it increases the soil cation-exchange capacity (the ability to attract and hold vital nutrients and moisture). Microorganisms' activities in organic matter provide the glue to bind soil particles into aggregates improving water infiltration, soil structure, and tilth. Organic matter is a food source for a diverse population of soil biota (the ecosystem of living organisms in soil). The soil biota promotes air and water movement within the ground and nutrient recycling. Organic material (and the surrounding soil biota) is the primary nitrogen and sulfur source (and supplies a significant part of the phosphorous requirements) for crops.

Soil Erosion
The start of soil erosion is evidenced by the formation of minor rivulets, called rills. Rills form when surface runoff's shear stress exceeds the soil's shear strength, limiting the soil's ability to resist forces acting across the surface. Water breaks up soil particles and carries them down the slope, causing the erosion process to begin.

Surface cover using mulch or cover crops are adequate preventers of erosion. Erosion can only occur if water can sufficiently accumulate on the surface to start flowing. The soil's water infiltration properties improve the rapid absorption of rain, again a product of compost addition. Roadside surface management technologies have vastly contributed to improved erosion control. Road construction often requires the travel surfaces to be lower than the surrounding landscape, leaving roadside slopes that require careful erosion management. Their research has shown that planting indigenous grass on composted surfaces is the quickest way to stabilize and strengthen soil's shear strength.

Soil Compaction

Sometimes life requires us to reach deep into our inner reserves for endurance, stamina, forgiveness, and resilience. Plants, too, need to go deep into the soil to be more drought resilient. Deep roots give the plant access to a broader spectrum of nutrients and better bind the ground for improved erosion prevention. Subsurface compaction limits the roots to the top few inches of soil in plants, leading to early seedling mortality. Soil compaction is measured in bulk density – the mass per volume ratio. Soil that has a higher bulk density is more densely packed. As the pore space in the soil is reduced, the weight of a given volume of soil increases. The soil's density values can predict plant root depth. Soil strength and loss of macro-porosity are just as crucial as bulk density.

The soil's tensile strength can be gauged using the flag test. Roots are most restricted by compaction when the soil is dry. Because of the compacted subsurface layers, less space is available for root development, air availability, and water penetration.

The solution is increased soil organic matter and soil biota (i.e. compost) – no surprise there. Increased soil organic matter can also be achieved by incorporating deep-root cover crops. During a regular freezing and thawing cycle, compacted soil fractures. Therefore, breaking compaction up is best done in early spring by adding compost to the affected area. Irrigate the site to allow soil biota to penetrate deeper into the freshly fractured subsurface compacted layers. Their presence will heal the ground, balance pH, develop aggregates and improve porosity.

Some compaction tests include using a section of wire. If using only your hands, you cannot push the wire into the ground for at least 18 inches after a good rainfall; you need to take the remedial steps detailed in the above paragraph.

Water Infiltration, Drainage, and Holding Capacity

After heavy rain, water infiltrates into the soil, causing it to become saturated. The porosity of the ground is an essential factor in water infiltration. Soil water movement and retention are determined by pores' number, length, and diameter. The majority of soil flow is caused by large pores (diameter greater than 1/16 inch). When it comes to water infiltration, texture and slope play a role. Sandy soils tend to be more efficient than siltier or clayey soils. Generally speaking, water drains more quickly from higher points in the landscape. Water infiltration is governed mainly by the structure of the ground. The clay particles that clog pores are caused by unstable soil aggregates disintegrate and dissolve in water. When soil is compacted, water cannot reach deeper subsoil layers, where it can be stored for use by plants.

Soil permeability refers to the ability of water or air to pass through the soil. Pore size, shape, and density are factors in determining how porous a given soil is. Soil surveys have traditionally referred to saturated hydraulic conductivity as permeability.

Available water refers to soil water accessed by plant roots and extracted from soil pores. This water resists evaporation and percolation due to suction forces within soil pores (CEC). Still, it is not so tightly held that roots cannot absorb it. The amount of water available to plants is known as the Available Water Capacity (AWC).

Soil organic matter content can be improved, but soil texture still plays a significant role in water holding capacity. By adding compost to the soil, soil water availability can be enhanced by reducing compaction and increasing the cation-exchange capacity (CEC). Any management strategy to raise infiltration and increase soil water storage by increasing the stability and number of fine aggregates is likely to be successful – a function of compost.

Soil Biodiversity

In the next section, we delve into the different organisms in the soil biota – just an introduction. An indicator of active soil biota is the presence of earthworms.

An abundance of life can thrive in the soil's complex ecosystem. Soil contains a wide variety of organisms. Organic residue degradation and nutrient cycling in soil are made possible by various soil life forms. The ground may include a wide variety of organisms. If this is the case, plant growth will have a better chance of accessing nutrients. Pests and diseases can be suppressed by the diversity and abundance of soil organisms. Earthworms are vital as a 'keystone' participant in the soil food web.

The soil is home to a variety of earthworm species. Deep burrows are made by some species, while others make shallow holes. Large amounts of organic and mineral soil are ingested and excreted as casts on the soil surface in some burrowing forms. More plant nutrients are available in casts of earthworms than in the surrounding soil. The passageways created by the movement of earthworms through the ground improve aeration and water infiltration and lubricate soil particles. Their excrement aids in the stability of aggregates. In no-till systems, the soil mixing that earthworms provide is essential for nutrient cycling and the decomposition of organic matter.

Gardeners have a direct impact on soil microbial populations. Diversity and abundance of soil life may be improved by using crop residues or cover crops. Conversely, larger species are culled by the indiscriminate use of pesticides in the simazine, triazine, and carbamate groups. Anhydrous ammonia fertilizers also negatively affect soil biota. Tillage is necessary to incorporate organic residues, but soil organisms' habitats can be disrupted due to tilling. Earthworm populations can be harmed if surface residue, which provides food and protection, is removed.

Soil biodiversity is a direct product of compost and mulching. Sometimes it's the small things that matter. In gardening, it's the creatures so small they're invisible to the naked eye – microorganisms. Composting is the fastest, cheapest, most effective microorganisms farming method. Farming and introducing microorganisms into your soil is the best possible soil health improvement measure you could take.

Plant and Root Growth

The health of individual plants in the field is a good indicator of plant vigor. Plant vigor is indicated by the uniformity of growth displayed by all crop plants in a given lot. Healthy soil increases germination rates, reduces seedling mortalities, ensures uniformity in development, and is the basis for better yields. The root system is essential to the plant's growth and development.

While photosynthesis is an essential part of a plant's food conversion process, building blocks are absorbed via the roots in the form of inorganic ions. The roots of healthy plants can be as extensive as the plant's above-ground growth. For that to be possible, soil structure and vitality are essential. Root system development can be hindered by compacted subsoil layers that reduce the effective root zone. The system is paradoxically both robust and delicate. The robustness of soil is a factor in the microorganism population's diversity. The system cannot control the proliferation of harmful bacteria, fungi, and nematodes without variety. Good soil structure is linked to a diverse range of soil organisms.

While healthy plants indicate healthy soil, unhealthy plants can result from poor care (late planting, insufficient irrigation or rainfall, etc.). It's critical to determine if the disease problem is linked to soil quality, remembering that poor drainage may contribute to root-borne diseases. A healthy soil structure improves healthy root growth, and compacted soil inhibits healthy root growth. Healthy roots are an indication of a plant's overall health and vitality.

Healthy Soil's Response to pH

Acidity and alkalinity are indicated in pH, a scale between 0 and 14. The scale is logarithmic, meaning that pH 5.0 is ten times more acid than soil with a pH reading of 6.0. A pH of 7.0 is neutral, zero most acidic, and 14 is purely alkaline. pH has a significant impact on plant nutrition, directly affecting plant growth.

Plant nutrient release by weathering, soil solubility, and cation-exchange capacity (CEC) are all influenced by the pH of a soil's environment. As a result, the pH level is an excellent indicator of plant nutrient deficiencies. At pH values between 5.8 and 7.5, the availability of all plant nutrients is generally adequate. Neutral and alkaline soils have pH values between 6.66 and 7.33, while acidic soils have values below 6.66. The primary benefit of soil pH is its information about the soil's other properties. CEC values, nutrient availability, and the release of toxic aluminum are all associated with pH.

Adding lime to acidic soils is a quick and straightforward way to raise the pH – typically, dolomitic limestone is used. The pH of the top inch or two of a field that isn't tillage-intensive needs to be closely monitored because it can change very quickly. Most crops prefer a pH of 5.8 to 6.5, and inactivation of some herbicides can occur at a pH lower than 5.8. Toxicity to plants can be caused by the release of aluminum and manganese at acidities of 5.2.

Acidity (or alkalinity) can be reduced by organic matter. Organic matter decomposes into humus, which has molecules that can absorb or release hydrogen ions depending on the surrounding soil's pH. As a result, this buffering effect keeps the soil's pH stable. Organic matter also decomposes and competes for aluminum ions (Al^+) in solution, reducing its toxicity to plants.

Nutrient Holding Capacity of Healthy Soil

Gardener's view nutrient holding capacity as a process in which the soil acts as both a sink and a source of nutrients. Essential considerations for gardeners and farmers are the storage capacity, the rate of release, and the ability of the soil to replenish itself and provide nutrients to subsequent crops.

Cation-Exchange Capacity (CEC) is the ability to hold, retain, and exchange positively charged ionic nutrients. CEC refers to the net surface charge of soil materials that enables them to hold and retain charged nutrient forms against leaching. While both negative and positive charges are present, negative charges usually dominate.

Increasing the pH of the soil solution or adding compost increases the CEC. Examples of positively charged (cations) are:

- Potassium (K^+)
- Ammonium (NH_4^+)
- Calcium (Ca^{2+})
- Magnesium (Mg^{2+})
- Aluminum (Al^{3+})

Negatively charged ions (anions) are not attracted to negative surface charges and thus are more subject to leaching. Examples include:

- Nitrate (NO_3^-)
- Chloride (Cl^-)
- Sulfate (SO_4^-)
- Phosphate ($H2PO_4^-$)

Phosphate and sulfate are not leached as readily as nitrate, particularly in soils with iron-coated clays. Phosphate is also less mobile in soils because it is not soluble and binds readily with clays. Factors critical to nutrient holding capacity are pH, amount and kind of organic matter, soil texture, and clay type.

Soil test results will help predict whether the soil will provide nutrients fast enough to meet the crop's future needs. Currently, soil tests are reliable for P, K, and Mg. While soils can be tested for other nutrients, interpretations are less reliable. Soil tests can be valuable over the long run as they can show which soils are building nutrient levels and which ones are dropping.

Applications of high levels of fertilizers can skew test results. While heavy fertilization can lead to short-term increased productivity, it can also lead to leaching and nutrient loss. This approach also does little to improve other aspects of the soil, such as tilth or infiltration. Nutrient holding capacity is best enhanced by increasing soil organic matter, which serves as both a sink and a source for plant nutrients. Organic matter also extends the release of nutrients over a longer period.

Soil Amendments

Soil additives are used to improve the health and condition of the soil. Incorporating organic matter, for example, into tight clay reduces soil bulk density, generates pore spaces for air and water, and improves soil structure and tilth, allowing roots to expand. Adding organic matter to sandy soil increases water and nutrient retention, feeds soil bacteria, and improves soil structure.

Warmer temperatures accelerate decomposition, and soils may require up to twice as much organic material as colder environments. It is a good idea to mulch regions after adding organic materials. Mulch is a substance laid on the soil to prevent evaporation and keep roots cool. Mulch also helps to prevent weed growth, soil compaction, and erosion. In the case of plant-based mulches, the addition of mulch increases the organic matter content of the soil.

Effective soil amendments include:

- Aerobic Compost
- Leaf Mold
- Vermicompost
- Organic Fertilizers

The Aerobic Composting Process

As a general rule, temperatures below 50°F are considered psychrophilic. In a mesophilic environment, the transitional temperature ranges from 50°F to 105°F. At 105°F and above, the thermophilic organisms thrive. Organisms are not definition bound and may thrive in a pile during the mesophilic, psychrophilic, and thermophilic phases. These ranges represent how certain microorganisms reach their maximum growth and productivity.

As the microbial population grows and diversifies, the temperature rises steadily through the psychrophilic and mesophilic temperature ranges. As they degrade highly available degradable material, heat is rapidly generated by microbial activity and their population expansion. The temperature of the compost pile builds up from the self-insulted center.

The thermophilic stage typically takes two to three days to reach its peak in the compost pile, depending on several factors. With temperatures in the thermophilic zone, the pile becomes populated by microbes at their most efficient and productive levels. Pathogens, fly larvae, and weed seeds are destroyed by the high levels of microbial activity and high temperatures.

Because of the microorganism diversity, complex and decay-resistant materials, such as cellulose and lignins, are more quickly and efficiently. Temperature can quickly reach temperatures of 130°F and 160°F. As available degradable material and oxygen decrease, so does the microbial activity.

At high temperatures, enzymes responsible for the breakdown of the material denature and become ineffective, preventing microorganisms from obtaining the nutrition they need to survive. Even though some organisms may withstand high temperatures, they may be less efficient and active. Another way that microorganisms respond to heat stress is by producing spores. Some microorganisms take the inactive form of spores to protect themselves from conditions detrimental to their survival, such as heat and dehydration. Once more favorable conditions are present, the spores begin to germinate.

As microbial activity decreases, the pile starts cooling. Different microorganisms return to the pile as the temperature cools from thermophilic levels, and spores germinate as the conditions become more favorable for survival, further aiding decomposition. The compost pile can remain in the thermophilic range for 10 to 60 days, depending on the operation.

Curing or reactivation of active composting can begin once temperatures fall below 105°F. There is no fixed point at which active composting is considered finished. Still, continuous cycles of reheating with lower peaks indicate that the pile is stabilizing. When the pile conditions are such that microbial activity cannot rise high enough to reheat the pile, it is considered finished.

Curing is an essential part of the composting process, even though microbial activity is lower and most organic material has already been degraded. A lower level of microbial activity characterizes curing, which stabilizes the products of active composting. It includes the further decomposition of organic acids and decay-resistant substances, humic compounds and nitrate-nitrogen formation, and stabilization. Some fungi can begin to grow in a batch during curing and help improve the compost's disease-fighting properties.

When pile temperatures remain low due to the decreased microbial activity and lower levels of heat generation, proper moisture and oxygen management are still necessary during the curing period to maintain microbial activity. During the curing process, it's essential to ensure that the batch isn't contaminated with weed seeds. Curing can be a time-consuming process, and a more extended curing period is needed if the compost is used for sensitive purposes like planting media. As soon as the pile cools down to room temperature, it's considered to have finished curing. Beware, those constant temperatures can also indicate a lack of oxygen or moisture.

Check out my Composting Masterclass for more information on creating effective compost.

Making Leaf Mold

There are many ways to manage leaves in the fall. You could mulch them with a mulching mower, collect them with a mower, blow or rake them into heaps, or use a vac-blower to shred and collect and store them for later use. Whatever way you choose, they're a fabulous resource.

Leaves are the tree's primary energy converters and heat regulators. Perennial trees shed their leaves annually. Shed leaves consist mainly of cellulose and lignin, and leaves with high lignin levels are slow to decompose.

Because leaves are high in cellulose and lignin, they are resistant to bacteria breakdown. Fungi do initial decomposition with bacteria taking over later in the process. This section reviews how straightforward it is to improve your soil with leaves often discarded without a second thought.

Like with all composting processes, there are five essential ingredients:

- **Carbon** for the microorganisms.
- **Nitrogen** for the microorganisms.
- **Water** to increase the mobility of microorganisms and act as an energy supply line. Water also helps regulate temperatures and provides fungi with oxygen and hydrogen.
- **Oxygen** to help with the oxidation process of the carbon-releasing CO2.
- **Heat** speeds up the process. Much of the heat is self-generated, and our role is merely to help prevent that generated heat from escaping. A study done by MIT showed a direct correlation between ambient temperature and decomposition rates.

Have you ever seen a fantasy ice castle – like the ones they put up on ice rinks? They're able to do that by minimizing the exposed area of the ice. If you took a BIG block of ice and waited for it to melt, it would take ages. If you took that same massive block of ice and broke it down into tiny pieces, the melting process will be accelerated. The ice block's surface area has increased and is now exposed to ambient temperature, causing the ice to melt faster.

The same applies to composting – the more surface area exposed, the more area upon which microorganisms can act, the faster the decomposition. Because the construction of leaves has evolved to balance weight and efficient light exposure, leaves are generally flat. Their flat shape creates a mat of leaves stuck to each other when wet. The flat structure also makes flight possible in windy conditions – similar to a butterfly wing.

It's therefore a good idea to shred the leaves before adding them to your compost pile. I shred my leaves four times before they are fine enough. You can use various methods to shred leaves, but here are three suggestions.

- Run over them with a lawnmower with a catch-bag – you might need to repeat the process a couple of times. You will see how fast ten bags of leaves can be reduced in volume to fit into a single bag.
- Vacuum them up with a blower-vac. A couple of years ago, while using this method, the static caused by the dry leaves created a conduit for a spark between the motor and my bare arm, and it wasn't fun. Lesson learned: always wear appropriate protective gear.
- Put them through a shredder. Personally, I think it's worth the investment.

You'll need the following to create leaf mold:
- Lots and lots of shredded leaves – enough to create a pile of no less than a 3-foot cube. A cubic yard of shredded leaves is about 40 garbage bags of leaves.
- Some* moist soil taken from a wooded area.
- Some* horse manure – good but not essential.
- Some urine mixed with water – urine is rich in uric acid – a rich form of nitrogen. Ideally, you'll make a 4-gallon mix, which I will explain below.
- A bin that can hold a cubic yard of leaves. Take a look at my video on making leaf mold and see what I did. Alternatively, use a 1-ton bulk bag. They're great for collecting leaves and as a holding unit for leaf mold/compost production.
- A couple of sheets of wet newspaper.

*The *some* referred to above is about a heaped spade full – or half a 4-gallon plastic shopping bag.

Making a nitrogen-rich wetting agent
To make a wetting agent loaded with nitrogen and microorganisms, you will need:

- A cotton bag or a commercial horticultural compost tea bag
- 5 cups of horse manure
- 5 cups of nutrient-rich soil from a wooded area
- A 2-gallon bucket filled with water and topped up with 2 cups of urine

Place the horse manure and soil in the compost tea bag and soak in the water/urine mix for 48 hours. If you have an air pump (like those used in fish tanks), pumping air into the mixture will speed up the diffusion and proliferation of microorganisms in the solution.

The end product is a solution loaded with nitrogen and microorganisms that radically speed decomposition.

Making leaf mold practical
- Start with a 6-inch layer of shredded leaves.
- Drizzle the layer with the urine mixture – wetting enough that a single drop can be squeezed out. Remember that the shredded leaves are electrostatically charged and hydrophobic, repelling water. Even though spraying the pile may seem to wet it, the layers beneath will still be dry. You will need to ensure all the layers are wet by agitating the pile and ensuring the WHOLE batch is moist.

- Spread a thin layer of horse manure/soil mixture.
- Cover with a wet sheet of newspaper.
- Repeat the previous steps until all the shredded leaves are used up.
- End with a layer of shredded damp leaves. Use a board or rake to compress the pile.

If you have an old rug, covering your pile will help it retain heat and speed the composting process up considerably. It could even reduce the time down to six months! That is 25% of what it usually would take (24 months).

What leaves are best for composting?

Leaves with a low lignin content are ideal for making leaf compost. Plant matter such as needles, which contain a lot of lignin (a vital building block), has a narrower decay rate than leafier plants, which have less lignin and more nutrients that attract microbes. Lignin protects organic compounds from degradation by acting as a shield.

Lignon-reduced leaves (with higher calcium and nitrogen levels) include ash, cherry, elm, linden, and maple. In six months, these leaves will be completely decomposed.

Beech, birch, oak, hornbeam, magnolia, holly, and sweet chestnut are unsuitable leaves because they are high in lignin and low in nitrogen. A typical two-year breakdown period is required. Trees like oaks, beech, and sycamore with thick leaves that stick around for a long time have high lignin levels and might leach nitrogen out the soil before giving any back.

How long does it take for leaves to compost?

Leaves vary in their decomposition times. The Long-term Intersite Decomposition Experiment Team (LIDET) study collected leaf litter from 27 North and Central America locations, from the Alaskan tundra to Panamanian rainforests. The research showed that leaves in warm and wet regions decomposed faster than those in cold and dry areas. Leaf-type was also a determinant – with needles (high-lignin) deteriorated much slower than leaves with low levels of lignin.

In nature, leaves take about two years to decompose. As discussed above, decomposition can be reduced to six months in controlled environments.

Do leaves compost quicker if shredded?

Leaves are decomposed by the activities of microorganisms – mainly fungi. Because these organisms are tiny, and their action is on the material's surface, maximizing the surface area maximizes their activity.

Consider a loaf of bread. The loaf has six surface areas – two ends, a top and a bottom, and two sides. Cutting six slices, increases the surface areas by 6 x 6 = 36 surface areas. The unsliced loaf will take a while to dry out (or grow mold), but the slices will dry out faster. Repeating the cutting process will increase the exposed surfaces exponentially.

Similarly, shredding your leaves increases the exposed surface area, thus increasing the fungi's activity on the leaves. Shredding and wetting your leaves can halve or even quarter the time required to make leaf mold – and it improves the quality of the end product.

Another handy way to speed up leaf composting is to create a wetting agent made from beer. By mixing a medium bottle of beer, a can of sugar-containing soda, and half a cup of ammonia with 2 gallons of water, you have an effective composting kick-starter.

What leaves should not be composted?

The general rule of thumb, non-scientific approach, is to stick to composting thinner leaves. The following is a list of trees and shrubs that have thicker leaves and are higher in lignin content:

- Birch
- Oak
- Hornbeam
- Sweet chestnut
- Magnolia
- Holly
- Sycamore
- Eucalyptus
- Beech (to a lesser extent)
- Black walnut

These leaves have high lignin content and might leach nitrogen out of your soil before giving any back when added. Black walnut also contains juglone, a natural fungicide that will stall your leaf-molding efforts. While lignin is strongly associated with retarded leaf decomposition rates, the leaves' C:N ratio has also been researched and may hold a more vital link to their slow decomposition. Either way, thicker leaves, even in accelerated environments, decompose slower.

What equipment do I need to make leaf compost?

Leaf Shredder
Some ways of shredding leaves are gathering them in low piles, going over them with a mower, or vacuuming them with a blower/vac shredder. Alternatively, you can get a leaf shredder. The benefit of a leaf shredder is that it will reduce effort and the volume of leaves. An electric shredder allows you to produce one bag of shredded leaves from several bags of leaves.

An advantage is that shredded leaves compost so much faster. I shred my leaves fine, and an electric shredder allows you to choose between coarse, medium, and fine shredding. Since most electric shredders come with a stand, you can fit a catchment bag to collect the shredded leaves.

You can also use the same shredder to shred paper, a handy additive to the composting processes.

Tarps
A tarp is a handy gardener's tool. You can use it to gather leaves rapidly, cover your compost pile to retain heat, and much more.

1-Ton Bulk Bag
A 1-ton bulk bag is another excellent investment I found helpful in cultivating leaf mold. The size is ideal – 35 x 35 inches square and 43 inches deep, and they are airtight and will prevent the compost from losing heat. Woven polypropylene bags are also handy for collecting leaves.

Leaf Scoops
I use scoops that fit my hands, converting them into big plastic shovels. Once you've raked your leaves into piles, use these to scoop the leaves into one of your 1-ton bags – ready for shredding.

Rake
It is easier to rake damp leaves than dry leaves, and it is much easier if you have a 30-inch broad leaf rake that is light to use. Rake in the direction of the wind to make it easier. Create multiple piles that you can gather with your hand scoops.

Watering Can
While I usually use a hose to wet my compost heaps, for my leaf compost/mold, I use one of the above wetting regimes. To spread the compost tea evenly, I like using a watering can.

Compost Tea Bags
A compost tea bag allows you to create compost tea without clogging your watering can's sprinkler. The instructions for how to do this are shared above.

How to use leaf compost
Leaf mold is a gold mine for gardeners, and it has a high mineral content and can grow plants naturally without additional fertilizer. Contrary to popular belief, leaf mold is beneficial to your lawn. Leaves are the product of the tree roots extracting minerals deep underground and transporting them to the leaves, loading them with many valuable trace minerals.

Leaf mold is one of the best soil conditioners you'll ever use, despite the negative connotations associated with 'mold.' A single leaf mold spore can hold five times its weight in water, and that's on par with peat moss, if not better. Because of this, leaf mold is an excellent mulch to use around the garden. Soil structure and texture are greatly improved when organic matter is added to sandy or clay soils.

Microbes and other beneficial organisms, such as earthworms, thrive in leaf mold environments. As a result, your garden's soil will be vibrant and alive. There's also the fact that it's free! Don't let the lack of leaves in your yard stop you from participating. People are always willing to let you drop off bags of leaves or let you rake some for them. Find out by talking to your friends and family! If you don't like cleaning up after the leaves in the fall, make friends with them.

It can be used as a mulch, a soil amendment, in containers and raised beds in place of peat moss, and in your compost bin as brown matter.

As a soil amendment, I turn leaf mold into the soil to a spade depth (about 8 to 11 inches). I also use between 2 and 3 inches of mulch around plants, careful not to mulch up to the plant's stem or base. Because leaf mold is so hygroscopic, the continuous moisture on the stem can provide an opportunity for diseases.

Vermicomposting

Vermicomposting is a highly effective bio-oxidative process that involves earthworms and microorganisms working together to break organic matter down into a potent soil amendment. While I've seen operations that produce tons of worm castings, we'll focus on residential operations. Essentially, the size of your vermicomposting operation depends on available space, the amount of worm food you have available, and the time you want to spend farming worms and collecting their castings.

Vermicomposting is a non-thermophilic biological oxidation process where select earthworm species, preferably *Eisenia fetida* (red wrigglers), enhance the conversion of organic waste to compost. Earthworms help influence the growth of specific microbial species that improve the soil's physical and chemical properties. The microbial population present in vermicompost plays an essential role in increasing crop productivity and maintaining the soil's structural stability.

Vermicompost highlights:

- There are approximately 9,000 earthworm species, of which seven, to varying degrees, are suitable for vermicomposting.
- Vermicomposting requires high feeders. Earthworms in your garden are unsuitable for vermicomposting; use red worms (*Eisenia fetida* and *E. Andrei*) instead.
- Worms are most active in moist environments at temperatures between 55^0F and 85^0F. Their living quarters must be dark and have enough air. Worms try to escape unsuitable environments.
- Earthworms are hermaphrodites, but two worms are required for reproduction, exchanging sperm as they lay alongside each other. Both get covered in the

process.
- Conditions permitting, your worm population can double every two months.
- Cocoons take four to six weeks to emerge, and the two to five worms from each cocoon take six to eight weeks to mature. Cocoons take longer to release the worms in colder conditions.
- Worms require some sand grains to strengthen their consumption capacities.
- Generally, vermicompost is equivalent to a 3:3:3 fertilizer with higher nitrate (NO_3^-).
- It is rich in microorganisms, as worms use bacteria in their gut to process food.
- A carbon-rich diet will increase fungi populations for regions that require better water retention.
- Worm castings are rich in enzymes.
- Worm mucus helps soil particles form aggregates.
- Improves root penetration, water usage, nutrient availability as a product of improved soil structure.
- Desirable microorganisms thrive, increasing resilience against pests and diseases.
- Earthworms feed on decaying organic matter and microorganisms, like nematodes. Underground they eat bacteria, algae, fungi, and nematodes, releasing the minerals consumed by these microorganisms into the soil.
- In worm bins, they consume kitchen waste and limited yard waste.
- Avoid
  - Animal products and by-products (cheese, yogurt, etcetera)
  - Some citrus fruits (orange peels and pineapples)
  - Glossy paper
  - Onions and garlic
  - Salt
  - Oily substances
- Advisable worm food for your worm farm
  - Fruits and vegetable scraps
  - Coffee grounds and filters (snip filters into smaller parts)
  - Grains – bread, crackers, cereals, even if they're moldy or stale
  - Leaves
  - Eggshells
  - Paper products, shredded cardboard
  - Grass clippings if not treated with pesticides in particular, but herbicides too.

- Worms live for about one year, and because their bodies are 90% water, their dead bodies dry up and become part of the compost. The cycle of life and death is seamless and unnoticeable, with populations remaining in balance with their environment.
- Approximately 800–1,000 mature worms (or 1 pound) can consume about half a pound of organic material each day.
- Bins can be customized depending on the volume of food scraps used to manufacture the castings.
- Useable castings take approximately three to four months to produce, depending on the bin size.

How to use worm castings in your garden

Worm castings are a slow-release nitrogen-rich fertilizer balanced with other essential minerals – generally equivalent to 3:3:3 NKP. You can safely spread it around potted plants, vegetables, and flowing plants. If you sift it finely, adding it to your lawn would replace your usual nitrogen needs. You can also incorporate it into the soil around shrubs and trees.

It's up to you whether you want to use your compost right away, store it for the gardening season, or use it at any time. Vermicompost can be added directly to potting soil or garden soil as a soil amendment, making nutrients more accessible to plants. It's possible to top dress your indoor or outdoor plants with the compost. You can also create a nutrient-loaded compost tea by straining the vermicompost in an aerated water tank for 24 hours. Don't confuse the leachate from the bottom of a poorly managed bin with composting tea. The leachate is loaded with nitrogen and should always be diluted and used with care. I advise that you test it on a single plant, review the reaction over a couple of days, and proceed if safe. Use leachate with caution, as it risks poisoning your plants.

Compost Teas

Artificial applications of the primary nutrients (nitrogen, phosphorous, and potassium) have long been promoted as the de facto route to crop yield increases. Billion-dollar marketing campaigns support the use of synthetic fertilizers, pesticides, herbicides, and fumigants. At ground level, though, the nutritional level of fresh produce is dropping.

Farmers find that input costs and volumes are escalating year on year, with diminishing yields. Increasingly farmers are turning to the sciences for solutions. Finally, the emergent appreciation of the role of soil biology in agriculture is affording the sector a turn-around strategy. The notable successes of grand-scale farmers as they move towards more sustainable practices have sparked investment for further research of the role of soil biota in crop production.

As the familiarity with the benefits of composting expands, extending its application is fast becoming the next generalist frontier. A growing number of gardeners are turning to water solutions of compost as a more natural method of boosting their plants' resilience, health, and productivity. Compost is the primary host of an assortment of microorganisms, enzymes, and minerals, and it can significantly benefit the soil.

Pesticides, herbicides, and fumigants are increasingly recognized as counter-productive, killing a range of beneficial microorganisms, and their application kills both the bad and the good. In the absence of beneficial microorganisms, the soil biota cannot increase water retention, stabilize pH, fight pathogens, and improve cation. While the general application of compost has enormous benefits, the specific needs of the soil (and plants) could be addressed if the broad diversity of microorganisms and pathogens were known.

While most gardeners are happy with the benefits compost provides the soil, studies show that those benefits can be extended to the rest of the plant. Aerobic microorganisms, primarily bacteria, fungi, nematodes, and protozoa, can be hosted in water for short periods – if the water is well aerated and agitated. In addition, the populations of either bacteria or fungi can be boosted through feeding regimes, depending on the application need. The water in which these microorganisms are hosted is actively aerated compost tea (AACT).

Healthy compost produces healthy AACT. Healthy AACT extends the benefits of compost:

- Beneficial microorganisms improve the surface protection of plant foliage. The attached microorganisms can defend the plant against disease-causing organisms.
- The representative microorganisms from the compost offer similar soil nutrition benefits – pH buffering, nutrient distribution, aggregate formation, aeration, water retention, etcetera.
- Microorganisms increase the nutrient availability where it's needed – at the roots. The soil food web's predator-prey interactions increase nutrient availability at the right time and at the right place.
- Beneficial microorganisms can neutralize the impact of chemical-based pesticides and herbicides.
- Beneficial microorganisms reduce the loss of moisture from the leaf surface.
- Improved tilth and soil structure – an exclusive soil biota function.

Compost tea contains all the soluble nutrients extracted from the compost and representative bacteria, fungi, protozoa, and nematodes. The compost quality used in compost tea is an essential factor in the tea's efficacy. It stands to reason that if the microorganisms and nutrients are absent in the source compost, they will not be present in the tea either. However, the populations of either bacteria or fungi can be boosted by adding food that will stimulate their individual growth. Humic acid boosts fungi growth, and molasses will boost the bacterial population.

Brewing an effective composting tea is dependent on several factors. Like most living organisms, including you and I, if the needs of the microorganisms are met, they thrive. Making compost tea is an evolving science, and different approaches have been developed to satisfy select organisms' needs fully. By closely monitoring the brewing environment, beneficial microorganisms can be kept alive and helped to thrive. Factors that influence the outcome are:

- the brewing temperature
- the added foods
- the levels of oxygenation during production
- the quality and microbial composition of the compost used
- the time microorganisms are immersed in water.

It's essential to remember that we're working with oxygen-dependent aerobic microorganisms. These organisms are essential to the soil, allow plants to grow unimpeded, and act as defenders of the realm. Merely soaking compost in water overnight is a good way to make humus-colored water, not compost tea. Ensure the microorganisms don't perish by maintaining an oxygen level of at least 5.5ppm.

Anything less might be counter-productive, producing microbes that could be detrimental to the plants and soil. The bacteria responsible for diseases in humans are almost exclusively anaerobic, and this scenario is less likely if your thermophilic process during composting was unquestionably effective.

Effective compost tea, like effective compost, is location specific. The best compost is produced by gardeners or farmers using local materials. This is because the organisms in a local system are best equipped to manage the requirements of the local pedosphere. Similarly, compost-tea-making should ideally be localized using localized compost. This is the best option, but not an absolute necessity.

If buying compost tea, remember that the shelf-life is exceptionally short (about 6 hours). If buying compost tea, your best option is to buy the compost and microorganisms food and brew it at home.

Compost Tea Variations

Actively Aerated Compost Tea (AACT)
- An aerated brew of unchlorinated water and compost extract.
- It is wholly representative of the nutrients and microorganisms in the original compost.
- Added food for targeted microbial growth.

Non-Aerated Compost Extract (NCE)
- A suspended compost extract is actively aerated in solution.
- It may contain some of the compost microorganisms.

- No added food to promote microbial growth.
- Soluble nutrients and enzymes are present if used soon after making.
- Very time sensitive due to lack of aeration.
- Rich in humic acid.

Actively aerated compost tea is actively aerated using a bubbler, blower, or any other device to force oxygen-laden air into the liquid containing a bag of compost extract. Alternatively, compost extracts are only occasionally stirred to re-suspend solid materials that have settled to the bottom, and this process is not actively aerated.

Making Active Aerated Compost Tea (AACT)

Resources Required:
- About a 7-gallon bucket with a cloth cover.
- Air pump (aquarium air pump will do).
- A length of tubing to fit the air pump – long enough to feed air into the bottom of the bucket.
- Aquarium airstones or bubblers.
- 5 gallons of dechlorinated water (rainwater is suitable).
- 3 cups of finely sieved compost.
- A porous bag – compost teabags are available online. Alternatively, use a sock.

Directions:
- Start aerating the water in the bucket.
- Put mature compost in the bag or sock, attach it to a weighted object, and place the bag and weight in the bucket.
- To remove air from the compost bag, gently massage it.
- Allow the bag containing water to be aerated for 24 hours.
- If you use the AACT in a sprayer, you will need to filter the liquid before using it – a cheesecloth will be adequate.
- Use the liquid within an hour after aeration stops.

Making Non-aerated Compost Extract (NCE)

Resources Required:
- About a 7-gallon bucket with a cloth cover.
- 5 gallons of dechlorinated water (rainwater is suitable).
- 3 cups of finely sieved compost contained in a porous bag – compost teabags are

available online. Alternatively, a sock or stocking will work.
- An implement to stir with.

Directions
- Place the compost-filled bag in the water.
- Help your tea draw by stirring the water and massaging the bag of compost.
- Repeat the above action twice a day for the next seven days.
- When done, filter the solution to avoid blocking your sprayer nozzles.
- Use the liquid as compost, drenching the soil around plants and spraying on foliage.

Composting Tea Review

I'm personally a fan of the AACT method. With the extended, non-aerated method, I imagine the microorganisms drowning, slowly growing weaker, until all I'm stirring are unresponsive microbodies. With the AACT method, my little divers get a chance to gulp air, have plenty of additional food, and are even reproducing.

But the proof is in the pudding, as they say. There is no set recipe for compost teas, and the above ones are mere guidelines. As a master gardener, you will develop what works for you, your soil, and your plants. If you want to be effective, find a lab that can analyze your soil – not for chemical content, but rather microbial diversity and population. That way, you can know what is abundant and in deficit. Diversity rules the earth – literally. The more diverse your population and balanced the predator-prey systems are, the healthier your soil and happier your plants are.

Speaking of diversity, we know the thermophilic phase of composting reaches unsuitable temperatures for many fungi species. While evolution has provided them with a survival strategy, it remains much easier to end with a batch of compost high in bacteria than fungi populations. Using the initial compost, AACT offers gardeners an easy way to boost the fungi populations in the soil.

Bacteria thrive on sugars, and fungi thrive on proteins. By adding a tiny amount of protein (fish hydrolysis or humic acid), you can boost your fungi population in the tea and, therefore, the soil. The amount is approximately two teaspoons to 5 gallons of water. Always use dechlorinated water when working with anything microbial. You can also fill a bucket of water from the tap and leave it in the sun for a day to neutralize the chlorine (or add some ascorbic acid).

Worthy of a special mention is the manufacturing of AACT using vermicompost. Vermicompost is the most nutritious version of compost, especially if the food supply is predominantly aerobic compost and leaf mold.

Organic Fertilizers[10]

The items listed below are typically allowed under the NOP for commercial organic growers unless otherwise specified.

Fertilizer	Primary Benefit	Average Analysis
Alfalfa meal	Organic matter	5-1-2
Algae	Organic matter	N/A
Amino acid (nonsynthetic)	Chelating agent	N/A
Ash	Liming effect, source of calcium, micronutrients	25% calcium carbonate; 9% potash
Basalt dust	Micronutrients	N/A
Blood meal (dried)	Nitrogen	10-0-0
Bone meal	Phosphate	3-15-0; 20% total phosphate; 24% calcium
Borax	Trace minerals	10% boron
Calcitic limestone	Calcium	65-80% calcium carbonate
Coffee grounds	Nitrogen	2-0.3-0.2
Colloidal phosphate	Phosphate	0-2-2
Compost	Organic matter	Varies with components added
Corn gluten meal	Nitrogen	9-0-0
Cottonseed meal	Nitrogen	6-4-1.5

---

10   https://content.ces.ncsu.edu/extension-gardener-handbook/17-organic-gardening

Cotton gin trash	Nitrogen, phosphorus, potash	14–10.5–41
Dolomite	Balancer, calcium, magnesium	51% calcium carbonate; 40% magnesium carbonate
Eggshell meal	Calcium	1.2–0.4–0.1
Elemental sulfur	Balancer, nutrient	99.5% sulfur
Epsom salts	Balancer, magnesium	10% magnesium; 13% sulfur
Feather meal	Nitrogen	11–0–0
Fish emulsion	Nitrogen	5–2–2
Fish meal	Nitrogen	10–6–2
Fish powder	Nitrogen	12–0.25–1
Fur	Nitrogen	12–0–0
Granite dust	Potash	4% potash
Greensand	Potash	7% total potash
Gypsum, mined	Calcium, balancer	22% calcium; 17% sulfur
Hair	Nitrogen	12–16% nitrogen
Horse manure	Organic matter	1.7–0.7–1.8
Hoof and horn meal	Nitrogen	12–2–0
Kelp meal	Potash	1.5–0.5–2.5; trace minerals
Leaf mulch	Organic matter	0.5–0.1–0.5
Magnesium rock	Magnesium	32–35% magnesium

Milk	Nitrogen	0.5–0.3–0.2
Oyster shells	Calcium	33.5% calcium
Peanut meal	Nitrogen	7.2–1.5–1.2
Peat moss	Organic matter	pH range 3.0–4.5
Potassium sulfate	Potassium, sulfur	22% potash; 23% sulfate
Poultry manure	Organic matter	4–4–2
Rabbit manure	Organic matter	1.5–1–1
Rock phosphate	Phosphate	0–3–0
Sawdust (untreated)	Organic matter	0.2–0–0.2
Sheep manure	Organic matter	4–1.4–3.5
Soybean meal	Nitrogen	7–0.5–2.3
Straw	Nitrogen, potash	0.2–0–0.2
Sulfur	Sulfur	50–100% sulfur
Sul-Po-Mag	Potash, magnesium	0–0–22; 11% magnesium; 22% sulfur
Wood ashes	Potash, micronutrients	0–2–6
Wood chips	Phosphorus	0–0.4–0.2
Worm castings	Organic matter	0.5–0.5–0.3

Mulches

Mulches give several advantages to plants, and the benefits vary depending on the material used, the kind of soil, the type of plant, and the cultural practices employed. Mulches can also make landscapes more appealing and useable and minimize the amount of maintenance labor required. Below are some of the benefits of mulch:

- Soil amendment
  - Improves soil granulation and aggregation
  - Increases water absorption and retention
  - It prevents soil compaction and improves aeration
- Surface insulation
  - Conserves moisture
  - Moderates extremes in temperature
  - Controls weed growth
- Beautification
  - It makes surface areas more attractive
  - Improves surface areas utility (paths, play, and sitting areas)
  - It makes maintaining areas easier

Organic Mulches

Material	Aesthetics	Resistance to wind blowing	Source of weeds and disease	Comments
Bark chunks	Excellent	Excellent	Excellent	Pricey, but worth it
Cocoa shells	Excellent	Good	Excellent	High potassium content may cause problems
Coconut coir	Excellent	Excellent	Good	Sustainable alternative to peat moss
Compost	Good	Excellent	Fair	Ensure it's cured
Corn cobs	Poor	Good	Poor	Not recommended
Cottonseed hulls	Fair	Poor	Good	Better incorporated

Hay	Fair	Good	Fair	Fire risk
Lawn clippings	Poor	Good	Fair	Better composted
Leaf mold	Good	Excellent	Fair	Hygroscopic – attracts and retains moisture
Leaves	Good	Poor	Good	Compost to improve the value
Manure (well rotted)	Fair	Excellent	Unsatisfactory	The odor may be a challenge
Pecan hulls	Excellent	Good	Excellent	A good alternative if available
Pine needles	Good	Good	Good	Acidic
Rice hulls	Fair	Poor	Fair	Better incorporated
Sawdust (coarse)	Fair	Good	Excellent	Will extract nitrogen for the soil
Sawdust (fine)	Fair	Poor	Excellent	Will extract nitrogen for the soil
Shredded bark	Excellent	Excellent	Excellent	Good option
Straw	Poor	Poor	Poor	Not advised – will extract nitrogen from the soil
Wood chips	Good	Excellent	Excellent	Will impoverish the soil.
Wood shavings	Good	Good	Excellent	Will extract nitrogen for the soil
Wood fibers	Fair	Good	Excellent	Will extract nitrogen for the soil

Inorganic Mulches

Material	Aesthetics	Resistance to wind blowing	Source of weeds and disease	Comments
Black plastic film	Unsatisfactory	Unsatisfactory	Excellent	It needs to be anchored. Unsightly.
Crushed rock	Good	Excellent	Excellent	Avoid crushed limestone
Geotextile weed barrier	Unsatisfactory	Unsatisfactory	Excellent	It needs to be anchored
Gravel	Good	Excellent	Excellent	Use sparingly
Volcanic rock	Good	Excellent	Excellent	Small sizes are moved by water
Perlite	Good	Poor	Excellent	Rather incorporate
Vermiculite	Fair	Poor	Excellent	Rather incorporate

Mulch may be made from a variety of biological and inorganic materials. Organic mulches can decompose in one season or fewer, or they might last over several seasons. The first kind is commonly seen in vegetable and flower gardens and freshly planted trees and bushes. By the conclusion of the growing season, they are typically degraded sufficiently to be spaded or plowed through, increasing the organic matter content of the soil and so improving soil structure. Mulch helps the soil even if it is not integrated because worms and soil bacteria carry it into the soil.

Inorganic mulches might be gravel, crushed stone, or a synthetic substance. Because they do not increase the structure or nutritional content of the soil, most of these materials are not as useful to plants as organic mulches. Although it is not advised for use in landscaping, black plastic mulch may be effective in the vegetable garden. Spun-bonded or woven landscape fabrics (geotextiles) are more suited for use in the landscape. Rather than being utilized alone, these textiles are usually covered with a more attractive mulch. However, soil structure may degrade because the organic mulch above geotextiles cannot permeate the soil.

Though they are not typically thought of as mulches, some low-growing groundcover plants provide many mulch benefits. They shade the soil surface, keeping it cool in the summer and avoiding evaporation.

Mulching Vegetables

The fundamental reason for mulching vegetable and flower gardens is to retain soil moisture. Beans, peppers, sweetcorn, tomatoes, vine crops, and other long-term summer crops with a lot of foliage are the best crops to mulch. Long-term crops planted in the chilly season, such as broccoli, cabbage, cauliflower, and potatoes, will produce more when mulched. Asparagus and rhubarb should be mulched continuously to maintain soil moisture and avoid weed issues.

Composts, straw, hay, and other materials that will be mostly decomposed by the end of the season are some of the best mulches for annual vegetable crops.

CHAPTER 6
PROPAGATION

Plant propagation is the practice of growing a new plant, either from seed or other means. It is both an art and a science, and success necessitates knowledge, talent, competence, and experience. Understanding why, when, and how to propagate necessitates a fundamental understanding of the growth and development of plants, plant anatomy and morphology, and plant physiology.

There are two forms of propagation in general: *sexual and asexual.* The reproduction of plants via seeds is known as sexual propagation. Pollination and fertilization combine the genetic material of two parents to produce offspring that are distinct from each parent. Asexual propagation (also known as vegetative propagation) takes vegetative elements of a plant (stems, roots, or leaves) and propagates a new plant. The resulting plant is genetically identical to the parent plant. Vegetative propagation can be done by cuttings, layering, division, separation, grafting, budding, and micropropagation.

Seed Propagation

Seeds
Seeds comprise three basic components: an embryo, endosperm (food storage) tissue, and a seed coat (protective tissue).

- The embryo is a tiny inactive plant – think yoke.
- The endosperm is a built-in food source found in most seeds – think albumen.
- The seed coat is a seed's protective outer coating – think shell. It protects seeds from mechanical damage as well as illnesses and insects. Furthermore, the seed coat normally prevents water from entering the seed until it is time to germinate. The seed coat permits seeds to be preserved for long periods.

The seed has to be of good quality for healthy plants to grow. Cultivars and hybrids are the product of cross-breeding and selection processes, often over many years, to produce a strain that offers specific size, color, resilience, and growth habits. Hybrids are generally pricy but offer better traits, features, vigor, and region-specific resilience. Most seeds deteriorate with age, so limit purchases to immediate needs.

Store seeds in a cool, dry area if they are received long ahead of the actual sowing date (or if they are extra seeds). Laminated or foil-wrapped containers aid in dry storage. Paper packages should be stored in firmly sealed containers at 40°F and in low humidity – an *airtight* container in the refrigerator would be a nice place to store it. Gardeners may save money while cultivating a pleasant pastime by preserving seeds from their plants. Open-pollinated seeds have been pollinated by an insect, an animal, the wind, or another natural pollination process. Open-pollinated plants may have distinct features from their parent plants, boosting biodiversity. This is especially true when storing hybrid seeds.

Germination

The restart of active embryo development following a latent phase is germination. For a seed to germinate, three criteria must be met:

The seed must be viable; that is, the embryo must be alive and capable of germination.

The seed's internal conditions must be favorable for germination; that is, any physical, chemical, or physiological barriers to germination must no longer be present.

The conditions for germination must be right – a combination of moisture, light (or the absence thereof, temperature, and oxygen.

The absorption of **water** is the initial stage in germination. An appropriate and consistent supply of moisture is required to activate germination. After germination has begun, a dry spell might be fatal to the embryo.

Some species' seed germination can be stimulated or inhibited by **light**. Seed catalogs and seed packs generally provide germination and cultural information for specific plants. Light-required seeds should be sown on the soil's surface. Fluorescent lamps hung 6 to 12 inches above the soil surface can give additional light – 16 hours a day on and 8 hours off.

Dormant seeds do not respire, although they require some **oxygen**. During germination, the rate of respiration rises. The media used to plant the seeds should be loose and properly aerated. Germination can be substantially slowed or impeded if the oxygen supply is limited or diminished during germination.

Temperature influences the percentage of germination and the speed of germination. Some seeds germinate over a wide range of temperatures, whereas others germinate at a small range. Many species germinate at minimum, maximum, and optimal temperatures. Tomato seeds, for example, have a minimum germination temperature of 50°F, a maximum germination temperature of 95°F, and an optimal germination temperature of 80°F. Suggested germination temperatures are generally indicators of the optimum – most seeds like soil temperatures ranging from 65°F to 75°F.

Dealing with Seed Dormancy

Some seeds may not germinate due to a seed-specific inhibitory factor. There are two forms of dormancy: (a) external dormancy (seed coat) and (b) internal (endogenous) dormancy. A seed can experience both types of dormancy. In dealing with external dormancy, scarification is used, and for internal dormancy, stratification is used.

Some species' seeds have twofold dormancy. This is a hybrid of two forms of dormancy: exterior and internal dormancy. To germinate these seeds, they must first be scarified and *then* stratified for the necessary time. The seeds will not germinate if the treatments are given in reverse order. After you've finished these procedures, place the seeds in the right setting for germination.

Seed Scarification

When a seed's hard seed coat becomes impermeable to water and gases, it enters external dormancy. The seed will not germinate unless the seed coat is physically changed. Scarification refers to any method of breaking, scraping, or mechanically modifying the seed coat to render it permeable to water and gases. In nature, this might happen during the winter when freezing temperatures shatter the seed coat or when microbial activity modifies the seed coat while the seed is in the soil. Scarification may also occur while the seed goes through an animal's digestive tract.

Scarification can be induced rather than waiting for nature to change the seed coverings. Scarifying seeds is a process used by commercial growers that involves immersing them in sulfuric acid. Depending on the species, seeds are put in a glass container, covered with sulfuric acid, gently agitated, and left to soak for 10 minutes to several hours. Sulfuric acid is highly acidic and inappropriate for domestic use. Vinegar is a safer alternative that can be used on some species; the procedure is the same as sulfuric acid.

Mechanical scarification involves filing seeds with a metal file, rubbing them with sandpaper, or gently cracking them with a hammer to weaken (break) the seed covering. Hot water scarification is another option. Bring the water to a boil, remove the saucepan from the heat and add the seeds. Soak the seeds until the water cools, then remove and dry.

Seed Stratification

The inner seed tissues manage the second form of enforced dormancy, internal dormancy. When environmental circumstances are not suitable for seedling survival, this dormancy inhibits many species' seeds from germinating. There are several forms of internal dormancy, and some varieties need a specific duration of moist-chilling or moist-warming periods.

Cold stratification (wet-chilling) keeps seeds in a refrigerator after combining them with an equivalent amount of moist media (such as sand or peat). Check the medium regularly to ensure that it is moist but not wet. The time necessary to break (remove) dormancy varies depending on the species; consult reference books for recommended times. This dormancy type may be achieved organically by sowing seeds outside in the fall. Warm stratification is identical to cold stratification, but, depending on the species, temperatures are maintained at 70°F to 86°F.

Growing Plants From Seeds

Some seeds can be sown in situ, while others do better if first grown in seedling containers. This section will review the essential elements of growing plants from seeds:

- Media
- Containers
- Sowing Seeds
- Water and Light
- Transplanting

Growing Media

Seeds can be germinated in a variety of mediums. With practice, you'll figure out what works best for you. The germination media should be fine and homogenous while properly aerated and loose. Insects, disease organisms, nematodes, weeds, and weed seeds should not be present. It should also be low in fertility and capable of retaining moisture while being properly drained. Purchase a commercial potting medium comprising fine-particle pine bark, coconut coir, and perlite, or mix these ingredients' equal proportions (by volume). Garden soil should not be used to start seedlings since it is not sterile, is too heavy, and generally does not drain effectively.

Containers

Plastic or polystyrene cell packs can be purchased or sanitized, and reused. Each cell in this arrangement houses a single plant. When transplanting, this procedure decreases the danger of root damage. Seedlings can also be grown in peat pellets, peat pots, or inflated foam cubes. Resourceful gardeners frequently utilize cottage cheese containers, the bottoms of milk cartons, or pie pans. Just make sure there are appropriate drainage holes on the bottoms of the containers and that they are sterile. It is impossible to overstate the necessity of utilizing sterile media and containers. Before using the containers, wash them to remove any dirt, then soak them for 5 minutes in a fresh solution of one part chlorine bleach to nine parts water and allow them to drip-dry.

Sowing Seeds

Seedlings are often started inside four to 12 weeks before the final spring frost. A typical error is to sow the seeds too early and keep the seedlings in a sterile environment, resulting in tall, weak, spindly plants that fare poorly in the garden. The directions that follow are general principles for planting seeds for transplants. However, it is critical to follow the directions on the seed packaging for more detailed information.

Fill the container to within three-quarters of an inch of the top with wet growth material when sowing seeds. Use a fine, screened media for very small seeds, such as ¼ inch layer of fine vermiculite. To create a smooth and level surface, firm the medium at the corners and edges with your fingers or a woodblock.

Make furrows 1 to 2 inches apart and 18 to 14 inches deep across the surface of the planting medium for medium and big seeds. Row planting promotes light and air movement, and if damping-off illness develops, it has a lower likelihood of spreading. At transplanting time, seedlings in rows are easier to identify and handle than those produced by disseminating seeds. Sow the seeds thinly and consistently in the rows by gently tapping the seed packet. Cover the seeds gently; a recommended planting depth is generally two to four times the seed's minimum diameter.

Extremely fine seeds, such as carrots and onions, should be dusted on the surface of the germination medium and watered with a thin mist rather than covered. If these seeds are spread, try to achieve a consistent stand by sowing half of the seeds in one direction and the remaining seeds in the other way.

Large seeds are typically put directly in a compact container or cell pack, obviating early transplantation requirements. Sow two or three seeds in each cell on average. Afterward, finishing them will allow just the most strong seedlings per cell to thrive.

Indoor and outdoor seed tapes are available at most garden stores and seed merchants. Seed tapes are made up of properly spaced seeds encased in an organic, water-soluble substance. When the tape is removed, the seeds germinate normally. Seed tapes are used for extremely tiny, difficult-to-handle seeds. Seed tapes provide consistent emergence, minimize overcrowding, and allow for straight row sowing. The tapes can be cut for multiple row plantings, and thinning is rarely required – tapes are convenient, but their per-seed cost is higher.

Water and Light Requirements
Before planting, properly moisten the planting media. After sowing, spray the containers with a fine mist or set them on a pan or tray with about 1 inch of warm water. Avoid splashing or severe flooding, which may cause little seeds to be displaced. Set the container aside to drain once the planting mix has been soaked. The soil should be damp but not soggy.

During the germination stage, the seed flats should be kept wet. On the other hand, excessive moisture might cause damping-off or other disease or pest issues. Place the entire flat or pot in a transparent plastic bag to keep the moisture in. The plastic should be placed at least 1 inch above the dirt. Keep the container away from direct sunshine; otherwise, the temperature will rise and harm the seeds. Instead of using a plastic bag, many home gardeners cover their flats with glass panes. When the first seedlings appear, remove the plastic bag or glass cover.

After the seeds have germinated, transfer the flats to a well-lit area maintaining temperatures between 65°F to 70°F during the day and 55°F to 60°F at night. This inhibits soft, leggy growth and reduces disease issues. Certain crops, of course, may require specific temperatures.

After germination, seedlings require strong light. Place them in a window that faces south or beneath fluorescent lights if a large, bright site is not available. Two 40-watt cool-white fluorescent bulbs or special plant development lights are recommended. Place the plants 6 inches below the light source and give them 16 hours of light every day. The lights should be increased as the seedlings develop.

Transplanting Seedlings
Plants that have not been sown separately must ultimately be moved into their pots as seedlings to allow them to grow properly. A typical blunder is leaving the seedlings on the flat for too long. When the first genuine leaves develop, it is time to transfer young seedlings.

With a knife or plastic plant label, carefully remove the little plants. Allow the seedlings to fall apart and pluck out individual plants. Allow them to separate gently to minimize root harm. Small seedlings should be handled by their leaves rather than their delicate stems. Punch a hole in the medium with a tiny instrument or your finger. Plant a seedling at the same depth that it grew in the seed flat, i.e. level to the growing medium. Firm the dirt with your hands and water carefully. Keep newly transplanted seedlings in the shade or under fluorescent lights for a few days. Place them away from direct heat sources. Continue to water and fertilize as you did with the seed flats.

Hardening Plants
The process of preparing a plant for outdoor development is known as hardening. If plants grown indoors are put outside without a hardening phase, their growth may be significantly hampered. When harsh weather circumstances are likely, early crops require the most hardening.

Hardening is performed by progressively lowering the temperature and relative humidity and reducing the amount of water. This method causes glucose buildup and cell wall thickening. Transitioning from soft, succulent growth to stiffer, tougher development is required.

The procedure should begin at least two weeks before planting plants. On warm days, place seedlings outside in a sheltered area and gradually increase the length of exposure. Tender seedlings should not be planted outside on windy days or when temperatures fall below 45°F. Even cold-hardy plants will be harmed if exposed to freezing temperatures before hardening.

The purpose of hardening is to slow plant development. Hardening, when taken to the extreme, can inflict substantial harm. Cauliflower, for example, generates thumb-sized heads and fails to develop further if too tough; cucumbers and melons cease developing totally.

Asexual Propagation
Vegetables are generally propagated by seed, but the following asexual propagation methods may be used for fruit trees and others. Herbs such as mint are also propagated asexually.

- Leaf cuttings
- Leaf bud cuttings
- Cane cuttings
- Stem cuttings
- Root cuttings
- Layering
- Separation and division
- Budding and crafting
- Micropropagation

I cover asexual propagation in my book on growing fruit.

CHAPTER 7
GROWING VEGETABLES

And now we get to the fun part – growing your vegetables. This chapter is divided into seven sections, grouping vegetable plants into families. The grouping is vital in managing soil nutrients and soil-borne diseases common to a given group of plants. By planting alternate families sequentially in a location, diseases and pests common to one group are interrupted, increasing your chance of a successful crop. The eight vegetable families are:

- **Amaranthaceae** – The Leafy-Roots Family
    - The Amaranth family includes beets, chard, spinach, sugar beets – and quinoa.
- **Brassicaceae** – The Mustard Family
    - The Brassica family – also known as the mustards, the crucifers, or the cabbage family includes broccoli, Brussels sprouts, cabbage, cauliflower, collards, kale, kohlrabi, mustard, radishes, rutabaga, and turnip.
- **Compositae** – The most highly evolved plants
    - The Composite family includes artichokes, endive, lettuce, and sunflowers.
- **Cucurbitaceae** – The Gourd Family
    - The Cucurbits family includes cucumbers, melons, squashes, pumpkins, and gourds.
- **Fabaceae** – The Pea Family
    - The Pea family consists of all the legumes – beans, peas, lentils, chickpeas, fava beans, lima beans, and soybeans.
- **Liliaceae** – The Lilly Family that includes the Allium Vegetables
    - The Lily family includes asparagus, chives, garlic, leeks, onions, scallions, and shallots.
- **Solanaceae** – The Nightshade Family
    - The Solanaceae family (nightshades) consists of eggplant, pepper, potato, and tomato.
- **Umbelliferae** – Fragrant plants with small flowers borne in umbels
    - The Umbellifers family consists of angelica, anise, caraway, carrot, celery, coriander, cumin, dill, fennel, lovage, parsley, and parsnip.

Of course, there has to be one that doesn't fit in any of the families – rhubarb – which belongs to the **Polygonaceae** family. Planting your first vegetable garden should be fun. I like planting my perennials in the ground and other veggies in raised beds, hills, or containers which help soils heat faster and provide better drainage and air circulation.

Container Planting

If you're planting in containers, great options include:

- Herbs
- Potatoes
- Tomatoes
- Swiss chard (and spinach)
- Eggplants
- Peppers
- Cucumbers
- Summer squash (zucchinis)
- Carrots
- Lettuce

Companion Planting

Several combo-garden options provide the ingredients you need for various dishes. You may choose to create a pizza planter – a tomato plant surrounded by basil and onions. Another traditional favorite is the three sisters: a sweetcorn plant, a pole bean, and summer squash. Other great combos include:

- Lettuce and herbs
- Adding the carrots to the three sisters – corn, beans, squash, *and* carrots
- Spinach, chard, onions, and turnips
- Beans and eggplants (aubergine)
- Beans with cucumber, peas, and lettuce
- Broccoli with onion
- Cauliflower with celery
- Eggplant and spinach
- Leeks with carrots
- Lettuce with strawberries or radishes

- Onions with bell pepper
- Squash with sweetcorn
- Swiss chard with onion
- Root crops (like radish) with other vegetables – kale and radish especially
- Marigolds repel Mexican bean beetles, squash bugs, thrips, tomato hornworms, whiteflies, and nematodes, so include them in any garden

If friends grow well together, there must be some that shouldn't be grown together. Below is a list of interplanting options that should be *avoided*:

- Beans and peas shouldn't be interplanted with allium plants (onions, garlic, etc.)
- Carrots shouldn't be planted with fennel or dill (family members)
- Asparagus and garlic
- Beets and beans
- Broccoli and beans
- Cabbage and strawberries
- Carrots and celery
- Corn and tomatoes
- Potatoes should always be a singular crop

Interplanting can maximize limited space, but whatever you choose to do – plan it, map it, and keep a log to learn what works in your unique environment. I have created a reference with the key information in easy-to-reference tables for each plant – color-coded for warm-season and cool-season vegetables.

Have fun.

Artichokes (*Cynara scolymus*)

Family	Season	Sun	Soil	Hardiness	pH
COMPOSITAE	Perennial	Full Sun	Organic, deep, well-drained	6 to 9	6.5-8.0
Height	**Spread**	**Tolerance**	**Ease-of-Care**	**Germination**	**Emergence**
3-6'	2-4'	Frost & Salt	Challenging	70°F–80°F	8-12 days

The **Composite family** includes artichokes, endive, lettuce, and sunflowers.

This *perennial* appreciated for its tasty 'hearts' is hardy to Zone 6 and (if properly mulched) Zone 5 in mild winters. Its bristly leaves offer an interesting texture to flower beds. In warmer regions, it's grown as a perennial – plant annually in cooler regions.

Perennial vegetables, such as asparagus and rhubarb, are picked in the spring but permitted to grow all year. Others, such as Jerusalem artichoke and horseradish, are picked fully at the end of the season, but a root or stem piece is kept for planting the following year. This latter group may be moved about the garden yearly, although asparagus and rhubarb remain in the same position for years.

Planting Artichokes

Planting Type	Depth (inches)	Initial Spacing	Row Spacing	Thinning
Division	2.5 to 3	2 to 3 ft	30 to 36 inches	-
Seed	Not recommended – seed-grown plants are generally inferior			

- Artichokes can be grown as ornamental annuals in cooler regions. Propagate by seed or division. Plant root divisions 2 to 3 feet apart in rows 2½ to 3 feet apart after the first frost. It is not recommended to plant from seed since the outcomes are varied and typically inferior to parent plants.
- There are advantages to using a low-nitrogen fertilizer (rich in phosphorus and potassium) before planting, remembering that plants seldom blossom in their first year.

Growing and Caring for Artichokes

Head back to 12 inches and insulate with leaves or an old carpet to boost the possibility of overwintering. Another option is to dig roots and keep them in a cool (but not freezing) place. Plant in pots for about a month before transplanting after the last frost. While individual plants can live for up to 15 years or more, it is recommended that you divide them every three years to maintain your plant's productivity.

Harvesting Artichokes

Harvest when the plants begin to die back after one or two mild frosts. Remove the stems before digging the tubers. To prevent this plant from becoming a weed, be as thorough as possible. Save a few tubers for the following year's harvest. The yield for a 10-foot row is estimated to be 7 pounds.

Potential Challenges to Growing Artichokes

Artichokes may have aphid challenges – encourage lady beetles, their natural enemy.

Asparagus (*Asparagus officianalis*)

Family	Season	Sun	Soil	Hardiness	pH
LILIACEAE	Perennial	Full Sun	Organic, deep, well-drained	2 to 8	6.8 to 7.2

Height	Spread	Tolerance	Ease-of-Care	Germination	Emergence
5-9'	2-2.5'	Frost & Salt	Easy	70°F-77°F	10-12 days

The **Lily family** includes asparagus, chives, garlic, leeks, onions, scallions, and shallots.

Plantings of this hardy perennial, one of the first harvests in spring, may continue for decades if carefully cared for. The exquisite leaves make it a natural for edible landscaping. When the sensitive spears are consumed as soon as possible after harvesting, they are at their best.

Asparagus is one of those perennials (with rhubarb) harvested each spring but allowed to stay in the ground all year. You must set aside a garden area for asparagus and rhubarb and place them so that their shadow does not affect your other vegetables.

Planting Asparagus

Planting Type	Depth	Initial Spacing	Row Spacing	Thinning
Crown	2 inches	18 inches	5 ft	-
Seed	Not Suggested			

- Asparagus can be propagated by seed, root division, or separation. If you don't have a plant, I suggest getting crowns for your first planting. Purchase disease-free, one-year-old crowns.

- Dig a trench 12 to 18 inches wide and 6 inches deep for the plants. The crowns should be separated by a foot minimally – 18 inches advised. Spread the roots evenly, crown bud side up, in an upright, centered posture that is somewhat higher than the roots. Cover the crown with 2 inches of dirt.
- During the first summer, gradually fill the remaining section of the trench as the plants grow higher. Asparagus plants tend to 'rise' as they age, with the crowns gradually rising closer to the soil surface. Many gardeners add 1 to 2 inches of soil from between the rows in subsequent years.
- A 5-foot gap between rows is commonly suggested. Asparagus grows swiftly and fills in nicely – the wider the space, the better the airflow and the lower the number of illnesses.
- After a week, you should start seeing leaves. Irrigate as needed during the planting season.
- The first year, do not harvest, permitting the root system to establish itself.

Growing and Caring for Asparagus
- Asparagus plants develop a mat of roots that grow horizontally rather than vertically. The top growth is spindly in the first year, and the stems of the plants get greater in diameter as they age.
- Asparagus plants are dioecious (either solely male or solely female). Female plants produce more spears or stems than male plants, but the diameter of the stems is less. New varieties are generally vigorous male plants that are highly productive. Remove the asparagus tops after the first freezing weather in the fall, decreasing the chances of rust disease overwintering on the foliage.
- Because asparagus remains in situ for years, proper soil preparation considerably benefits future output. It is good to include green manure crops, compost, manure, or other organic elements into the planned bed well before planting. For the first three years, asparagus should be fertilized in the same manner as the rest of the garden. Apply 10-10-10 fertilizer at 2 pounds per 100 square feet in the spring and mix it in. After harvesting, add a further 2 ounces per 100 square feet.
- The biggest challenge with asparagus is weeds and grasses, which compete with the emerging spears, creating a disordered area in the garden, and severely reducing productivity and quality. Begin regular, gentle, shallow cultivation early in the spring in both fresh plants and older patches that are being harvested.
- Once established, asparagus is typically drought resistant – control weeds by hand weeding.

Harvesting Asparagus
- Asparagus plants' new shoots (the spears) are gathered when they appear in the spring. Do not harvest them the same year you grow them. In the second year, harvest softly for no more than three to four weeks, and in the third year, harvest gently for four to six weeks. Following that, a complete harvest of six to eight weeks is feasible.
- Harvest the first spears that appear, and then continue to harvest regularly. This will improve the yield by encouraging the growth of additional spears. If the spears are less than three-quarters of an inch in length, stop harvesting. When you've finished harvesting, snap all spears off at ground level. Shoots that develop after harvest will become the plant's summer leaves.
- Expect a yield of 3 to 4 pounds per 10-foot row.

Potential Challenges to Growing Asparagus
- Asparagus beetles (common and spotted) – handpick in small plantings.
- Diseases include fusarium wilt, crown rot, and rust.

Beans – Bush (*Phaseolus vulgaris*)

Family	Season	Sun	Soil	Hardiness	pH
FABACEAE	Warm	Full Sun	Consistently moist	6 to 13	6.0 to 6.8
Height	Spread	Tolerance	Ease-of-Care	Germination	Emergence
1–3'	1–2'	Average Fertility	Easy	70°F–80°F	8–10 days

Also known as French, filet, haricot, green bean, wax bean, and string bean. The **Pea family** consists of all the legumes – beans, peas, lentils, chickpeas, fava beans, lima beans, and soybeans.

Planting Bush Beans

Planting Type	Depth (inches)	Initial Spacing	Row Spacing	Comments
Seed in situ	1 to 1.5	2 to 3 inches	>18 inches	Repeat Planting

- Propagate by seed, remembering that beans do not like to be transplanted.
- Plant seeds directly in the soil after it has warmed to 60°F, usually a week or fortnight after the last frost date. If soil is too cold, germination will be slow,

and the seed may rot. Seeds can be purchased pre-treated with a fungicide to minimize the risk of this happening.
- Plant 1 inch deep in heavy soils or 1½ inches in sandy soils. Mulching lightly with compost or sand will help seedlings emerge in heavier soils.

Growing and Caring for Beans
- Plant beans in succession until mid to late July for a consistent supply.
- Beans require even moisture – approximately 1 inch per week – especially when flowering and producing pods. When watering, avoid soaking the leaves, as this promotes disease.
- Water early in the day to allow the foliage to dry rapidly.
- When the second set of true leaves appears, add mulch to retain moisture. Nitrogen fertilizers should not be used, and inoculating seed with *Rhizobium* bacteria may boost yields, particularly in soils where beans have never been cultivated.
- When temperatures rise to above 90°F, pod sets deteriorate. Deformed pods can be caused by a lack of moisture, insufficient soil fertility, or insect damage during blossoming. A three-year rotation reduces some illnesses.

- Beans have shallow roots. Avoid cultivating or picking beans while the foliage or beans are moist. Bean bacterial blight is a dangerous disease that spreads more easily when the plants are wet.

Potential Challenges to Growing Beans
- Pests include aphids, leafhoppers, seedcorn maggot, spider mites, bean flea beetles, and Mexican bean beetles.
- Diseases include bacterial blight, white mold, bean mosaic disease.

Beans – Pole (*Beta vulgaris*)

Family	Season	Sun	Soil	Hardiness	pH
FABACEAE	Warm	Full Sun	Consistently moist	6 to 13	6.0 to 6.8
Height	**Spread**	**Tolerance**	**Ease-of-Care**	**Germination**	**Emergence**
5-10'	1-2'	Average Fertility	Easy	70°F–80°F	8-10 days

The **Pea family** consists of all the legumes - beans, peas, lentils, chickpeas, fava beans, lima beans, and soybeans.

Also known as French, filet, haricot, green bean, wax bean, and string bean, bush beans are a variant of pole beans, cultivated not to require vining. Growing pole beans can thripple your harvest if you have limited space for the same square footage a bush bean plant will deliver. Plant and grow as you would bush beans.

The treatment and requirements are identical to the bush variety, except the spacing should be increased to 4 to 6 inches and the row-spacing to 24 inches.

Planting Type	Depth (inches)	Initial Spacing	Row Spacing	Comments
Seed in situ	1 to 1.5	4 to 6 inches	>24 inches	Two Repeat Plantings

Beet (*Beta vulgaris* subsp. *vulgaris*)

Family	Season	Sun	Soil	Hardiness	pH
AMARANTHACEAE	Cool	Full Sun Part Shade	Well-drained sandy loam	2 to 11	6.5 to 7.0
Height	**Spread**	**Tolerance**	**Ease-of-Care**	**Germination**	**Emergence**
1'	0.5'	Low Fertility	Easy	50°F–85°F	5–8 days

The **Amaranth family** includes beets, chard, spinach, sugar beets – and quinoa.

The table beet (also known as the garden beet, blood turnip, or red beet) is a common garden vegetable in the United States. The tops of beets are high in vitamin A, whereas the roots are high in vitamin C. The tops are cooked or eaten fresh as greens, while the roots can be pickled for salads or cooked whole before being sliced or diced. Beet juice is a key component in Russian borscht. Garden beets are relatives of sugar beets, Swiss chard, and spinach.

Planting Beet

Planting Type	Depth	Initial Spacing	Row Spacing	Thinning
Seeds in situ	0.5	1 inch	12 to 18 inches	3 to 4 inches

- Propagate by seed – can be transplanted as soon as the soil can be worked in early spring, plant seeds ¾ inches deep and 2 inches apart – ideal for square-

foot planting. Plant every three weeks until mid-summer to provide a continual crop. Sow crop around ten weeks before heavy frost for winter storage.
- Because the wrinkled 'seedball' normally contains two to four viable seeds, thin to 3 to 4-inch spacings if you want to harvest young, tiny, or cylindrical-shaped roots, or 6-inch spacings if you plan to harvest bigger roots for winter storage.
- Thinning should begin when seedlings are approximately 4 to 5 inches tall, and thinnings should be eaten. To prevent harming the roots of adjacent plants, cut rather than pull plants while thinning.
- Though it's uncommon, beets actually may be transplanted. Some care must be taken to get the roots vertically oriented so that the beets can develop properly.

Beet Maintenance and Care
- Use floating row covers to keep insects at bay early in the season and keep the garden well-weeded. Beets can become stringy and harsh due to competition and inconsistent irrigation, and beets are cousins to Swiss chard and spinach. In a rotation, avoid following these crops.
- Beets can withstand average to low fertility, and too much nitrogen promotes top growth at the price of root development.
- Color and taste develop best in cold temperatures and direct sunlight. When beets develop in warm temperatures, they become lighter in color, contain less sugar, and exhibit more intense color zoning in the roots. White zone rings in roots are caused by changing weather conditions.
- Beets are biennial plants. During their first season, they often generate a larger root, and they then grow a flower stalk after overwintering. A flower stalk may bolt if exposed to temperatures below 45°F for two to three weeks after establishing many genuine leaves during its first season. Many newer kinds are less susceptible to this issue.

Potential Challenges to Growing Beet
- Beet's main pest is the leafminer.
- Diseases include Cercospora leaf spot, scab, root rot.

Bok/Pak Choi (*Brassica rapa var. chinensis*)

Family	Season	Sun	Soil	Hardiness	pH
BRASSICACEAE	Cool	Full Sun Part Shade	Well-drained composted, moist	2 to 11	6.0 to 7.5
Height	**Spread**	**Tolerance**	**Ease-of-Care**	**Germination**	**Emergence**
1-2'	1.5"	Slight Alkalinity, Frost	Moderately Challenging	50°F – 80°F	4-7 days

The **Brassica family** – also known as the mustards, the crucifers, or the cabbage family includes broccoli, Brussels sprouts, cabbage, cauliflower, collards, kale, kohlrabi, mustard, radishes, rutabaga, and turnip.

They are also known as Bok choi, Pak choi, Yu Tsai. Bok choi by any name has a mild taste that is essential for stir fries. It isn't as sensitive to heat and cold as Chinese cabbage, and its eye-catching white petioles and green leaves make it a must-have for edible landscaping.

Growing Pak Choi

Planting Type	Depth	Initial Spacing	Row Spacing	Thinning
Seed	0.25 to 0.5 inches	1 inch	18 to 30 inches	6 to 12 inches

- Propagate by seed in situ.
- Spring crops may bolt if young plants are exposed to frost or nighttime temperatures drop to below 50°F.
- Wait until after the last frost date to seed in situ or transplant out.
- Begin transplanting indoors four to six weeks before the final frost date – plant in rows 18 to 30 inches apart, 6 to 12 inches apart. Closer spacings should be used for smaller cultivars.
- Direct-seeded spring crops should be planted 14 to 12 inches deep and 1 inch apart in rows 18 to 30 inches apart.
- Thin to 6 to 12-inch intervals. The thinnings are delicious in salads.
- Mulch fall crops thickly to keep them damp and help avoid early bolting.

Harvesting Bok Choi

Harvesting of bok choi takes place all year. Sow seeds every two weeks until the summer heat arrives for a steady bok choi supply. Row coverings will provide some shade from the hot heat and may assist in lengthening the harvest. When harvesting bok choi for the complete plant, cut the plant off at the soil level.

Broccoli (*Brassica oleracea var. italica*)

Family	Season	Sun	Soil	Hardiness	pH
BRASSICACEAE	Cool	Full Sun Min. Shade	Well-drained composted, moist	2 to 11	6.0 to 7.5
Height	**Spread**	**Tolerance**	**Ease-of-Care**	**Germination**	**Emergence**
2-3'	2-3'	Slight Alkalinity, Frost	Moderately Challenging	45°F –85°F	4-7 days

The **Brassica family** – also known as the mustards, the crucifers, or the cabbage family includes broccoli, Brussels sprouts, cabbage, cauliflower, collards, kale, kohlrabi, mustard, radishes, rutabaga, and turnip.

In the northern cooler regions, transplant broccoli seedlings by mid-July. In warmer regions, you should wait until mid-August before transplanting broccoli seedlings. In the desert Southwest, broccoli should be grown as a winter crop. Broccoli is rich in vitamins A and D but requires constant attention to do well. This cool-season crop thrives at temperatures in the 60s°F during the day. Grow in spring and fall, but avoid crops in the middle of summer since hot temperatures can promote early bolting. Romanesco varieties are very appealing for edible landscaping.

Planting Broccoli

Planting Type	Depth	Initial Spacing	Row Spacing	Thinning
Seed	0.25 to 0.5 inch	10 inches	>36 inches	-

- Broccoli requires constant feeding.
- Seeds should be used within three years.
- Plant seeds in situ or use seedlings. In situ planting should be done in July (shallow seeds spaced about 10 inches), and seeds for seedlings can be planted indoors as early as April.
- Keep soil moist and thin by cutting – broccoli needs constant attention during the seedling stage.
- If started indoors for transplanting, start as early as April using perlite or other sterile seedling mix, plant seeds ¼ inch deep.
- There's no need for heating mats. Seeds germinate between 45°F and 85°F, and seeds will even germinate at soil temperatures of 40°F.
- Seeds take between 6 to 14 days to germinate. You can boost seedling growth with growth lights and weekly applications of half-strength starter solutions (high in P and low in N and K).
- When the seedling has four leaves, gradually expose them to the sun, protecting them from wind and keeping them well hydrated. More mature seedlings (more than five leaves) will bolt if exposed to cold in the garden, so the hardening process is essential.

- Seedlings are ready for transplanting when there are four or five established leaves (usually five to seven weeks after seeding). Space them 10 inches apart in a fall-composted bed – water with a starter solution high in phosphorus and low in nitrogen and potassium.

Growing and Caring for Broccoli
- From Hardiness Zone 7 upwards, fall-planted broccoli crops can overwinter.
- Use fertilizers low in nitrogen and high in phosphorus at planting as excessive nitrogen may result in hollow stems.
- Broccoli plants have shallow root systems, so avoid cultivation. Mulch to protect roots, reduce weed growth, and aid moisture retention.
- The use of floating row covers will help protect the crop from early insect infestations.
- Three weeks after transplanting, when rapid growth begins, side-dress with 0.1 pounds of actual nitrogen per 100 square feet.
- Make sure plants receive at least 1 inch of water a week while heads are forming – test depth of water penetration and, if less than 4 inches, increase watering regime.

Harvesting Broccoli
- The edible parts of broccoli are compact clusters of *unopened* flower buds and the attached portion of the stem.
- Cut the central head with a short stem after the head is fully developed but before it begins to loosen and separate.
- Removing the central head stimulates the development of side shoots along the stem left for harvesting later. You can usually continue harvesting broccoli for several weeks.
- The first harvest is about 55 to 60 days from transplanting, though following the above guidelines is more accurate than counting days.
- Expect a yield of 10 pounds per 10-foot row.

Potential Challenges to Growing Broccoli
- Floating row covers are strongly recommended as they can protect plants from cabbage maggots, flea beetles, and diamondback moths when the plant is most vulnerable in the early stages. Wash aphids off using a forceful water spray. Be careful not to remove the aphid's natural enemy – the lady beetles and lacewings. Their larvae may be on the plant. Remove row covers before season temperatures rise too high.

- Cabbage maggots, flea beetles, slugs and snails, and cutwork are also potential pests that may be found on broccoli.
- Diseases include clubroot if pH drops too low.

Brussels sprouts (*Brassica oleracea var. gemmifera*)

Family	Season	Sun	Soil	Hardiness	pH
BRASSICACEAE	Cool	Full Sun Min. Shade	Well-drained composted, moist	2 to 11	6.0 to 7.5
Height	**Spread**	**Tolerance**	**Ease-of-Care**	**Germination**	**Emergence**
2–3'	1.5–2'	Slight Alkalinity, Frost	Moderately Challenging	45°F–85°F	5–8 days

The **Brassica family** – also known as the mustards, the crucifers, or the cabbage family includes broccoli, Brussels sprouts, cabbage, cauliflower, collards, kale, kohlrabi, mustard, radishes, rutabaga, and turnip.

Brussels sprouts are hardy, long-seasoned members of the cabbage family. They can be grown with reasonable success almost anywhere in the cooler season – as long as temperatures are above 20°F. The sprouts may overwinter in temperate areas or where snow cover is deep. In the northern states, you can plan to harvest in September.

Summers are usually too warm for growing Brussels sprouts from spring plantings in central and southern states. Here, plants set out in late spring to early summer grow well and produce high-quality sprouts when the fall weather cools.

Planting Brussels Sprouts

Planting Type	Depth	Initial Spacing	Row Spacing	Thinning
Seed	0.25 to 0.5 inch	10 inches	>24 inches	14–24 inches

- Grow from seed. Plant seeds a quarter to ½ inch deep.
- They will be ready for transplanting in four to five weeks. You may also be able to purchase transplants.
- If you try a spring planting, put transplants out early, in March or early April.
- Summer planting for fall harvest is more common.
- Practice crop rotation. Do not plant the same area with a brassica crop two years running

Growing and Caring for Brussels Sprouts

- When the direct-seeded plants are 4 to 5 inches tall, thin them to 14 to 24 inches apart.
- Use a balanced fertilizer to side-dress plants once a month during the growing season.
- Mulch to conserve moisture in the summer heat and to eliminate weeds.
- When sprouts reach half their ideal size, cut the plant's lowest leaves to allow the sprouts to grow to their full potential.
- Pinch out the developing tip sprouts that have grown on 10 or 12 inches of the stem to stimulate early maturity. This focusses the plant's energy toward producing more leaves, fewer stalks, and larger, earlier sprouts.
- If planting in spring (into cold soil), a starter fertilizer may help the plants become established.
- Make sure plants receive 1 inch to 1½ of water per week.
- Side-dress with 2 ounces of actual nitrogen per 100 square feet about three weeks after transplanting when rapid growth has begun.

Potential Challenges to Growing Brussels Sprouts

- Several caterpillars attack Brussels sprouts, feeding on stems and leaves – cabbage loopers, imported cabbageworm, diamondback moth, cabbage webworm, and corn earworm. Cabbage aphids can be a problem, and flea beetles can damage small seedlings.
- Brussels Sprout yellows is a fungal disease that causes leaves to yellow and fall off. Black rot is a bacterial disease common to the cole family.

Cabbage (*Brassica oleracea var. capitata*)

Family	Season	Sun	Soil	Hardiness	pH
BRASSICACEAE	Cool	Full Sun Min. Shade	Well-drained composted, moist	2 to 11	6.0 to 7.5
Height	**Spread**	**Tolerance**	**Ease-of-Care**	**Germination**	**Emergence**
1–2 '	1.5–3'	Frost (limited)	Moderately Challenging	45°F –85°F	4–7 days

The **Brassica family** – also known as the mustards, the crucifers, or the cabbage family includes broccoli, Brussels sprouts, cabbage, cauliflower, collards, kale, kohlrabi, mustard, radishes, rutabaga, and turnip.

Cabbage is a robust vegetable that thrives in well-drained soil. Greens in various colors, as well as red and purple varieties, are available. The most common head form is round, but it can also be flattened or pointed. The leaves of most cultivars are smooth, but the Savoy variety has crinkly textured leaves.

Cabbage is simple to cultivate if you choose the right kinds and follow proper culture and insect management practices. Cabbage has long been acknowledged as a rich source of vitamins and is becoming increasingly popular for its disease-prevention characteristics.

How to Plant Cabbage

Planting Type	Depth	Initial Spacing	Row Spacing	Thinning
Seed	0.25 to 0.5 inch	Seedling Trays	>18 inches	18–24 inches

- Seeds should be sown ¼ to ½ inch deep. Seeds are normally started indoors, but they can be planted directly in the ground for the fall crop. At 70°F to 80°F, seeds germinate in about a week. Grow at 60°F to 70°F throughout the day, with colder temps at night.
- When transplants with less than four genuine leaves are placed outdoors, they are more susceptible to cold than larger transplants. Older transplants with more than six leaves may produce weaker crops or blossom too soon.
- Planting dates in the spring are typically two to six weeks ahead of the average last frost date. Early plantings are risky since the plant will bolt if there is a lengthy cold snap. A hard frost could kill the fragile core leaves while leaving the outer leaves seeming healthy. Before transplanting, wait until the soil temperature reaches 40°F.
- Crop rotation is important. Do not grow a cole crop in the same spot for two successive years – a gap of four years is advised.
- Plant spacing depends on cultivar and desired head-size – between 1 foot and 2 feet apart. In general, recent varieties are spaced 12 inches apart in all directions as they grow to about 3 pounds, and older varieties are known to produce heads weighing up to 8 pounds.

Growing and Caring for Cabbage
- Thin or transplant cabbages when they reach 4 to 5 inches in height, spacing them 18 to 24 inches apart.
- To assist the retention of moisture, apply a thick layer of mulch.
- To keep weeds at bay, cultivate shallowly. To grow healthy cabbages, you'll need enough soil moisture throughout the growing season.
- To protect your crop from early pests, use a floating row cover.

- When grown, heads are prone to splitting in reaction to any stress or rain after a period of drought. Choose types that are resistant to splitting, plant them close, cut roots on one side about 6 inches from the plant with a spade, or twist plants after the heads have firmed to break part of the roots.
- There is a disease risk to planting cabbage or other cole crops in the same site more than once every three years.

Potential Challenges to Growing Cabbages
- Cabbage pests include cabbage, cabbage root maggot, cabbage worms, flea beetles, cutworms, cabbage loopers, slugs, and nematodes.
- Diseases include clubroot, purple blotch (*Alternaria porri*), cabbage yellows, black rot, blackleg.

Carrots (*Daucus carota var. sativus*)

Family	Season	Sun	Soil	Hardiness	pH
UMBELLIFERAE	Cool	Full Sun Shade	Well-drained, deep, composted, moist	3 to 8b	6.0 to 6.8
Height	Spread	Tolerance	Ease-of-Care	Germination	Emergence
1–2'	1'	Shade, Acidity	Easy	50°F–85°F	7–21 days

The **Umbellifers family** consists of angelica, anise, caraway, carrot, celery, coriander, cumin, dill, fennel, lovage, parsley, and parsnip.

Carrots are a cool-season root vegetable available in various colors and are packed with beta carotene, a substance converted to vitamin A in the body. A half-cup serving of cooked carrots contains four times the recommended daily intake of vitamin A. Beta carotene is also a potent antioxidant effective in fighting against different cancers.

Carrots need soil free of rocks up to 8 inches – sandy loam is ideal. Raised beds with sieved soil work well. The easier it is for the root to penetrate the soil, the better the root quality. Plant shorter variants if your soil is heavier. Avoid excessive nitrogen as your roots will have fingers.

Planting Carrots

Planting Type	Depth	Initial Spacing	Row Spacing	Thinning
Seed	0.25 to 0.5 inches	2–3 seeds per inch	12 inches	See below

- For easier germination, DO NOT use seeds *older* than three years.
- Carrots are generally not suitable for containers unless deep enough and well-drained.
- Propagate by seed in situ and thin later. Germination is often irregular and needs a light covering – consider perlite to cover seeds.
- Thin seedlings when plants are about 1 inch high. The variety and intended use determine the spacing:
  - Space them three-per-inch if harvesting as finger carrots.
  - Space one to two per inch if harvested young.
  - Space 1 to 2 inches apart if carrots will be allowed to grow to full size.
- Plant in spring, two to three weeks after the last frost, ½ inch deep, 1 inch apart, in rows 12 to 24 inches apart. Staggered planting allows a year-long harvest.
- Keep the soil damp. Carrots will germinate faster (in a week) if the soil temperature is in the region of 75°F. Remember, lower is slower, but seeds will germinate at soil temperatures of between 50°F and 85°F.
- Plants take between a week and three weeks to emerge.
- Cover the bed with a board to retain soil moisture until seeds germinate in dry weather. Remove the board as soon as the plants start emerging.

Growing and Caring for Carrots

- Thin to minimize competition from neighboring plants. Depending on the desired root size, thin to a spacing of 1 to 4 inches before the plant is 2 inches tall. Tinning by pinching off the shoots reduces the risk of disturbing the remaining plants.
- Mixing seed with sand or fine perlite can reduce seed wastage and thinning requirements.
- Mulch keeps the soil cool and conserves moisture while keeping carrot's 'shoulders' from burning, causing them to turn green and become bitter. Alternatively, hill soil over the emerging roots to prevent sunburn.
- Stagger plantings every three weeks through mid-summer for a continuous supply of fresh carrots.
- Your carrot quality will improve if you maintain soil temperatures between 60°F and 70°F and moisture levels constantly damp.

- To prevent diseases, allow a three-year gap between using a bed for carrots. Keeping a gardening diary makes it easier to track where what was planted when.

Potential Challenges to Growing Carrots
- Generally, no severe disease or insect problems if beds are not used for carrots successively. Possible pests may include carrot rust fly, carrot weevil, root maggots, leafhopper, and slugs.
- Diseases may include aster yellows

Cauliflower (*Brassica oleracea var. botrytis*)

Family	Season	Sun	Soil	Hardiness	pH
BRASSICACEAE	Cool	Full Sun Min. Shade	Well-drained composted, moist	2 to 11	6.0 to 7.5
Height	**Spread**	**Tolerance**	**Ease-of-Care**	**Germination**	**Emergence**
1–2'	1.2–3'	Frost (limited)	Moderately Challenging	45°F –85°F	5–21 days

The **Brassica family** – also known as the mustards, the crucifers, or the cabbage family includes broccoli, Brussels sprouts, cabbage, cauliflower, collards, kale, kohlrabi, mustard, radishes, rutabaga, and turnip.

Cauliflower is a tough biennial plant. The curd, or head, is comprised of latent flower buds. The curd is often white (snowball type), blanched during development by drawing the leaves over the head. Broccoli and cauliflower hybrids with purple or green heads are called *broccoflower*. Purple cauliflower tastes like broccoli when picked before frost and like cauliflower when picked after frost. During cooking, the purple hue fades.

Plant Cauliflower

Planting Type	Depth	Initial Spacing	Row Spacing	Thinning
Seed	0.25 to 0.5 inches	Seedling Trays	>24 inches	18–24 inches

- Sow seeds a quarter to ½ inch deep. Seeds are usually started indoors but may be planted in soil for the fall crop. Seeds germinate in five to six days at 70°F to 80°F and grow at 60°F to 70°F with cooler night temperatures.
- If using seedlings, don't let them get too large before transplanting. However, plants with less than four pairs of true leaves are sensitive to frost – too early, and the frost will get them; too late, and they'll be stunted.
- For spring planting, transplant seedlings two to three weeks before the average last frost when soil temperatures reach 50°F. Do not plant so late that the curd matures in the heat of the summer. If growing from seed, plant indoors five to seven weeks earlier. Space plants about 2 feet apart.
- For fall harvest, plant transplants seven to nine weeks before the average first frost date and put transplants further apart than the spacing listed for spring plantings.
- Cauliflower is ready for harvest 50 to 55 days from transplanting for early season cultivars and 70 to 80 days for late-season varieties. Harvest by cutting far enough below the head to include several leaves to help hold the head together. Each plant produces only one head. You can expect a 10-pound yield of cauliflower per 10-foot row.
- Practice crop rotation. Do not plant the same area with a cole crop two (or even three) years running

Growing and Caring for Cauliflower

- Cauliflower plants should be nurtured in good health from seedling to harvest. The growth of the edible component can be halted by any disruption (severe cold, heat, drought, or plant injury). Large plants that never produce a head are a huge letdown. Cauliflower needs a steady supply of moisture in the soil, so side-dress nitrogen fertilizer when the plants are half-grown.
- Cauliflowers are the fussiest of the cole family crops. In hot or dry conditions, heads will not develop well – so timing is key. Cauliflowers can withstand cold compared to other cole crops in the spring, but mature heads are less immune to strong frost.
- Overexposure to the sun, heat, or nitrogen fertilizer can result in *ricey* heads, in which the curd separates into tiny, rice-like grains.

- A starter fertilizer may aid in establishing plants when in lower-temperature soils.
- A side-dress of 2 ounces of nitrogen per 100 square feet three weeks after transplanting will boost development – if the soil needs it based on soil tests.
- For optimum head development, cauliflower needs to grow at a consistent rate. If there isn't enough rain, irrigate to ensure a constant weekly 1-inch watering.
- Blanching your cauliflower improves the whiteness of your curds. Fold the leaves below the head up over the curd and bind them when it is 2 to 3 inches in diameter (try a rubber band or toothpicks). The curd grows swiftly, reaching a diameter of 6 to 8 inches in three to four days in warm weather and two weeks in chilly conditions.

Potential Challenges to Growing Cauliflower
- Be aware of the following pests common to the cole family: cabbageworms, flea beetles, cabbage root maggot, cabbage aphids, slugs, snails, and cutworms.
- Diseases to be aware of are: clubroot, purple blotch, black rot, blackleg, and cabbage yellows.

Celery (*Apium graviolens var. dulce*)

Family	Season	Sun	Soil	Hardiness	pH
UMBELLIFERAE	Cool	Full Sun Part Shade	Composted, moist, fertile soil	3 to 10b	6.0 to 7.0
Height	**Spread**	**Tolerance**	**Ease-of-Care**	**Germination**	**Emergence**
2.5'	1.2'	Wet Feet	Challenging	70°F–75°F	14–21 days

The **Umbellifers family** includes angelica, anise, caraway, carrot, celery, coriander, cumin, dill, fennel, lovage, parsley, and parsnip.

This cool-season vegetable requires soil rich in organic matter and is kept consistently moist. Plants bolt in response to cold, so wait until temperatures are in the 58°F to 80°F range before transplanting. Seeds sprout slowly and need proper water, while older seeds germinate quicker. Celery is a European wetlands native acclimatized to utilize higher soil moisture than other vegetables. Celery is a low-calorie meal high in fiber, calcium, and potassium, but it is a labor-intensive plant that will put your gardening talents to the test.

Growing Celery

Planting Type	Depth	Initial Spacing	Row Spacing	Thinning
Seed	0.25 to 0.5 inches	Seedling Trays	18 to 36 inches	6 to 12 inches

- Seeds *older* than three years give the best results. Older seeds germinate better and are less prone to blight.
- Propagate by seed indoor, planting in plug trays filled with a good germination mix.
- Celery takes a while to germinate, but temperatures of 70°F to 75°F should be sustained. Once plants emerge, the plant can handle temperatures of 60°F to 70°F.
- Celery seeds need ample light to germinate, so don't cover the seeds too deeply and use additional artificial light for 16 hours a day. They take a while to pop up, so be patient – two to three weeks.
- Seeds can be saved for five years and are best used after three.
- Plants will withstand light frost, but ten days with night temperatures below 40°F and days below 55°F can cause bolting.
- Set out transplants 6 to 12 inches apart in rows 18 to 36 inches apart, about two weeks before the average last frost date.

- Plants are shallow-rooted and require consistent moisture. Lack of water will cause the stalks to be fibrous and bitter. Mulch with straw to retain moisture and suppress weeds.
- Avoid disturbing roots when cultivating.
- Celery is ready to harvest in 75 to 120 days after transplanting or when they're about 30 inches tall.
- Harvest the outer stalks once they're 6 to 8 inches tall, leaving the inner stalks to grow.
- Harvest all stalks before the first frost date.
- Spring plantings are more common in the Midwest, but you might try a fall crop planted in June or July if you can provide ample water.
- Time planting so that the last harvest is on the average first frost date. *Mature* celery can withstand a severe frost.
- If you wait too long to harvest, the stalks will be stringy and tough.
- Expect a yield of 10 pounds per 10-foot row.

Potential Challenges to Growing Celery
- The celery you waited patiently for to germinate may get infested with aphids, tarnished plant bugs, cabbage loopers, whiteflies, and cutworms. Protect them using collars and floating row covers.
- Celery is not disease-prone, but keep an eye out for leaf blight, celery mosaic, and black heart (a calcium deficiency).

Chives (*Allium schoenoprasum*)

Family	Season	Sun	Soil	Hardiness	pH
LILIACEAE	Cool Perennial	Full Sun Part Shade	Not fussy, slight acidity	3 to 9	6.2 to 6.8
Height	**Spread**	**Tolerance**	**Ease-of-Care**	**Germination**	**Emergence**
0.5–1'	1'	General	Easy	45°F –95°F	7–21 days

The **Lily family** includes asparagus, chives, garlic, leeks, onions, scallions, and shallots.

This easy-to-grow allium's pinkish-lavender blossoms make a lovely border in flower beds and are great for dressing potatoes and sprucing salads up. Both chives and garlic chives are perennials harvested for their leaves, which grow to about a foot.

They produce small bulbs, but these are not eaten. Chives produce purple to pink flowers in early summer, and garlic chives have white flowers in late summer.

Chive flowers are edible and can be harvested just as they begin to open – the more you pick, the more the plant will produce. Chive flowers have a mild onion flavor and can be added to salads, eggs, and other dishes.

Growing Chives

Planting Type	Depth	Initial Spacing	Row Spacing	Thinning
Seed	Sowing – light cover	Plugs	Grow as clumps	Grow as clumps
Bulb clusters	To cover roots	Cluster of 4	Grow as clumps	Grow as clumps

- Chives can be grown from seed or by vegetative propagation (division). You can plant indoor and transplant when the soil is above 50°F.
- Chives will take a week to three to emerge – patience is required.
- Space plants about a foot apart in the sun (or part shade) after the danger of frost is past. Start seeds indoors six to eight weeks earlier.
- Direct seed onto a well-prepared seedbed (lightly cover) or transfer mature plants in the spring or fall. (Plants won't be ready to harvest for at least a year if

you start from seed.)
- Cutting plants keeps them strong and healthy and encourages them to spread. To avoid dormancy in the summer, keep flowers picked.
- If cultivated in adequately fertile soil, no fertilizer is required. Nitrogen top-dressing is beneficial to plants that are frequently harvested.
- Every three to five years, divide and replant the cluster in new soil.
- Planting rooted clumps in the spring after the threat of frost has passed is the easiest and most successful method of cultivating chives.
- Chives can be grown readily inside in a bright, sunny setting.
- You can start harvesting when plants are 6 inches tall. Cut down to 2 inches as needed and use the leaves fresh. It is unnecessary to cut all the leaves in a clump – leave some for a later harvest.

Harvesting Chives
Harvest chives throughout the season to encourage the formation of new bulblets and to prevent the leaves from becoming tough. Cut leaves about 1 inch above the soil. Flowers can also be used as an edible garnish. Ideally, leaves are used fresh but can be frozen for later use.

Potential Challenges to Growing Chives
- Chives are impervious to pests and diseases.

Collard Greens (*Brassica oleracea var. acephala*)

Family	Season	Sun	Soil	Hardiness	pH
BRASSICACEAE	Cool	Full Sun Min. Shade	Well-drained composted, moist	2 to 11	6.0 to 7.5
Height	**Spread**	**Tolerance**	**Ease-of-Care**	**Germination**	**Emergence**
1.5–3'	1–2'	Frost improves crop	Easy	45°F–85°F	4–7 days

The **Brassica family** – also known as the mustards, the crucifers, or the cabbage family includes broccoli, Brussels sprouts, cabbage, cauliflower, collards, kale, kohlrabi, mustard, radishes, rutabaga, and turnip.

Frost enhances the taste of this traditional herb from the South. Collards are very cold resistant (harvesting may continue through snow) and one of the most heat tolerant cole crops.

Growing Collards

Planting Type	Depth	Initial Spacing	Row Spacing	Thinning
Seed	0.25 to 0.5 inches	6 inches	18 to 24 inches	12 inches

- Plant three months before the first forecast fall frost. Plant seeds 1 inch apart in rows 18 to 30 inches apart, 14 to 12 inches deep. 12 to 18-inch spacings are thin, and thinnings can be eaten or transplanted.
- Plants should be started indoors approximately eight weeks before the last frost and transplanted for spring crops at six weeks old. Plants should be spaced 12 inches apart, and rows should be 18 to 24 inches apart.
- Plant direct-seeded crops three weeks before the final frost, ½ inch deep and 3 inches apart. Thin to about a foot apart. If you wish to overwinter your collards, mulch the beds.
- Pests don't bother collards as much as they do other cole crops. To prevent early pest infestations, use floating row coverings.
- Plant collards or other cole crops in the same bed no more than once every four years to help prevent illness.

Harvesting Collards

Harvest a few of the biggest leaves every few days. If the plant is well-cared for, it will continue to produce until frost. You may also want the harvest the entire crop when the plant reaches 6 to 10 inches. Plants are generally ready to be harvested in 50 to 80 days. If their leaves are getting tough, replant.

Potential Challenges to Growing Collards

- Cole crops attract their own army of pests, but not collards. Diseases like clubfoot, black rot, black leg, and *Alternaria* also seem not to affect collards.

Corn – Sweet (*Zea mays*)

Family	Season	Sun	Soil	Hardiness	pH
GRAMINEAE	Warm	Full Sun	Deep, well-drained composted, fertile	6 to 11	6.0 to 6.8

Height	Spread	Tolerance	Ease-of-Care	Germination	Emergence
4–6′	1–1.5′	Frost (limited)	Moderately Challenging	65°F –85°F	4–7 days

Sweetcorn comes from the ubiquitous grass family, the six major types of maize are dent corn, flint corn, pod corn, popcorn, flour corn, and sweetcorn. Corn is wind-pollinated and requires cross-pollination to yield a crop.

Few plants are more widely produced or used in more diverse ways than maize. It's becoming more significant as fodder, spreading into chilly temperate zones where summers aren't generally warm enough to grow the grain crop. In Central and South America and many portions of Africa, corn is a staple crop for human consumption.

Growing Sweetcorn

Planting Type	Depth	Initial Spacing	Row Spacing	Thinning
Seed	1 inch	4 to 6 inches	18 to 24 inches	8 inches

- Corn grows best on soil that is lush and fertile. In the fall, add compost or well-rotted manure. To fulfill the nutritional demands of this heavy feeder, consider growing a legume cover crop the season before corn. Legumes form symbiotic relationships with mycorrhizal fungi, known to nitrify the soil.
- Plant the first time after the last frost date. For quick germination, the soil temperature should be at least 65°F. (Corn will not germinate if the soil temperature is below 55°F.) Consider covering the soil with black plastic for several weeks before planting to speed up the temperature rise.
- Plant only a singly hybrid per bed for optimum pollination and well-filled ears.
- Plant seeds 1 inch deep and 4 to 6 inches apart. When the plants are 3 to 4 inches tall, thin them out to a spacing of 8 inches; if the soil is not yet warm, increase sowing rates to guarantee a solid stand.
- Make the initial planting with an early hybrid for a sequential harvest. Plant another early hybrid block and blocks of mid and late-season hybrids two weeks later. Depending on the duration of your growing season, you can continue to plant until late June.
- You can intercrop corn with early-harvested cool-season crops to conserve space.
- Corn plants have a lot of roots at the surface, so cultivate carefully around them. To bury tiny weeds in the row and give the corn a greater grip, mound soil up around the base of the stalks as they develop. Corn may be mulched once the soil has warmed up to help control weeds and maintain moisture.
- Suckers do not need to be removed (side sprouts growing from the plant base). According to studies, removing them can diminish yields.
- Corn is a strong feeder, especially nitrogen, and may require many fertilizer side dressings to get optimal yields. Look for nutritional deficit symptoms – purple-tinged leaves indicate phosphorus deficiency, and pale green leaves show a lack of nitrogen.
- Plant seeds 2 to 4 inches apart for tiny or baby corn and harvest as silks emerge from the ear or pick secondary ears from evenly spaced plantings as the main ear matures. Also, hybrids designed expressly for early baby corn harvest should be considered.

Potential Challenges to Growing Corn
- Pests most common on corn are European corn borer, corn earworms, and seedcorn maggots.
- Diseases to look out for are rust and smut, but both can be avoided by choosing the hybrids cultivated to be resistant.

Cucumber (*Cucumis sativus*)

Family	Season	Sun	Soil	Hardiness	pH
CUCURBITACEAE	Warm	Full Sun	Well-drained composted, fertile	4 to 11	6.8 to 7.2
Height	Spread	Tolerance	Ease-of-Care	Germination	Emergence
1–6'	1–6'		Easy	60°F–105°F	7–21 days

The **Cucurbits family** includes cucumbers, melons, squashes, pumpkins, and gourds.

Cucumbers, whether for pickling or slicing, are simple to cultivate, provided you provide them with excellent soil, full light, and enough moisture, and wait for the weather to warm before planting.

How to Grow Cucumbers

Planting Type	Depth	Initial Spacing	Row Spacing	Thinning
Seed – Rows	0.5 to 1 inch	4 to 6 inches	>48 inches	12 to 24 inches
Hills	Transplant	3 plants	-	36 inches

- Cucumbers are often cultivated from seeds directly sown in the garden – plant in the spring when the soil temperature has risen over 65°F. Warm soil is necessary for plant germination and growth. Cucumbers thrive in hot, humid summer weather when the soil is moist. A second planting for autumn harvest may be undertaken in the mid to late summer.
- Cucumbers may be replanted for early harvest. Three to four weeks before the frost-free date, sow two or three seeds in peat pots, peat pellets, or other containers. Remove the weaker plants, leaving a single plant in each container. When the transplants have two to four genuine leaves, space them 1 to 2 feet apart in rows 3 to 5 feet apart. Allowing transplants to grow too big in containers will cause them to transfer poorly. Cucumbers do not transfer well when plucked as bare-root plants like other vine crops.

- Plant seeds ½ inch deep, then thin seedlings to a plant every 12 inches, or three plants spaced 36 inches apart in a hill system. If you're using transplants, space them 12 to 24 inches apart in a row in warm soil. Space rows at least 4 feet apart.

Growing and Caring for Cucumbers
- Cucumber plants have shallow roots and need enough moisture in the soil at all stages of development. Proper moisture becomes more important when the fruit starts to set and mature. Before planting, mix with compost or well-rotted manure for the greatest results. Cucumbers react well to mulching with soil-warming plastic in the early spring and organic materials in the summer. Using a black plastic mulch in the early season heats the soil and may result in earlier yields, particularly when paired with floating row coverings.
- When the plants start to vine, apply a side-dressing with nitrogen fertilizer. Cucumber beetles should be managed with the emergence of new plants from the soil.

- Vine may be trained on a trellis or fence in small gardens. Cucumbers hang free and produce straight fruits when the long, burpless kinds are supported. Vertical training may be rendered impracticable by strong winds battering the plants. Wire cages may also be utilized to support the plants. When the plants are moist, do not touch, harvest, or work with them.

Harvesting Cucumbers
- Cucumbers should be picked before the seeds harden – most prefer theirs young. The application and diversity determine the ideal size. Pickles should be selected when they are no more than 2 inches long, dills 4 to 6 inches long, and slicing types when they are 6 to 8 inches long.
- When the cucumber is evenly green, firm, and crisp, it is of the finest quality. Cucumbers should be 1 inch to 1½ in diameter and up to 10 inches in length, and some types may grow to be huge.
- Remove any fruits approaching ripening off the vine so that the young fruits may continue to grow. Cucumber fruit matures quickly and should be plucked at least every other day.

Potential Challenges to Growing Cucumbers
- Pests attracted to cucumbers are striped and spotted cucumber beetles, aphids, and vine borers.
- Diseases may include bacterial wilt caused by striped or spotted cucumber beetles, powdery mildew, scabs, cucumber mosaic virus, anthracnose, leaf spot, and downy.

Eggplant (*Solanum melongena*)

Family	Season	Sun	Soil	Hardiness	pH
SOLANACEAE	Warm	Full Sun	Well-drained composted, fertile	11 to 13	5.8 to 7.0
Height	Spread	Tolerance	Ease-of-Care	Germination	Emergence
3'	3'		Moderately Challenging	60°F–95°F	7–10 days

The **Solanaceae family** (nightshades) consists of eggplant, pepper, potato, and tomato.

This heat-loving annual's dramatic foliage and vivid fruits (deep purple, green, cream, and other hues) make it a superb option for decorative beds and veggie gardens. It takes at least two months with nighttime temperatures in the 70s. Eggplant plants are much larger than pepper plants and should be spaced farther apart, and good production of eggplant needs close care. Containers may be used to grow small-fruited, exotic-colored, and ornamental varieties.

Planting Eggplant (Aubergines)
- Eggplant is best begun through transplanting, and it is critical to get the plant started properly. Choose plants with well-developed roots in the soil ball. Planting should not begin too soon. Plant once the soil has warmed and the threat of frost has gone. Eggplants are more vulnerable to cold weather than tomato plants.
- Begin inside approximately six weeks before the final frost date (or eight weeks before expected transplanting). Plant flats or cell-type pots ¼ inch deep. Keep the soil warm (ideally between 80°F and 90°F) till emergence. In chilly soil, eggplant will not germinate.
- Consider using raised beds or black plastic mulch to warm the soil and accelerate

early-season development. Do not add organic mulches to help retain moisture until the soil has warmed.
- Reduce temperature and water to harden off plants before transplanting properly.

How to Grow and Care for Eggplants

Planting Type	Depth	Initial Spacing	Row Spacing	Thinning
Seed	0.25 inch	6 inches	>24 inches	18 to 24 inches

- Plants may be protected from pests by using row coverings.
- The fruit set may be irregular if the season is chilly. Staking is beneficial to plants that produce a lot of fruit.
- Eggplants are voracious eaters, but they should avoid high-nitrogen fertilizers. They may promote luxuriant foliage growth at the price of fruit production.
- Pinch off flowers 2 to 4 weeks before the first forecast frost to direct plant energy toward ripening existing fruit rather than developing new ones.
- Avoid planting eggplants (or other nightshade crops) in the same site no more than once every three or four years to help prevent illness.
- For transplanting, use starting fertilizer – side-dress nitrogen fertilizer when the plants are half-grown and again soon after the first fruits are harvested. In the heat of summer, eggplant flourishes if given enough moisture and fertility. After they are well established, the plants can withstand dry weather, but they need to be watered during lengthy dry times to maintain top output.
- Begin inside approximately six weeks before the final frost date (or about eight weeks before expected transplanting). Plant flats or cell-type pots ¼ inch deep. Keep the soil warm (ideally between 80°F and 90°F) till emergence. In chilly soil, eggplant will not germinate.
- When the first fruits have set, side-dress with 2 ounces of nitrogen per 100 square feet.
- Eggplants like it heated. Eggplants thrive in temperatures ranging from 80°F to 85°F during the day and around 70°F at night. Flowering and fruit set are halted when the temperature falls below 65°F.
- If rain isn't falling, water the plants to keep them wet. Eggplants need 1 inch of water each week for development and up to 2 inches for fruit sets. Water deficiency during fruit sets might limit production, and a lack of continuous moisture may cause blossom-end rot.

Eggplant Harvesting
- Fruit that is picked too soon may contain solanine, a poisonous chemical. If the fruit is firm and your thumb cannot create an imprint on it, it is still immature. It is ready when an indentation produced by pushing your thumb into the skin springs back. It is overripe if the fruit is spongy and your thumbprint is still visible.
- Fruit size, when harvested, might range from third to full size, depending on the variety. It should be firm and have gleaming skin.
- Fruit that has become dull, discolored, or spongy is no longer edible. Take it away from the plant.
- If the fruit is collected regularly, the plant will continue to yield until frost. Any overripe fruit should be removed as soon as possible.
- The stem of the fruit is woody and sometimes spiky. Remove the fruit off the plant by cutting it rather than pulling it. Allow approximately an inch of the stalk to remain connected to the fruit.
- When the fruits are 6 to 8 inches long and still glossy, they are ready to harvest. Instead of breaking or twisting the stems, use a knife or pruning shears. Many eggplant types contain little painful thorns on the stem and calyx, so pick with care or gloves. Allow the huge (typically green) calyx to remain connected to the fruit.
- When the fruits become dull or brown, they are too ripe to be used in cooking and should be cut off and thrown. Overripe fruits are spongy, seedy, and may be bitter. Even correctly picked fruits do not keep well and should be used as soon as possible after harvesting. Large, robust plants may produce four to six fruits at the height of the season.

Potential Challenges to Growing Eggplant
- Pests that may challenge eggplant growers include aphids, flea beetles, Colorado potato beetles, cutworms.
- Diseases common to eggplants can be avoided by not using beds where any of the nightshade plants have grown for consecutive annual plantings. Verticillium wilt is the most common disease with eggplants.

Endive (*Cichorium endiva*)

Family	Season	Sun	Soil	Hardiness	pH
COMPOSITAE	Cool	Full Sun / Part Shade	Well-drained composted, fertile	5 to 9	6.8 to 7.2
Height	**Spread**	**Tolerance**	**Ease-of-Care**	**Germination**	**Emergence**
0.5-2'	10-24"	Frost improves flavor	Moderately Challenging	35°F–85°F	5–7 days

The **Composite family** includes artichokes, endive, lettuce, and sunflowers.

Endive is a cool-weather green with a unique, clear, crisp flavor. It's available in most grocery stores' vegetable sections, but it's pricey. It does not enjoy hot conditions, but it can withstand strong frosts. So it's a wonderful winter green in the South, where the temperatures are moderate. It is exclusively cultivated in the north as a spring or autumn crop.

Growing Endive

Planting Type	Depth	Initial Spacing	Row Spacing	Thinning
Seed – Direct	0.25 inch	4 to 6 inches	>24 inches	18 to 24 inches

- Plant seeds straight into the bed three weeks before the usual last frost, approximately a ¼ inch deep and 18 inches apart. Planting is staggered to guarantee a continual supply. Thin by trimming to achieve a 9-inch gap between plants.
- Maintain a wet environment in the soil until they emerge.
- Start seeds indoors six to eight weeks before the latest frost date for extra-early harvests. Plant in the garden approximately two weeks before the final frost.
- When temperatures rise over 75°F, keep plants well-watered and protected to prevent them from going to seed (bolting). Mulch to keep moisture in and weeds out. Direct seed in the garden around two to three months before projected autumn frost for fall crops. A little frost improves the taste.
- Endive, like other greens, tastes best when it grows swiftly and persistently. Ensure that it receives enough water and fertilizer.
- Endive's bitterness may be reduced by cutting off the light to the heads or 'blanching' them approximately a week before harvesting. Gather the plant's leaves and knot them above the head, or cut the tops and bottoms of milk cartons and put these improvised blanching tubes over the plants.
- To have a milder taste, blanch the heading varieties. Pull outer leaves over the head and tie a week before harvest. To prevent decay, make sure the leaves are completely dry. Other blanching options include covering the plant with a flower pot, cardboard disk, or plastic container. There are self-blanching variants available. Self-blanching is encouraged by close plant spacing of around 8 inches.

Potential Challenges to Growing Endive
- Aphids are the only pests that may challenge your endive crop.

Garlic (*Allium sativum*)

Family	Season	Sun	Soil	Hardiness	pH
LILIACEAE	Warm	Full Sun	Well-drained, composted, fertile	11 to 13	6.2 to 6.8
Height	**Spread**	**Tolerance**	**Ease-of-Care**	**Germination**	**Emergence**
1–2'	6–12"	Frost	Easy	60°F–95°F	7–10 days

The **Lily family** includes asparagus, chives, garlic, leeks, onions, scallions, and shallots.

Garlic comes in three varieties: elephant, softneck, and hardneck. Elephant garlic is a bulbing leek that produces huge, mild-flavored bunches that may weigh up to a pound and contain four to six huge cloves. Hardneck garlic produces bulbs with six to 12 cloves, and softneck garlic produces bulbs with eight to 24 smaller cloves. Hardneck garlic thrives in cold winter climes, while softneck garlic thrives in moderate winter temperatures.

Planting Garlic

Planting Type	Depth	Initial Spacing	Row Spacing	Thinning
Unpeeled Clove	1 to 2 inches	3 to 6 inches	>12 inches	12 inches

- Garlic, like onions, is ideal for wide-row cultivation. Plant the cloves 3 or 4 inches apart, at the entire depth of the bulb, and firm the soil. Make a row that is 10 to 12 inches broad.
- Plant the cloves in late autumn to produce large garlic bulbs. They'll reach maturity the following summer. If you reside in the north, you may mulch garlic during the winter, but keep an eye out for seed stalks and pluck them off as soon as they appear.

- If you have a long growing season, you may plant the cloves as soon as the ground can be worked in the spring. However, the resultant heads will be smaller than those produced by fall-planted garlic.
- If you reside in the South or Southwest, you may plant the garlic anytime from autumn to early April. Garlic dislikes hot temperatures, so plant it early to get a harvest before it heats up.
- Cloves must be exposed to temperatures below 65°F, or they will fail to develop bulbs when planted. Plants may produce flowers; however, they are typically sterile.
- Plant garlic cloves 2 to 3 inches deep in the autumn, with the tip of the clove sticking up. Bulbs should be spaced 12 inches apart.
- Allow 90 to 100 days for maturation. Garlic is mature when two-thirds of the leaves (tops) start to dry out or turn yellow. Tie the tops together and hang them in a cool, dry location for two weeks after taking them from the soil. Garlic is now ready to be stored. Expect yields of up to 25 pounds per 100-square-foot area.

Growing and Caring for Garlic
- Keep your garlic mulched and well-watered from spring through early summer, and eradicate any competitive weed growth. If you see any flower stems sprouting, cut them off as soon as they emerge. Removing flower stems will aid in the redirection of energy to the bulb.
- A few hardneck types have a scape (a flower stem) that may blossom or produce little aerial bulbs called bulbils. These are the hardiest kinds.
- Remove the scape as soon as it starts to curl to increase the development of hardneck kinds (they can be eaten). These cultivars do not preserve as well as softneck cultivars.
- Garlic requires loose soil that is consistently wet and fertile. Per 100 square feet, apply 3 pounds of 10-10-10 or an equivalent.
- Garlic requires a cold season to yield the biggest bulbs; thus, it is often planted around October (like ornamental spring-flowering bulbs).
- That autumn, roots will sprout, and leaf growth will begin when the earth warms in early spring. With the long days of June, bulbs begin to develop. Huge plants in June will yield large bulbs, while little plants will produce small bulbs.

Harvesting Garlic
- Harvest garlic when the tops begin to fall, but there are still five green leaves left, normally in July or August. Plants old enough to harvest should have plainly visible and readily separated cloves, but the outer sheath should not have broken. Because the changeover is very quick (approximately two weeks), keep an eye on development as the leaves begin to die back.
- Bulbs with a split sheath are more difficult to harvest and keep poorly.
- Before storing garlic, dry it well in a dark, airy area.
- Expect a yield of 4 pounds per 10-foot row.

Potential Challenges to Growing Garlic
- Expect few or no insect problems but watch out for too much water that could cause root rot. Do not plant where other lily family crops have been grown in the past three years.

Gourd (*lagenaria siceraria*)

Family	Season	Sun	Soil	Hardiness	pH
CUCURBITACEAE	Warm	Full Sun	Well-drained, composted, fertile	8 to 13	5.8 to 6.8
Height	**Spread**	**Tolerance**	**Ease-of-Care**	**Germination**	**Emergence**
1.5–3'	5–15'		Easy	60°F–105°F	5–10 days

The **Cururbits family** of plants includes cucumbers, melons, squashes, pumpkins, and gourds.

Hard-shelled gourd, birdhouse gourd, bottle gourd, calabash, bottle gourd, opo squash, and long melon are other names for gourds. *Cucurbita*, *Lagenaria*, and *Luffa* are the three principal gourd genera. Gourds are commonly grown for mature aesthetic fruit, while immature fruits are edible in small quantities. *Cucurbita* varieties are the most prevalent, and they come in various colors and shapes. Bottle or dipper gourds are common names for the *Lagenaria* species. *Luffa* sponges are manufactured from dried luffa.

How to Plant Grounds

Planting Type	Depth	Initial Spacing	Row Spacing	Thinning
Hill Planting	1 inch	4 to 8 feet	-	-
Trellis	1 inch or less	18 inches	-	36 inches

- Seeds should be planted 1 inch deep or less if the seeds are small. Plant two to three plants per hill. The distance between hills should be at least 6 to 8 feet.

Growing and Caring for Gourds

- Gourds can be grown in the same way as other cucurbits.
- Planting gourd vines in full sun and good soil will yield the best results. Mulch will assist in conserving water and keep weeds at bay around these shallow-rooted plants by providing a regular water source throughout the growing season. Give plants one or two side dressings of a complete fertilizer throughout the season, but hold off on feeding near the end of the season and minimize watering as the gourds' shells harden.
- Gourds prefer warm soil and are quite susceptible to frost. So don't rush into planting in the spring. Wait until the danger of frost has passed and the soil temperature has reached around 70°F or about two weeks after the last frost date.
- There's no need to start gourds inside unless you're trying to grow a long-season variety in an area that experiences early frosts. Instead, sow four to five seeds 1½ inch deep onto hills or rows. Depending on the size of the vine, space hills 4 to 8 feet apart. Thin to three plants per hill when the plants are 2 to 3 inches tall, snipping off undesired plants without damaging the roots of the existing ones. Sow seeds 6 inches apart in rows 9 feet apart; thin plants to one plant every 18 to 36 inches by snipping them off.
- In colder regions, plant inside in 3-inch pots or cells a month before transplanting outside if you need to start seedlings early. Sow three or four seeds per pot, then thin to one or two plants by snipping out the weaker ones to prevent injuring the roots of the ones that remain. Reduce the amount of water and the temperature before transplanting to harden the plant. After all risk of frost has gone, plant transplants in the garden at the same final spacings as above.
- Black plastic mulch can help plants grow faster, particularly in chilly, short-season climates. To prevent mildew, remove or till in vines at the end of the season. Early in the season, use row covers to protect plants and prevent insect infestations. Remove before flowering to allow insect pollination or when the weather warms up.

- Mulching plants keeps moisture in and weeds at bay. Squash borers are discouraged from depositing eggs by mounding soil at the base of the plants.

Harvesting Gourds
- When the stems and tendrils sprouting from them are dry, you'll know your gourds are fully ripe.
- The gourd's skins may still be green when frost kills the vines in shorter-season areas of the county, but they are ready to harvest if the stems and tendrils are dry and the surface is hard. Harvest as soon as possible before heavy frost.
- Carefully clip the gourds from the vine, keeping a few inches of stem attached, and handle them lightly to avoid bruises. Uncured gourds are heavy, so don't lift them by their stems, which could break.
- To eliminate dirt and fungi, wash the shells with a disinfectant solution of EM1®. Then, in a dry, well-ventilated area, spread the gourds out on a high screen, ensuring they don't touch. As they dry, turn them frequently.
- The time it takes to dry a gourd depends on its size, but it normally takes at least four weeks for thin-shelled gourds and even longer for hard-shelled gourds. When the gourd shell is completely dry, you'll be able to hear the seeds rattle inside, and it will feel light. Clean the surface with rubbing alcohol after the gourd has dried, then seal with floor wax or paint.
- Gourds for consumption should be harvested every alternating day, while the fruits are small and sensitive, just like summer squash.

Potential Challenges to Growing Gourds
- The pests that may bother your gourd crop include aphids, squash bugs, spider mites, squash vine borers, and striped cucumber beetles.
- Diseases may include powdery mildew, bacterial wilt, scab, viral diseases, and downy mildew.

Horseradish (*Armoracia rusticana*)

Family	Season	Sun	Soil	Hardiness	pH
BRASSICACEAE	Cool	Full Sun	Deep, rich, moist, loam	3 to 8b	6.1 to 8.4
Height	Spread	Tolerance	Ease-of-Care	Germination	Emergence
2–3'	6–12"	Slight Alkalinity, Frost	Easy	Vegetative	4–7 days

The **Brassica family** – also known as the mustards, the crucifers, or the cabbage family includes broccoli, Brussels sprouts, cabbage, cauliflower, collards, kale, kohlrabi, mustard, radishes, rutabaga, and turnip.

There are only a few perennial vegetables of which asparagus and rhubarb generally become a garden feature – able to grow for decades. Others, such as Jerusalem artichoke and horseradish, are picked fully at the end of the season, but a root or stem piece is kept for planting the following year. This latter group may be moved about the garden each year. Remember that horseradish can become invasive, so make sure that you containerize the roots, preventing them from spreading to the rest of your garden.

Planting Horseradish

Planting Type	Depth	Initial Spacing	Row Spacing	Thinning
Root stock	Cover 2–3 inches	12 inches	>30 inches	-

- Spade or rototill the soil to 8 to 10 inches before planting horseradish.
- Turn it beneath or mix in a lot of well-decayed compost or other organic material.
- Incorporate a complete garden fertilizer (10-10-10) at 1 pound per 100 square feet into the soil or a significant quantity of quality compost.
- Allow a few days for the worked-up soil to settle before planting.

- Get some root cuttings from a garden shop, a seed business, or a neighbor who already has some growing to start cultivating horseradish. These straight, thin roots are sections cut from a bigger root that has been collected for consumption.
- In rows 30 inches apart, place root portions, normally about 1 foot long, approximately 1 foot apart at a 45-degree angle in the soil, deep enough to be covered by 2 to 3 inches of dirt.
- The plants will grow to reach 2 to 3 feet tall. Expect a yield of 4 pounds per 10 foot.
- Weed management is particularly critical early in the season when the plants are tiny.

Growing and Caring for Horseradish
- You may attempt 'suckering' or 'lifting' to acquire the biggest roots possible. Suckering is accomplished by eliminating all but one or two shoots as they grow, and lifting is simply digging below the top of the plant and lifting to break the side roots.
- Lift twice, once early in the season and once in the middle of the season. Suckering and lifting can result in a huge root that may weigh up to 2 pounds.
- Postpone autumn harvesting until just before the ground freezes.
- Horseradish may rapidly become a weed if allowed to grow as a perennial. Instead, harvest all of the roots in the autumn, before the ground freezes, in October or early November.
- Picking and replanting yearly enhances the taste. Side roots the size of a pencil should be saved for growing next year's crop. Refrigerate after wrapping in plastic.

Harvesting Horseradish
- If you're beginning a fresh bed, don't pick your first horseradish until the following spring. Even if you have a well-established bed, the optimum time to harvest is in the spring, when the horseradish is at its peak.
- Weed management is particularly critical early in the season when the plants are tiny.
- It is advisable to cultivate in the same direction as planted sets.
- Mulch organic material around each plant, such as compost or leaves. It will aid the plants by holding moisture in the soil, keeping the soil colder, and controlling weeds.

- You may dig up some roots in the autumn and store them like carrots or beets, or you can keep horseradish right in the garden (year-round if you wish), digging up a root whenever you want some fresh.
- Expect yields of up to 5 pounds per 10-foot row.

Potential Challenges to Growing Horseradish
- Pests that may challenge your horseradish crop are the flea beetle – some wood ash will repel them.
- Diseases to be on the lookout for are root rot – rotate your site if you find any.

Kale (*Brassica oleracea var. acephala*)

Family	Season	Sun	Soil	Hardiness	pH
BRASSICACEAE	Cool	Full Sun Light Shade	Well-drained composted, fertile	2 to 11	6.0 to 7.5
Height	**Spread**	**Tolerance**	**Ease-of-Care**	**Germination**	**Emergence**
1.5–3'	1–3'	Frost for taste	Easy	45°F–85°F	4–7 days

The **Brassica family** – also known as the mustards, the crucifers, or the cabbage family includes broccoli, Brussels sprouts, cabbage, cauliflower, collards, kale, kohlrabi, mustard, radishes, rutabaga, and turnip.

These fast-growing plants' tender young leaves can be eaten fresh or cooked in soups or stir fries. Harvesting can continue even if there is snow on the ground. Many colored variants are beautiful additions to ornamental gardens and stunning garnishes.

The leaves are similar in size to collards, but they have extremely frilled borders. The color is a rich green, and the texture is gritty and sharp – certain decorative cultivars include colorful red, white, and green mixes. The seeds resemble cabbage.

Planting Kale

Planting Type	Depth	Initial Spacing	Row Spacing	Thinning
Seed	0.25 to 0.5 inches	3 inches	18 inches	9 inches

- Plant seed straight into the garden 4 to 6 weeks before the typical last frost date and continue till then. Seeds can also be started indoors five to seven weeks before transplanting. Fall planting begins in the north in mid-July and in the south in early September.
- Planting should be completed six to eight weeks before the typical first frost date. In 18-inch rows, place 9 inches apart. Within a wide row, the spacing is 16 inches. When the plants are about one-third grown, a side dressing of 2 ounces of nitrogen per 100 square feet should be administered.

Growing and Caring for Kale

- Kale can withstand chilly temperatures but not as much heat as collards. It's best to plant it in the spring and then again in the fall. You'll most likely be able to harvest until the ground hardens in early winter. The flavor is enhanced by frost exposure.
- Planting in the spring will result in a yield that matures in the summer. Plant growth is slowed by high temperatures, and the leaves become stiff and bitter. Kale may be grown in partial shade.

Harvesting Kale

- Expect to harvest about 50 days after seeding – before leaves become fibrous and tough.
- You can harvest the most mature leaves or the whole plant. Kale can tolerate mid-20s temperatures.
- Expect yields in the region of 4 pounds per 10-foot row.

Potential Challenges to Growing Kale

- Kale, like collards, is less susceptible to pests than the other plants in the brassica family. Using floating row covers is a good gardening habit.
- Diseases, though rare, may include clubroot, black rot, black leg, and Alternaria. In keeping with the brassica rule, give beds a three-year gap between brassica plantings.

Kohlrabi (*Brassica oleracea var. gongylodes*)

Family	Season	Sun	Soil	Hardiness	pH
BRASSICACEAE	Cool	Full Sun Min. Shade	Well-drained composted, moist	2 to 11	6.0 to 7.5
Height	**Spread**	**Tolerance**	**Ease-of-Care**	**Germination**	**Emergence**
1–1.5 '	1–1.5'	Slight Alkalinity	Easy	45°F–85°F	4–7 days

The **Brassica family** – also known as the mustards, the crucifers, or the cabbage family includes broccoli, Brussels sprouts, cabbage, cauliflower, collards, kale, kohlrabi, mustard, radishes, rutabaga, and turnip.

Just above ground level, the leaves emerge from turnip-like enlargements of the stem. The pale green or purple stem is swollen. The leaves resemble collards but are smaller, and the seeds resemble cabbage.

Seedlings develop a stem swelling just above the ground – referred to as a bulb. The leaves protrude like spokes, and the plant grows around 18 inches tall. With white flesh, the bulb can be light green or purple. Kohlrabi has a sweet, mild turnip flavor and, like all brassica crops, grows best when grown in colder conditions.

Planting Kohlrabi

Planting Type	Depth	Initial Spacing	Row Spacing	Thinning
Seed	0.25 to 0.5 inch	Seedling Trays	>18 inches	3–26 inches

- Plant seeds directly into the garden for a spring crop, ¼ to ½ inch deep, starting about four weeks before the average last frost date.
- Thin to a spacing 12 inches all around for a square-foot intensive garden.
- Start seeds indoors four to six weeks earlier to gain some harvesting time. There is only one bulb per plant, so make several plantings a few weeks apart to maximize the harvesting period.
- Kohlrabi is more tolerant of heat than other brassica crops, so you may be able to extend the planting (and harvesting) season by as much as a month. For fall harvest, plant seeds in mid-summer.
- Because kohlrabi can withstand a frost, even temps into the mid-20s, plan your last crop to mature a week or two after the normal first frost date – subtract 38 to 55 days from that date to determine your planting date.

Growing and Caring for Kohlrabi

- Kohlrabi prefers cool weather – in the 60s (Fahrenheit). Plants are sensitive to extreme cold, and brief exposure to freezing temperatures can cause plants to bolt. A week of temperatures below 50°F can also induce flowering.
- Fertilize kohlrabi with 2 ounces of nitrogen per 100 square feet in the middle of the season.
- If there isn't enough rain, water the bulbs to keep them from becoming rough, woody, and poor quality – about 1 inch a week is needed.
- Insects and illnesses are typically minor issues, and the harvest is not harmed by a few caterpillars eating on the leaves.

Harvesting Kohlrabi

- Kohlrabi is best harvested when the swollen stem is small, and the flavor is mild. Larger bulbs are more likely to be harsh and woody.
- Harvest when it reaches a diameter of 1 inch and continue till it reaches the desired size for the variety.
- The yield per 10-foot row is estimated to be 8 pounds.

Potential Challenges to Growing Kohlrabi
- Like most plants in the brassica family, kohlrabi may be challenged by cutworms, cabbage loopers, cabbage worms, flea beetles, cabbage root maggots, cabbage aphids, slugs, snails, and nematodes. An early coving with a floating cover will aid your fight against these pests.
- The diseases common to the brassica family (except collards, kale, and radishes) are clubroot, black rot, black leg, Alternaria, and cabbage yellows.

Leeks (*Allium ampeloprasum var. porrum*)

Family	Season	Sun	Soil	Hardiness	pH
LILIACEAE	Cool	Full Sun Part Shade	Well-drained, fertile, composted	3 to 9	6.2 to 6.8
Height	**Spread**	**Tolerance**	**Ease-of-Care**	**Germination**	**Emergence**
2–3'	1'	Frost	Moderately Challenging	45°F –95°F	5–7 days

The **Lily family** includes asparagus, chives, garlic, leeks, onions, scallions, and shallots.

In soups, braised meals, casseroles, and quiche, leeks have a subtle onion flavor. The white shaft and the green leaves are both tasty. Leeks resemble overgrown green onions and have a long, cylindrical white stem with thick, broad, and folded leaves. Plants may grow 2 to 3 feet tall and 2 inches wide.

Leeks are grown for their enlarged leaf bases near the bottom of the sturdy stem. Because no bulbs form, the leek has a bland flavor and is often used as a green onion. Seeds or transplants may be used to grow leeks; sow seeds inside early in the season to get a head start. Cut off the tips of the seedlings when they reach 8 inches tall and replant them 5 inches apart in the garden.

Planting Leeks

Planting Type	Depth	Initial Spacing	Row Spacing	Thinning
Seed	0.25 to 0.5 inch	Seedling Trays	>12 inches	3 to 5 inches

- Apply phosphorus (P) and potassium (K) according to soil test recommendations, and use a low- or non-phosphorus fertilizer unless your soil test report expressly advises extra phosphorus.
- Compost may be added to your soil in the spring or fall to improve its organic matter content. Fresh manure should not be used because it may contain harmful bacteria and may exacerbate weed problems.
- Seeds should be started inside and transplanted in the early spring.
- Plant in a furrow and fill it in to produce a longer white shaft, or hill the plants to produce a long white shaft.
- After the last frost, transplant 4 to 6-week-old plants. Plants should be spaced 2 to 6 inches apart.
- When transplants are planted in the garden, they should be no older than ten to 15 weeks old.
- Before transplanting, put the plants in a cold frame for five to seven days to harden them off. If you don't have a cold frame, leave them outside – starting at 2 hours a day and increasing the exposure daily, then bring them back inside at night.
- Transplant leeks as soon as the weather has calmed down in early spring and daytime temperatures are at least 45°F.
- A half-strength 10-10-10 fertilizer solution will help the plants get off to a strong start.
- Some gardeners grow leeks in furrows to generate long white shafts. Set transplants in a 6-inch deep furrow at the bottom. Raise the soil level along the stems to the leaves as the plants grow, eventually filling the furrow.
- Another option is to hill the plants by planting them at normal soil level and then mounding compost or soil around them throughout the growing season.

Growing and Caring for Leeks
- Pick a weed-free, well-drained spot. Raised beds are the best option – intercropping leeks with other garden plants, particularly early-maturing spring greens. Planting should not be done in areas where other onion family crops have been cultivated in the previous three years.

- As the leeks develop, hill or mound earth around the stems to blanch them. (When plants are young, a single massive hilling might cause them to decay.) Alternatively, wrap a piece of cardboard paper towel around the lowest section of the stem.
- Because leeks have shallow root systems, they require constant hydration and weed control. Water regularly and mulch to keep moisture in and weeds out if the weather is dry.
- Weeds should be removed by frequent, shallow cultivation before they become an issue.
- The roots of the leek are fibrous and shallow. Avoid hoeing too near to the plant to avoid damaging it.
- Cultivate just deep enough to kill the weeds below the soil's surface.
- Mulching to a depth of 3 to 4 inches with herbicide-free grass clippings, weed-free straw, or other organic material will help prevent weed development and reduce frequent maintenance.
- The root systems of leeks are shallow, and they will provide the highest yields and quality if they are given enough water, whether from rainfall or irrigation.
- During dry times, plan to irrigate. Fungal illnesses can be caused by overwatering the foliage. Ensure the plants get an inch of water every week.
- Sandy soil will be wet to a depth of 10 inches with an inch of water, whereas heavy clay soil will be wet to 6 inches. If your soil is sandy, you should water more frequently than once a week. To determine how deep down the soil is damp, use a trowel. Keep the water going if it's only an inch or two.

Harvesting Leeks
- When the stem width of a leek variety exceeds 1 inch, it is completely developed. Some of the lesser kinds reach maturity with a diameter of ½ to ¾ inch. A good leek should have a 3-inch-long, sturdy white stem section. Bulbing, or swelling at the base, is not a good thing.
- Leek tops do not die back as the crop grows, unlike onion and shallot relatives. The flag, or top growth, should be dark blue-green.
- Leeks can be harvested by twisting and tugging them carefully from the ground or digging and lifting them. If desired, harvest the leaves and trim them to a more manageable length.
- Before cooking, wash the leeks well. Because there is typically a tiny bit of dirt trapped between the leek layers, slice it lengthwise, separate the layers, and rinse well to remove any soil.

- Because leeks are frost-tolerant, you may wait until the first frosts to harvest them, and some cultivars may thrive in temperatures as low as 20°F. Protect your leeks with a layer of mulch, and you'll be able to dig fresh veggies from your garden until late in the season.
- From transplanting to the time of maturity, allow at least 90 days. After the stem diameter surpasses 1 inch and the length exceeds 4 inches, leeks can be picked.
- About 30 plants may be grown in a 10-foot row.

Potential Challenges to Growing Leeks
- Leeks and onions have common pest problems – thrips and onion maggots. The use of floating row covers should be a gardener's default go-to when planting new crops of any vegetable.
- Diseases common to the lily family include purple blotch (*Alternaria porri*), and botrytis leaf blight.

Lettuce (*Lactuca sativa*)

Family	Season	Sun	Soil	Hardiness	pH
COMPOSITAE	Cool	Full Sun	Organic, deep, well-drained	6 to 9	6.2 - 6.8
Height	**Spread**	**Tolerance**	**Ease-of-Care**	**Germination**	**Emergence**
0.5–2'	6–24"	Light Frost	Easy	40°F–85°F	2–15 days

The **Composite family** includes artichokes, endive, lettuce, and sunflowers.

Salads may never be the same again, thanks to the wide range of colors, shapes, and tastes. Lettuce can thrive in various environments but prefers to be kept cold, between 40°F and 75°F. Grow in the spring and fall, and shade summer harvests to prevent bolting. Lettuce virtually seldom pollinates each other, and it has beautiful blooms that self-pollinate before blooming.

Planting Lettuce

Planting Type	Depth	Initial Spacing	Row Spacing	Thinning
Direct Seed	Sow and light cover	1 inch	12–18 inches	12 inches

- Seeds can be planted in beds or flats indoors. If the soil temperature is between 60°F and 70°F, germination is fast. However, if the temperature is below 40°F, it will not germinate.
- For these salad crops to succeed, proper soil preparation is important.
- The tiny horizontal roots close to the surface absorb virtually all of the water and nutrients consumed by the plant, despite forming a lengthy taproot. Plants may struggle to develop if the upper soil gets dry or is deficient in nutrients, affecting the quality of the harvest.
- Choose types with a short growth cycle and suited to cold climates.
- Direct seeding: sow seeds 1/8 inch deep, 1 inch apart in rows 12 to 18 inches apart. Thin to 12-inch spacings for crisphead kinds and 6 to 10 inches for other types when plants have two or three real leaves. Instead of a row, you might softly distribute seed (especially looseleaf kinds) in a patch.
- Transplants: 3 to 4 weeks before transplanting outside, sow in 1-inch cells. Reduce water and temperature for three days before transplanting plants to harden them. Plants that have been hardened should be able to withstand temperatures of 20°F. Crisphead transplants should be spaced 12 inches apart in rows 18 inches apart, and other types should be spaced 6 to 10 inches apart in rows 12 to 18 inches apart. Because seeds require light to germinate, do not plant them too deeply.

Growing Lettuce

- Fertilize the soil to promote rapid development and keep it wet.
- Start seeds indoors in July and transplant in August for a late-season yield.
- Leaves should be harvested regularly for fresh salads.
- Use row covers to protect seedlings and plants from cold conditions.
- Plantings in succession should be done every week or two. Grow a variety of types with varying maturity dates to provide a steady supply.
- The root system of lettuce is shallow. Keep the soil wet to ensure that the plants continue to develop. Mulch keeps moisture in the soil and weeds at bay (unless slugs are a problem).
- Bolting is aided by moisture stress and high temperatures, especially at night. Plant additional bolt-resistant types as the season continue. Plants should

be placed where they will be partially covered by surrounding taller plants, latticework, or other screens.
- Row covers can be used to protect extremely early plantings from the cold, protect immature plants from insects, and shade crops as the weather warms up (with the help of hoops). Harvest fall crops at the time of the first forecasted frost. Seedlings are more resistant to cold than mature plants.

Potential Challenges to Growing Lettuce
- Potential pests may include aphids, cabbage loopers, cutworms, leafminers, leafhoppers, wireworms, and slugs.
- Potential diseases include damping off, downy mildew, mosaic, and Fusarium.

Lima beans (*Phaseolus lunatus*)

Family	Season	Sun	Soil	Hardiness	pH
FABACEAE	Warm	Full Sun	Consistently moist	6 to 13	6.0 to 6.8
Height	Spread	Tolerance	Ease-of-Care	Germination	Emergence
1–3'	1–2'	Average Ferility	Easy	70°F–80°F	8–10 days

The **Pea family** consists of all the legumes – beans, peas, lentils, chickpeas, fava beans, lima beans, and soybeans.

Lima beans are a classic garden delicacy that may be shelled or let develop and dry. Compared to ordinary beans, mild soils, warm temperatures, and a little longer growing season are required, and they will do badly if the weather is colder than usual.

Lima beans should not be eaten uncooked as toxic glucosides may be present in low concentrations. Cooking lima beans eliminates any poisons that may be present, even though most current cultivars have little or none.

Vegetable soybeans or shelled common beans can substitute for fresh limas in colder climates since they function better in the cold. Some lima bean types require less heat and a shorter season for gardeners who adore the buttery lima flavor. To identify the best types for your garden, examine seed catalogs or seek out a garden shop with a large seed selection.

Limas may be grown as pole or bush plants, and they are grown similarly to regular beans. While a well-drained clay loam is suitable for common beans, lima bean plants need a coarser-textured, sandier soil. When the seed color has changed to cream or white, and the pods are beginning to swell in the shape of the seed, it's time to harvest fresh-shelled beans. Allow dried lima pods to dry completely before threshing as regular beans.

Limas are fragile perennials that are cultivated as annuals. Unlike snap beans, the mature, still soft lima bean is eaten, not the pod. Lima beans come in two sizes: baby limas, sometimes known as butter beans, and bigger lima beans (Fordhook is a common variety).

How to Plant Lima Beans

Planting Type	Depth	Initial Spacing	Row Spacing	Thinning
Direct Seed	0.5 inch	3-4 inches	>24 inches	6 inches

- Plant seeds in the garden two to three weeks after the average last frost date or when the soil temperature reaches 65°F. Lima beans are more susceptible to cold than snap beans.
- Baby limas: small plants (18 inches); short harvest season, therefore plant until mid-summer for continuous harvest (at least 65 days before the first frost); space 3 to 4 inches apart, rows a minimum of 24 inches apart, and spacing inside a broad row is 4 inches all around.
- Bush-type large limas: short plants (18 inches); short harvest period, so plant until mid-summer for continuous harvest (at least 65 days before the first frost); spacing 6 inches, rows a minimum of 24 inches apart, spacing within a wide row is 6 inches all around; first harvest 65 to 80 days after seeds are planted. The yield per 10-foot row is estimated to be 2 to 3 pounds shelled.

- Pole-type large limas: tall plants to support height; longer harvest than bush types; space 10 to 12 inches apart, rows a minimum of 36 inches apart, both long linear and tepee-like supports can be used.

Growing and Caring for Lima Beans
- Excess soil nitrogen encourages leaf growth at the price of bean growth. At the start of the season, keep nitrogen applications to a minimum. Per row foot, use one teaspoon of 5-10-5.
- Beans have a shallow root system. Carefully cultivate.
- When the leaves or beans are damp, do not grow or pluck them. Bean bacterial blight is a dangerous disease that spreads quickly when the plants are damp.
- Lima bean blossoms can drop due to a cold, rainy spell and overly hot and dry ones, lowering production. This condition is less common in baby limas.

Harvesting Lima Beans
- Harvest, shell, and eat the delicate beans inside the pods (about 65–75 days after planting). It's best if the pods are plump and firm. Taste a couple to ensure that the beans are at the correct growth stage. Mealy and tough-skinned beans are past their prime – pick any pods that have progressed past this stage. Flowering will be limited, and future yield will diminish if let mature.
- When the pods or leaves are damp, do not pluck them. Hold on to the stem as you peel the pods off to prevent shattering it.
- Typically, bush kinds are gathered in two or three pickings. Pole beans produce many minor harvests, which can last until winter. Remove the beans as soon as they reach their peak.
- After 65 to 80 days, you should be able to harvest your first batch.
- The yield per 10-foot row is estimated to be 4 pounds shelled.

Potential Challenges to Growing Lima Beans
- Pests include aphids, leafhoppers, seedcorn maggot, spider mites, bean flea beetles, and Mexican bean beetles.
- Diseases include bacterial blight, white mold, bean mosaic disease.

Melon (*Cucumis melo*)

Family	Season	Sun	Soil	Hardiness	pH
CUCURBITACEAE	Warm	Full Sun	Well-drained composted, moist	6 to 11	6.5 to 7.5
Height	**Spread**	**Tolerance**	**Ease-of-Carev**	**Germination**	**Emergence**
1–1.5′	3–12′		Easy	60°F–95°F	3–10 days

The **Cucurbits family** includes cucumbers, melons, squashes, pumpkins, and gourds.

The garden muskmelon generates the grocery store fruit known as cantaloupe. In the United States, true cantaloupe, with its hard, warty rind and green flesh, is rarely cultivated. The rind of a muskmelon (cantaloupe from the supermarket) is netted. Honeydew, Crenshaw, and Casaba are similar to muskmelon in that they are grown similarly, but they take considerably longer to develop.

Planting Melons

Planting Type	Depth	Initial Spacing	Row Spacing	Thinned
Direct Seed	1 inch	3–4 inches	>48 inches	18–24 inches

- Place three plants every 4 feet in hills if planting in hills. The rows are still spaced 4 feet apart.
- Fruit quality and integrity can be harmed by too much or too little rain during ripening. If there isn't enough rain, irrigate. As they get closer to maturity, melons prefer a drier soil.

Growing and Caring for Melons
- Fruit is heavy enough to be supported if the plant is growing vertically. Stockings or cheesecloth slings work wonderfully.

Harvesting Melons
- Each plant should yield several fruits. The earliest muskmelon cultivars develop in around 70 days, but the majority mature in 80–90 days, and Honeydew takes 85–95 days to develop, whereas Casaba Golden Beauty takes 110 days. A muskmelon needs 42–46 days to mature after being fertilized.
- When the rind between the netting goes from green to tan or yellow, the muskmelons are ready to eat. Lift the melon gently. The stem should easily detach from the fruit (the fruit should 'slide' the vine, for example).
- When Honeydew and Crenshaw have become entirely yellow, they are removed off the vine. They will continue to improve if stored at room temperature. When the blossom end (non-stem end) is soft to the touch, they are completely ripe.
- When the plants are dry, harvest early in the day. As the fruit approaches ripeness, check it regularly, every other day early in the season, and every day later on.
- The yield per 10-foot row is estimated to be ten melons.

Potential Challenges to Growing Melons
- Avoid planting cucurbit family crops (melons, squash, pumpkins) in the same spot for two successive years to reduce challenges. Pests common to cucurbit crops include striped and spotted cucumber beetles, aphids, squash vine borer, squash bugs, and flea beetles.
- Diseases often caused by these pests include powdery mildew, bacterial wilt (Fusarium), fungal leaf spot, cucumber mosaic virus, and scab.
- It should be common practice to use floating covers on newly planted crops – it helps prevent challenges to your efforts.

Mustard (*Brassica juncea*)

Family	Season	Sun	Soil	Hardiness	pH
BRASSICACEAE	Cool	Full Sun Min. Shade	Well-drained composted, moist	2 to 11	6.0 to 7.5
Height	**Spread**	**Tolerance**	**Ease-of-Care**	**Germination**	**Emergence**
0.5–2'	1–2'	Slight Alkalinity, Light Frost	Easy	45°F–85°F	4–7 days

The **Brassica family** – also known as the mustards, the crucifers, or the cabbage family includes broccoli, Brussels sprouts, cabbage, cauliflower, collards, kale, kohlrabi, mustard, radishes, rutabaga, and turnip.

Mustard (also known as mustard greens, spinach, leaf mustard, and white mustard) is a cool-season food that matures quickly and is easy to grow. Although mustard is frequently associated with the Deep South, it is also good for gardens in the central and northern United States during the chilly seasons. Vitamins A and C are abundant in mustard greens.

Mustard is a plant grown for its leaves, which are used to form 'greens' when cooked. It's a cool-season crop that will bolt (flower) and become highly flavorful as the temperature warms up. Both curly and flat-leaved types may be available, and both reach a height of 18 to 24 inches.

Planting Mustard Greens

Planting Type	Depth	Initial Spacing	Row Spacing	Thinned
Direct Seed	Sow and cover with perlite	1 inch	6–8 inches	6 inches

- Plant three weeks before the frost-free period in the spring and again three weeks later. For an autumn crop, start planting in mid-summer. Fall plantings are typical of greater quality because they mature under milder temperatures in most places.

- Seeds should be sown 1/3 to ½ inch deep, and seedlings should be spaced 3 to 5 inches apart. Thinnings are edible.
- Plant every two weeks to ensure a steady supply of produce. Certain plants may bolt swiftly in reaction to rising temperatures and day length. Peppery flavor is enhanced by high temperatures and a lack of moisture.

Growing and Caring for Mustard Greens
- Growth comes to a stop as the weather warms up. Plant again in mid-late summer for fall harvest, be sure to time the last planting to maturity before the typical first frost date.
- Mustard can withstand frost. Take precautions if the temperature is expected to drop into the upper 20s.
- When the plants are about one-third grown, side-dress with 2 ounces of nitrogen per 100 square feet.
- If there isn't enough rain, irrigate to ensure your plants get 1 inch of water a week. To measure 1 inch, use an inch-deep tuna can under your sprayer.

Harvesting Mustard Greens
- When the leaves are young and fragile, harvest them. Leaves that are withered or yellowed should not be used. You may either chop the plant down to the ground or harvest individual leaves as they grow. The leaf texture becomes tougher in the summer, and the flavor becomes more intense.
- You may harvest by removing a few outer leaves every few days or cutting the entire plant off at ground level, as with other leafy greens (maturity is 40–50 days).
- The yield per 10-foot row is estimated to be 4–8 pounds.

Potential Challenges to Growing Mustard Greens
- Protect your crop with a floating cover from flea beetles, whiteflies, and aphids. When the plant has strengthened, remove the cover to encourage beneficial insects – lady beetles and parasite wasps. Mustards are generally less challenging than other brassica crops for pests and diseases.

Onions (*Allium cepa*)

Family	Season	Sun	Soil	Hardiness	pH
LILIACEAE	Cool	Full Sun Part Shade	Well-drained, fertile, composted, moist	3 to 9	6.2 to 6.8
Height	Spread	Tolerance	Ease-of-Care	Germination	Emergence
1–3'	0.5–1'	Frost	Moderately Challenging	45°F–95°F	4–5 days

The **Lily family** includes asparagus, chives, garlic, leeks, onions, scallions, and shallots.

Onions can be spicy or mild – white, yellow, or red. Green onions are onions that have been collected when they are still young. Short-day, long-day, and day-neutral onion types are available and should thrive well.

Planting Onions

Planting Type	Depth	Initial Spacing	Row Spacing	Thinned
Seed Trays	Sow and cover with perlite	1 inch	6–8 inches	Wanted size
Set Bulbs	1.5 inches	1 to 2 inches	6–8 inches	Wanted size

- Well-drained soil is essential for healthy onions.
- Direct-seeding, transplants begun inside, or sets (tiny bulbs approximately 12 inches in diameter produced from seed the previous season) are all options.
- In mid-summer, sow seeds thickly in a block to grow your own onion sets. Roll down the tops around two months after planting to force the plants to create little bulbs. Clip the tips off once they've dried, leaving approximately 12 inches of stem. Cure and store like you would eat onions for eating in a cold, dry location. The next spring, plant your seedlings.
- Long-day, short-day, and day-neutral onion types are available. This is the length of the day that causes bulb development. Shortly after the spring equinox, short-day types begin bulb production early in the season when days are 12 to 13 hours long. On that day, onion plants in Indiana will still be tiny and have few leaves. As a result, the resulting bulbs will be tiny. When the days are 14 to 16 hours long, long-day types begin to develop bulbs later in the summer. The plants are big, and the bulbs are generously proportioned.
- Sets are very little onion bulbs (imagine half-grown onions) that may be obtained at garden stores or by mail order. Plant them and water them regularly, and green leaves will grow quickly. One onion is produced by one set, so seeding is more economical.
- If feasible, buy sets with a diameter of less than a dime. These onions will grow to be huge and preserve nicely. Sets with a diameter bigger than a dime have a higher chance of bolting (flowering prematurely) before the bulbs reach maturity. Instead of dried onions, they should be utilized for green onions. The bulbs will change form as the sets expand. Round sets produce flattened top and bottom onions, whereas elongated sets produce more spherical bulbs.
- Regrettably, you may not know the specific variety of sets available at a garden shop. Plant sets begin approximately six weeks before the typical last frost date to mid-May. Sets of green onions should be 1½ inches deep and so close together that they touch. Place 1 inch deep and 2 inches apart for dry onions. Space rows a foot apart to promote ventilation. Within a wide row, the spacing should be 3 inches all the way around.

Growing and Caring for Onions
- Onions require continuous hydration and weed control due to their shallow root systems. Water regularly and mulch to keep moisture in and weeds out if the weather is dry.

- Pick a weed-free, well-drained spot. Raised beds are the best option, intercropping onions with other garden plants, particularly early-maturing spring greens. Planting should not be done in areas where other onion family crops have been cultivated in the previous three years.

Harvesting Onions
- Onions may be eaten at any stage of their development. If you're harvesting for storage, you'll want to pay attention to the growth stage, harvest carefully, and dry them well (cure) before storing them.
- When the tops of the onions fall over, they are ripe and may be collected for storing. For each plant, this does not occur at the same time. Harvest all the onions once the tops of at least two-thirds of the plant (ideally more) have fallen over.
- Carefully dig onions, taking care not to damage or pierce them. Do not chop off the tips of the plant; instead, harvest the entire plant.
- Before storing onions, they must be dried. Spread them out to dry in a well-ventilated, out-of-the-way location. Plants should not be stacked on top of each other. Place on a screen or hang in tiny bunches to encourage airflow and hasten drying. This might take up to two weeks.
- After the onions have dried completely, cut off all but an inch of the tops (do not cut flush with the bulb) and store them in a dark, dry location. Temperatures should be kept below 40°F, but not below freezing. The bulbs will most likely sprout if the temperature rises over 40°F.
- If the plant has bloomed, onions will not keep well.
- It's a delicious cultivar with a short growing season.
- Suppose you harvested before they reached full maturity; green onions should be kept refrigerated and used within seven days.
- If the onion has a thick, rather than a narrow, neck, it will dry well.
- If the top is chopped flush with the bulb, an entryway for disease organisms is created.

Potential Challenges to Growing Onions
- Your onion crop's potential challengers (pests) are predominantly thrips and onion maggots. Crop rotation and good sanitation (removing all onion bulbs and leaves from the garden at the end of the season and removing all nearby wild onion plants) will help. Row covers used immediately after planting will help keep the adults from laying eggs near your onion plants.

- Diseases common to onions include fungal diseases (Fusarium basal rot, purple blotch (*Alternaria porri*), and Botrytis leaf blight). Avoid wetting foliage if possible and allow space for air to circulate by removing weeds around plants and garden areas.

Parsnips (*Pastinaca sativa*)

Family	Season	Sun	Soil	Hardiness	pH
UMBELLIFERAE	Cool	Full Sun Part Shade	Well-drained, deep, composted, moist	3 to 8b	6.0 to 7.0
Height	**Spread**	**Tolerance**	**Ease-of-Care**	**Germination**	**Emergence**
2–3'	0.5–1'	Frost	Moderately Challenging	50°F–85°F	10–28 days

The **Umbellifers family** consists of angelica, anise, caraway, carrot, celery, coriander, cumin, dill, fennel, lovage, parsley, and parsnip.

Perhaps the hardiest of all garden crops is this cool-season member of the carrot family. Parsnips can take up to 130 days to develop, and their sweet, nutty flavor comes only after two to four weeks of frost exposure (or overwintered). Parsnip is a biennial plant produced every year, and wild parsnip is considered a weed in several US states.

Some people are sensitive to parsnip leaves, so exercise caution (skin rash, blisters). When working with parsnips, wear long trousers and a shirt with long sleeves.

Planting Parsnips

Planting Type	Depth	Initial Spacing	Row Spacing	Thinned
Seed in situ	0.5–7.5 inch	2–3 seeds per inch	>18 inches	2 to 4 inches

- Create a raised bed with ample compost mixed with some sand – the height should be about 6 inches. Add 1½ pounds of 10-10-10 fertilizer per 100-square-feet just before you plant your seeds.
- Use fresh seeds and soak them for 24 hours before planting.
- Mix parsnip seeds with radishes to help mark the area where they're planted. Radishes germinate fast, helping break any crust that may have formed.
- Sow the seeds in early spring, ½ inch deep and about 1 inch apart – separate rows about 18 inches. Seeds germinate slowly, taking two to three weeks (longer in cooler soils). To speed germination, keep the soil moist.
- Thin to 4-inch spacing in the row, trimming rather than pulling. Suppose you have planted wide rows, then space all plants 4 inches apart.
- Germination temperature is between 50°F and 85° F – the upper-temperature range will see faster germination.
- Germination may take up to three to four weeks with lower soil temperature. Planting with radishes helps break the crust that may form, and mulching also helps prevent crusting.
- Always use fresh seeds that are less than a year old and obtained that spring.

Growing and Caring for Parsnips

- Mulch to suppress weeds and retain moisture.
- Keep the bed weeded with shallow cultivation – take care not to damage the roots.
- Hill soil around the base of plants to prevent greening of root shoulders (called sunburning).
- Refertilize with a 5-10-10 side-dress six weeks after planting, using about one cup per 25 feet of row length. Always avoid fertilizers that contain pesticides or herbicides.
- Plan to plant your parsnips 120 days (four months) before the first frost. Leave the parsnips in the ground in late fall for three to four weeks to allow the plant to convert starches into sugars and significantly improve the quality of your parsnips.

Harvesting Parsnips
- Harvest before the ground freezes for the best-tasting parsnips, but after a few touches of frost.
- Alternatively, you may leave them in the ground through the winter but cover them with a thick layer of organic mulch. You should harvest as soon as the ground thaws.
- You can expect a yield of between 10 and 12 pounds per 10-foot row.

Potential Challenges to Growing Parsnips
- Parsnips are hardy plants and not prone to diseases.
- Carrot weevil – remove garden debris in the fall or purchase beneficial nematodes. Carrot weevil is also common in parsley and celery crops, though it's more common in the eastern United States and southeastern Canada.
- Leafhopper – spreads aster yellows, a bacterial disease.

Peas (*Pisum sativum*)

Family	Season	Sun	Soil	Hardiness	pH
FABACEAE	Warm	Full Sun Partial Shade	Well-Drained, Composted	6 to 13	6.0 to 7.0
Height	**Spread**	**Tolerance**	**Ease-of-Care**	**Germination**	**Emergence**
1–8'	0.5–1'	Average Fertility	Easy	60°F–85°F	9–13 days

The **Pea family** consists of all the legumes – beans, peas, lentils, chickpeas, fava beans, lima beans, and soybeans.

Peas, like sweetcorn, are at their best right after harvest. Whether shell or edible pod, peas grow best in the spring and early summer when temperatures are between 60°F and 75°F.

Planting Peas

Planting Type	Depth	Initial Spacing	Row Spacing	Thinned
Seed Direct	1 to 1.5 inches	1 to 2 inches	12 inches	-

- Seed into the garden directly once soil temperatures are above 60°F.
- Sow seed as soon as the soil tilth allows you to cultivate it in the spring, as early as late March or early April, depending on how rapidly the soil warms and dries.

Peas put in 40°F soil take a long time to germinate. When the soil is 60°F (or higher), seedlings can catch up fast to those planted earlier in colder soil – so nothing is gained. If your soil is reluctant to drain, use raised beds.
- Increase harvest time by making extra plantings from early to mid-May or planting types with varied maturity dates.
- Plant seeds in rows 18 inches apart, 1 to 2 inches deep, and 1 to 4 inches apart. Alternatively, sow 1 inch apart in a 3-inch-wide belt (about 25 seeds per foot). When the soil is chilly and damp, shallow planting is optimal. If the earth is dry, plant deeper. Making a furrow or trench with a hoe, placing the seed in the furrow, covering, and firming it is a rapid technique to sow.

Growing and Caring for Peas
- Using a garden cloth, chicken wire, or other suitable trellis material, erect a trellis for tall-growing, vining kinds at planting. Increase row spacing if trellising (4 to 6 feet).
- Maintain moist soil, but avoid overwatering during flowering to avoid interfering with pollination.
- Intercrop peas with cool-season crops that develop quickly, such as spinach or radishes. After the final harvest, plant late squash or cool-season vegetables harvested in the fall, such as broccoli, leeks, or potatoes.
- Fall crops should be planted eight to ten weeks before the first frost date. If the scorching weather continues, fall crops may be disappointing. The best kinds for

fall harvests are resistant to powdery mildew.
- High-nitrogen fertilizers should be avoided. You'll get lush foliage but poor blooming and fruiting if you use too much nitrogen. If peas have never been cultivated, rhizobia bacteria inoculation may be useful.
- Peas should not be planted in the same spot more than once every four years. Avoid planting peas in areas where the roots have already succumbed to root rot.

Harvesting Peas
- Garden peas should be harvested when the pods swell. Take a sample every day or two to capture them at the correct stage – the pods towards the bottom of the plant mature earliest. The harvest lasts roughly a week, with three pickings in most cases. When the harvest is complete, remove the plant from the garden.
- Allow garden peas to remain on the vine until the pods have withered and turned brown for dried split peas. Harvest them, shell them, and dry them for three weeks.
- Snap peas should be harvested when the pods begin to fatten but before the seeds get huge. When broken, pods should snap. If you miss the deadline, pick and shell the peas before eating them.
- Five to seven days after flowering, harvest snow peas before the individual peas have grown to the size of a grain of rice and the pods are still flat.
- To maintain the plants flowering and producing, remove any missed pods in earlier pickings. Snap and snow peas that have outgrown their shells should be shelled before eating.
- Snap and snow pea vines will continue to grow higher and yield peas as long as the plant is healthy and the temperature is mild.
- Peas should be used within 24 hours of being picked – they soon lose their sweetness after being picked.

Potential Challenges to Growing Peas
- You may encounter some pea aphids.
- Look out for Fusarium wilt, powdery mildew, damping-off of seedlings, and root rot, as these can be a problem.

Peppers (*Capsicum annuum*)

Family	Season	Sun	Soil	Hardiness	pH
SOLANACEAE	Warm	Full Sun	Well-drained composted, fertile	11 to 13	5.8 to 7.0
Height	Spread	Tolerance	Ease-of-Care	Germination	Emergence
1–3′	1–3′		Moderately Challenging	60°F–95°F	7–10 days

The **Solanaceae family** (nightshades) consists of eggplant, pepper, potato, and tomato.

Pepper plants are an ornamental and delicious addition to the garden, thanks to their gleaming green foliage and the rainbow of hues of maturing peppers — red, yellow, orange, green, brown, or purple. Sweet bell peppers go nicely with almost everything and are delicious straight from the garden, while spicier types provide heat to various dishes. Peppers do well as stuffed peppers, pickled peppers, and fried peppers. Wait until the soil and air temperatures warm up before planting peppers.

Planting Peppers

Planting Type	Depth	Raised Beds	Row Spacing	Thinned
Seed Plugs	0.5 inches			-
Transplants	Cover roots	14 to 16 inches	24–36 inches	12–24 inches

- Eight to ten weeks before you need to transplant outside, sow seeds and cover with ¼ inch vermiculite or perlite in flats, peat pots, or cell packs inside. Seed germinates best when the soil temperature is 80°F or greater, and it will not germinate below 55°F.
- Plants should be kept in a warm (70°F during the day, 65°F at night) and sunny place indoors. Lack of light will result in transplants that are lanky and unproductive.
- Don't hurry into transplanting outside. Plants can be weakened by cold weather, and they may never fully recover. Plants can be hardened, and transplant shock decreased by spending a few days at 60°F to 65°F with less water. After transplanting, over-hardened plants develop slowly.
- Choose a location that gets light abundantly and has well-drained soil. Prepare the garden bed by loosening the soil to a depth of 12 to 15 inches using a garden fork or tiller, then mixing in a 2- to 4-inch layer of compost.
- Pepper plants may be grown from seeds planted indoors or purchased as transplants. Many gardeners take advantage of the large range of peppers and chilis available in garden centers because they come in various forms, hues, and levels of hotness. Buy plants 4–6 inches tall with a good green color.
- When the soil has warmed, and the weather has settled, set plants out two to three weeks after the average last frost. Plant them 12 to 24 inches apart, in rows 24 to 36 inches apart, or in raised beds about 14 to 16 inches apart.
- Peppers do not withstand temperatures below 50°F for lengthy periods and do not thrive in cold, moist soil. Plant your peppers and chilis later in the season.

Growing and Caring for Peppers

- To hasten soil warming and early growth, use black plastic or row covers. Row coverings should be used with caution to avoid overheating plants and causing them to shed their flowers.
- When they are fully established, and the soil has warmed, if not using black plastic, mulch plants to retain moisture and suppress weeds.
- When it comes to laying fruit, peppers can be fickle if the weather is too hot or too cold. Temperatures lower than 60°F or above 75°F might inhibit the fruit set – it's a narrow variance.

- A high nitrogen fertilizer level might result in abundant vegetative growth but fewer fruits. Phosphorus fertilizer is typically beneficial to peppers.
- Tall types should be staked for an earlier and bigger yield.
- For the greatest results, peppers require consistent wetness. A consistent supply can help prevent blossom end rot caused by a lack of calcium.
- Provide 1 inch to 1½ inch of water every week, but don't overwater. Blossom end rot can be caused by insufficient soil moisture, although saturated soils can cause the plant to shed blooms and little fruit.

Harvesting Peppers
- Fruit begins to develop 60 to 90 days after transplanting for most varieties. After pollination, a single fruit grows to the green stage in 45 to 55 days and the colorful stage in 60 to 70 days.
- Green or ripe sweet peppers can be harvested (when they are red or the color for your variety). When they reach a size that you consider suitable, you may start selecting. If you wait until they turn color, the flavor will usually be sweeter.
- Harvesting peppers and chilis should be done with extreme caution. A yank can remove a whole part of a plant. Use clippers or one hand to hold the plant securely while the other snaps off the fruit. On the fruit, leave about 1 inch of stem.
- Because fruit does not ripen evenly, pick it regularly, typically every seven to ten days. If you store green fruit over 50°F, it will turn red.

Potential Challenges to Growing Peppers
- Several viruses infect peppers – select varieties labeled as resistant. Some varieties are also resistant to bacterial leaf spot. Practice crop rotation and don't plant a nightshade family member in the same spot for two years successively. Be on the lookout for cucumber mosaic virus if you didn't buy the resistant variant.
- Pests common to peppers include aphids, borers, and tarnish plant bugs. Look out for the tell-tale evidence of aphids' (and other pests) natural enemies – the lacewing and lady beetles. Look out for gray-brown or bloated parasitized aphids and the presence of alligator-like larvae.

Potatoes (*Solanum tuberosum*)

Family	Season	Sun	Soil	Hardiness	pH
SOLANACEAE	Warm	Full Sun	Well-drained, deep, composted, acidic	6 to 11	4.5 to 5.5
Height 1.5–3'	Spread 1.5–3'	Tolerance	Ease-of-Care Easy	Germination 42°F–95°F	Emergence 14–28 days

The **Solanaceae family** (nightshades) consists of eggplant, pepper, potato, and tomato.

Homegrown potatoes are gaining popularity again, especially now that they come in a wide range of colors, shapes, and flavors. Most gardeners plant 'seed' potatoes, which is a misnomer because they are little potato tubers rather than seeds. Try some odd potato cultivars like fingerlings or blue potatoes. Potatoes are a nutritional gold mine that is simple to cultivate if given full sun, temperate temperatures, and a light, rich, acidic, well-drained soil.

Planting Potatoes

Planting Type	Depth	Initial Spacing	Row Spacing	Thinned
'Seed' Direct	2 to 3 inches	-	24 inches	9–12 inches

- Choose a location that gets abundant light and has deep, well-drained soil. Prepare the garden bed by loosening the soil to 12 to 15 inches using a garden fork or tiller, then mixing in a 4-inch layer of quality cured compost.
- Potatoes, unlike other crops, thrive in acidic soil with a pH of 4.8 to 5.5. Scab-resistant cultivars with a pH greater than 6.0 should be used. Unless you commit one portion of your garden to growing potatoes in rotation with cover crops, it's typically not possible to cultivate potatoes in their optimal pH range because most other garden vegetables thrive best at near-neutral pH.
- Get disease-free seed potatoes from garden centers or online or mail-order catalogs for optimum results. If you're saving your own seed potatoes, those that exhibit indications of illness should be discarded. Potatoes from the shop should not be planted since they may have been treated with sprout inhibitors, and they may also be weaker and more susceptible to sickness.
- Seed potatoes bigger than a chicken egg should be cut into 1 inch or slightly larger chunks. At least one 'eye' (the bud from which the stem will develop) should be present on each piece, ideally two. Tubers that are egg-sized or smaller can be planted intact.
- Cut seed potato pieces are traditionally allowed to cure for a few days to a few weeks before planting. Because sliced potatoes recover fast, they require high humidity, plenty of oxygen, and temperatures between 50°F and 65°F. You can plant the seed pieces without curing if you have great, well-drained soil that fits those parameters, but the seed potatoes will rot in the ground if the circumstances aren't suitable.
- A popular method for planting potatoes is to use a hoe to dig a shallow trench approximately 4 inches deep. Replace the dirt in the trench and set the seed potato pieces with their eyes up (cut sides down) approximately 8 to 12 inches apart. Trenches should be around 2 to 3 feet apart. Depending on the soil temperature, stems and leaves should develop in two to four weeks.
- Put roughly 5 pounds of sliced potatoes in a big shopping bag and fold the top closed for a less dangerous method. Allow the bag to sit at room temperature for two or three days before shaking it to separate any bits that may have been stuck together. Allow for another two to three days before planting.

- Keep the bag of sliced potatoes at room temperature until sprouts develop if you want quick emergence. Before planting, some types require a two to four-week 'pre-warming' period to break dormancy, and others germinate in a few days.
- Plant two to four weeks before the latest frost date in your area. The temperature of the soil should be at least 40°F. Do not plant where potatoes, tomatoes, peppers, or eggplant were produced in the previous two years.

Growing and Caring for Potatoes
- When the potatoes are approximately 6 to 8 inches tall, 'hill' them by hoeing dirt loosely around the base of the plants from both sides of the row to within about an inch of the bottom leaves – repeat the process every two to three weeks. You may wish to add more hillings along the row, eventually producing a 6 to 8-inch ridge. Hilling protects the developing potatoes from the sun, which causes them to turn green and bitter – Solanine, a toxin found in green potatoes, is hazardous in big doses.
- Alternatively, bury seed pieces shallowly in the soil and cover them with a thick weed-free straw or mulch layer. To block light from reaching the potatoes, use extra mulch as needed. (Mulch may be needed in the amount of a foot or more.) Tubers produced in this manner may be readily picked after the plants have died by pulling back the mulch.
- If you have good potato-growing soil, a third option is to sow seed potatoes 7 to 8 inches deep and avoid hilling or heavy mulching. Although the potatoes take longer to sprout, this approach demands less work throughout the growing season. Deep planting is ineffective in cold, wet soils, and digging the potatoes at harvest is more difficult.
- Potatoes require at least 1 inch of water each week, coming from rain or deep watering. Mulching improves soil moisture retention, and scab may be reduced by preventing the soil from drying up.
- Use row coverings to keep Colorado potato beetles, leaf hoppers, and flea beetles at bay. On the undersides of leaves, crush the golden eggs of Colorado potato bugs, and adults must be removed by hand.

Harvesting Potatoes
- Around the time of flowering, tubers begin to form. Flowering does not affect tuber production; it's only a handy technique to estimate when tubers will start to grow.
- The number of days till maturity: early varieties are 70 to 90 days old, mid-season variants are 90 to 120 days old, and late varieties are 120 to 140 days old.

- When potatoes are large enough for you to utilize, as tiny as 1 inch in diameter for baby potatoes, they are ready to harvest. The deepest tubers are the first to sprout. You may dig into the mound cautiously, harvesting the larger potatoes while leaving the tiniest to mature for subsequent harvest. Because these 'young potatoes' don't keep well, only pick as much as you'll need in the next week or two. If you are cautious not to harm the plant, you can continue harvesting until the leaves have died back throughout the season.
- When the foliage dies down, the potatoes are ready to harvest. If the tops aren't dying back and you're ready to harvest, simply snip them off – harvest by gently digging out the potatoes and removing the top growth. Mid- and late-season cultivars are often harvested in August or September. After the tops have died back, you can allow the potatoes to cure in the ground for two weeks. This causes the skin to harden, reducing the risk of rot during storage. If the weather is very warm and rainy, don't leave potatoes in the ground (tubers may begin to sprout or rot).
- Late plantings will reach maturity around the time of the first frost. The frost will kill the tops, but the tubers will be unharmed. Two weeks after the last frost, dig the tubers before a harsh freeze. Potatoes allowed to freeze in the ground can rot in storage, so choose late-season types. Digging should be done with caution so as not to harm the skin. For many weeks, store in the dark at room temperature. Skins should harden to the point where they are tough to remove with your thumb. Store in the dark between 38°F and 40°F with high humidity during the winter. Tubers that are chopped, damaged or diseased should not be stored. Avoid storing with fruit. Potatoes sprout when gas from the fruit (the plant hormone ethylene) is released.

Potential Challenges to Growing Potatoes
- When exposed to sunshine, the exposed sections of a potato tuber turn green. This is chlorophyll, which is a completely safe substance. Unfortunately, a substance called solanine builds up in this location as well. Solanine is a bitter and toxic substance – mound earth over the potatoes as they develop to avoid the issue. Harvested potatoes should be stored in the dark. By peeling and cutting away any green bits, solanine may be eliminated.
- Scab on potatoes is a dangerous illness, and it may be avoided by reducing the pH of the soil from 4.8 to 5.2. The best solution is to use scab-resistant types and grow potatoes at a regular vegetable garden pH of 6.0 to 7.0. Adding organic matter to the soil in the fall rather than the spring and irrigating dry soils, especially while the plants produce tubers, are two more ways to decrease

potato scab (at flowering and for the next six weeks).
- Using only entire certified seed potatoes, such as aster yellows, will help control a variety of illnesses. Crop rotation is important, and planting potatoes, tomatoes, peppers, or eggplant (any of the nightshades) in the same spot for two years in a row is not recommended.
- Late blight may decimate a potato planting if the conditions are ideal, killing the plants in two weeks. Tomatoes are also infected, and this is the sickness that caused the potato famine in Ireland. Late blight is a fungal disease that affects the leaves and forms dark, water-soaked patches. Tubers can become infected and decompose if infected. In chilly, damp conditions, late blight is more likely. Crop rotation, cleanliness, and not watering from above can all assist. A few late-season cultivars have some disease resistance. Fungicides are an option but should be the last resort as they will impact the health of your soil for future crops.
- In hot, humid conditions, early blight can be an issue. It affects older leaves on older plants, resulting in black circular marks. Although late infections may not reduce yield, fungicide treatment may be necessary if symptoms appear before or during blooming. Some cultivars are resistant to the disease.
- The Colorado potato beetle eats potatoes and allied plants such as tomato, eggplant, and pepper. It is Indiana's most destructive potato insect pest, capable of entirely defoliating the plant. Adults are chosen by hand. When the larvae of the Colorado potato beetle are little, pesticides specialized for the beetle are available and effective. Insecticide resistance may develop in this bug.
- The creation of a cavity in the core of the tuber, known as *hollow heart*, is produced by uneven growth induced by unequal soil moisture.

Pumpkin (*Cucurbita pepo*)

Family	Season	Sun	Soil	Hardiness	pH
CUCURBITACEAE	Warm	Full Sun	Well-drained, composted, fertile	8 to 13	5.8 to 6.8
Height	**Spread**	**Tolerance**	**Ease-of-Care**	**Germination**	**Emergence**
1.5–3'	5–15'		Easy	60°F–105°F	5–10 days

The **Cururbits family** of plants includes cucumbers, melons, squashes, pumpkins, and gourds.

Pumpkins come in a wide range of colors, shapes, sizes, and species. Grow pie pumpkins for cooking, huge pumpkins for cooking and carving, giant kinds for county and state fairs, and naked-seeded varieties for roasted seeds (these varieties bear large, hull-less seeds).

Planting Pumpkins

Planting Type	Depth	Initial Spacing	Row Spacing	Thinned
Seed Direct	1 inch	6 inches	8 feet	24 to 48 inches

- Plant seeds 1 inch deep in rows 6 feet apart, with a final spacing of 2 to 4 feet for shrub kinds. Vining pumpkins need between 50 and 100 square feet per hill to grow. Allow 5 to 6 feet between hills with two to three plants and at least 10 feet between rows for vining kinds. Thin to two to three plants per hill, 4 feet between hills, and 8 feet between rows for bush-vine kinds. Plant tiny varieties in rows with 2 feet between plants and at least 6 feet between rows.
- Pumpkins prefer warm soil and are quite vulnerable to frost. So don't hurry into planting in the spring. Wait until the threat of frost has gone and the soil temperature has reached around 70°F or approximately two weeks after the last frost date.
- There's no need to start pumpkins inside unless you're attempting to produce a long-season variety in an area that experiences early frosts. Instead, direct seed onto hills or rows 1 to 1½ inches deep. Four to five seeds per hill should be sown. Depending on the size of the vine, space hills 4 to 8 feet apart. (Even the mini-fruited pumpkins have long vines.) Thin to two to three plants per hill when the plants are 2 to 3 inches tall, snipping out undesired plants without damaging the roots of the existing ones.
- Plant inside in 4-inch pots three to four weeks before transplanting outside if you need to start seedlings early. Sow three or four seeds per pot, then trim to one or two plants by snipping out the weaker ones to prevent injuring the roots of the ones that remain. Reduce the amount of water and the temperature before transplanting to harden the plant. After all risk of frost has gone, plant transplants in the garden at the same final spacings as above.

Growing and Caring for Pumpkins

- Black plastic mulch can help plants grow faster, particularly in chilly, short-season climates. To prevent mildew, remove or till in vines at the end of the season. Early in the season, use row covers to protect plants and avoid pest infestations. Remove before flowering to allow insect pollination or when the weather warms up.

- Mulching plants keeps moisture in the soil and keeps weeds at bay. Squash borers are discouraged from depositing eggs by mounding dirt at the base of the plants.

Harvesting Pumpkins
- They're ready to harvest when pumpkins have a rich, solid hue. It is important to know how your variety should appear since it might be orange, tan, white, or striped. The rind should be thick and tough. Pumpkins can be covered to protect them from minor frosts, but they must be harvested before strong frosts. Harvested pumpkins will spoil quickly.
- Harvest with care to avoid damaging the fruit. Using a sharp knife or pruning shears, cut the pumpkin from the vine, leaving 3 to 4 inches of stem intact. Keep dry at 50°F to 55°F. The yield per 10-foot row is estimated to be 40 pounds.
- The majority of cultivars need 100 to 110 days to reach maturity. It takes 120 days for jumbo pumpkins (*Cucurbita maxima* variants) to mature. Pumpkins will mature around 65 to 90 days after pollination, depending on the cultivar. Only one or two huge pumpkins will be produced per plant. A dozen miniature pumpkins (approximately 3 inches in diameter) can be harvested from a single plant of miniature pumpkins.
- Pumpkins may be picked when the rind is firm, and the color is a rich, solid hue (orange for most kinds).
- Harvest in late September or early October, before hard frosts, if the vines are still robust. Harvest the full fruit and keep it in a reasonably warm, dry area until Halloween if the vines die early due to illness or other circumstances.
- Using pruning shears or a sharp knife, gently cut pumpkins from the vines, leaving 3 to 4 inches of stem intact. Many 'handles' are damaged or missing when stems are snapped off vines.
- Pumpkins without stems don't keep very well. When picking fruit, use gloves since many types have stinging prickles on their stems.
- When handling pumpkins, avoid cutting or bruising them.
- Fruits that are not fully developed have been harmed or were exposed to extreme cold do not keep.
- Keep it in a dry place at a temperature between 50°F and 55°F.

Potential Challenges to Growing Pumpkins
- Pumpkins are prone to the diseases common to the Cucurbit family – cucumber beetles and squash bugs.
- Diseases include powdery mildew.

Growing a Champion Pumpkin

Whether you want to break the world record for pumpkin size (over 1,000 pounds) or just have fun cultivating a giant pumpkin, it will require a lot of water, healthy soil, pampering, and care. Follow these steps if you wish to go for it.

- Make the dirt ready. Apply 3 to 5 yards of composted manure per 30-foot-diameter circle where each pumpkin seedling will be planted.
- Plant seeds. Four weeks before your final frost date, start 'Atlantic Giant' seeds indoors in 6-inch peat pots. Keep the soil temperature between 80°F and 90°F for optimal germination.
- Seedlings should be transplanted. Transplant the seedlings into the garden after the roots have shown through the peat containers.
- Seedlings should be protected. Cover them with a heated hat to protect seedlings from wind and cold. Remove the hot caps once the seedlings have outgrown them and erect a temporary fence around the patch to keep raccoons and other animals away from the vines.
- Flowers should be pollinated. Pollinate the blooms by hand. Pumpkins may grow longer and larger if you get them to set fruit as soon as possible.
- Fertilize. Once a week, apply a 15-30-15 water-soluble fertilizer to seedlings. After the fruits have set, switch to a 20-20-20 fertilizer. Until harvest, fertilize at 2 ounces per week per plant. Throughout the season, keep the plants mulched and thoroughly watered.
- Choose the most delicious fruit. Choose a young plant that is very tall and appears to be growing at a rapid rate. Remove anything else.
- Pollinated pumpkins should be repositioned. It's crucial to arrange pumpkin fruits once they've begun to grow. The stems growing at right angles to the main vine produce the biggest pumpkins. Gently train the stem of the fruit you've picked to the right-angled position over a week.
- Prune vines 10 to 12 feet beyond the fruit you've picked. To decrease water loss and nutritional requirements, trim any side shoots (shoots that grow between the main vine and a side stem) back to 8 feet long and bury the ends of the vines.

Radish (*Raphanus sativus*)

Family	Season	Sun	Soil	Hardiness	pH
BRASSICACEAE	Cool	Full Sun Part Shade	Well-drained composted, loose	2 to 11	5.8 to 6.8
Height	Spread	Tolerance	Ease-of-Care	Germination	Emergence
0.5–1.5'	0.5–1.75'	Frost	Easy	55°F–85°F	3–4 days

The **Brassica family** – also known as the mustards, the crucifers, or the cabbage family includes broccoli, Brussels sprouts, cabbage, cauliflower, collards, kale, kohlrabi, mustard, radishes, rutabaga, and turnip.

Radish is a cool-season vegetable that matures quickly and is simple to grow – a reason they are often used to prevent soil crusting for slower germinating plants like carrots and parsnip. Garden radishes may be cultivated in any location with enough light and moist, healthy soil, even on the tiniest city lot. Although early types thrive in the chilly days of early spring, certain later-maturing kinds may be planted in the summer.

If watered regularly, the French Breakfast variety stands up and grows better than other early kinds in the summer heat. Additional spring sowings can start in late summer and develop in the colder, wetter autumn days. Winter radishes, like fall turnips, are planted in the middle to late summer. They take longer to mature than spring radishes, and they grow much larger, stay crisper for longer, are generally more aromatic, and last longer in the ground or storage.

Planting Radish

Planting Type	Depth	Initial Spacing	Row Spacing	Thinned
Seed Direct	¼ to ½ inch	3 per inch	12 inches	1 to 3 inches

- Choose a location that receives full sun to moderate shade and has well-drained soil. Prepare the garden bed by loosening the soil to 12 to 15 inches using a garden fork or tiller, then mixing in a 4-inch layer of compost.
- Spring radishes may be planted directly next to rows of larger, slower-growing crops since they grow so swiftly; there's no need to establish a separate radish bed. Radishes may be sown directly in the garden.
- Radishes should be planted ¼ to ½ inch deep. Spring radishes should be spaced 1 to 3 inches apart, while winter radishes should be spaced around 6 inches apart (seedlings can be eaten). Make sure you thin it out. Radishes that are overcrowded do not generate healthy roots.
- If planted in rows, the minimum row spacing for winter radishes is 12 inches, maybe slightly wider. Spring radishes should be spaced approximately 3 inches apart within a broad row.
- Spring radishes are frequently planted with carrots and parsnips, between slower developing cold crops or little tomato and pepper plants since they mature fast.

Growing and Caring for Radish

- Thin young radishes to 2 to 3 inches apart when they reach 1 inch in height. Water in a consistent manner. Heat and insufficient or irregular irrigation can produce harsh, pithy, and extremely hot radishes. Contact your local County Extension office for information on how to control common radish pests like root maggots.
- Make additional plantings every other week until temperatures average in the mid-60s for continuous harvest or plant types with varied maturity dates in a single planting for a continuous harvest. As temperatures drop in the fall, you can resume planting.
- Most winter types should be planted to mature around the first frost date in the fall. (Most winter types benefit from the addition of frost to increase flavor and texture.) Winter types require more room than spring kinds, so space them out to around 6-inch intervals, depending on the variety.
- Keep the soil wet for optimal quality and development.
- Applying nitrogen fertilizer or manure high in nitrogen at the time of planting might result in luxuriant crowns and tiny roots.

- Carrots, parsley, parsnips, and other slow-germinating crops can be seeded in the same row. For the weaker and later-germinating crops, the radishes assist in breaking the soil crust.
- Radishes make a good intercrop with slower-growing crops like other cabbage family crops or tomato- or squash-family crops since they develop fast. Alternatively, radish harvest might be followed by summer succession crops like beans or fall-harvested crops.
- Planting radishes or other cole crops in the same site more than once every three or four years will assist in minimizing illness.

Harvesting Radish
- If you miss the perfect harvesting window, spring radishes get hot and pithy rapidly. When the roots are no longer than 1½ inches, harvest them (smaller is better). White radishes should have a diameter of no more than ¾ inch. Pull the plant out of the ground to harvest.
- The harvest window for winter radishes is longer, and the cold weather enhances the taste.
- If temperatures drop below the 30s, harvest or protect any late-planted radishes. Before the ground freezes, harvest the mulched radishes.
- Before storing radishes, remove the green tips and long, thin roots.

Potential Challenges to Growing Radish
- Like most plants in the brassica family, radishes may be challenged by cabbage root maggots, cabbage aphids, cutworm, cabbage loopers, cabbage worms, flea beetles, slugs, snails, and nematodes. An early coving with a floating cover will aid your fight against these pests.
- The diseases common to the brassica family infect radishes to a lesser extent; Alternaria, clubroot, black rot, black leg, and cabbage yellows.

Rhubarb (*Rheum rhabarbarum*)

Family	Season	Sun	Soil	Hardiness	pH
POLYGONACEAE	Perennial	Full Sun	Well-drained composted, acidic	3 to 8	5.1 to 6.5
Height	Spread	Tolerance	Ease-of-Care	Germination	Emergence
2–3'	3–4'	Drought Frost	Easy	Vegetative	

Rhubarb is one of the four perennial vegetables we covered; artichokes, asparagus, horseradish are the other three. This tart, easy-to-grow perennial is particularly good in pies and jams combined with strawberries. It blooms when the temperature reaches the 40s (Fahrenheit), making it one of the first spring crops.

Rhubarb thrives in climates with cool, wet summers and harsh winters that freeze the ground several inches below the surface. Rhubarb grows nicely in Indiana as long as the drainage is good. The color of the leaf stalks can be determined in part by the climatic circumstances after development begins in the spring, especially for older cultivars. When the temperature is chilly, the stalks turn a lovely pink to scarlet hue, which fades as the weather warms.

Planting Rhubarb

Planting Type	Depth	Initial Spacing	Row Spacing	Thinned
Crowns	Exposed two buds 2" above the soil	-	5 foot	3 foot

- To avoid crown rot, ensure rhubarb has sufficient drainage. Grow rhubarb on a raised bed if your soil doesn't drain well.
- Rhubarb does not germinate well from seed and takes a long time to establish. Thus, crowns (rhizomes with buds) are used instead. Plant four to six weeks before the typical last frost date.
- Apply fertilizer as directed by a soil test before planting. Cover the area with 2–3

inches of properly decomposed manure and work it into the soil if available.
- You may either buy crowns or divide existing plants. At least two big buds should be present on crowns for transplantation. Plant the crowns 3 feet apart, with a 5-foot minimum row spacing. Each plant will require 12 to 15 square feet of space. Crowns should be placed such that the buds are barely 2 inches below the surface.

Rhubarb Growing and Caring
- Side-dress with 2 ounces nitrogen per 100 square feet after harvest. If there isn't enough rain, there isn't enough water, and weeds should not be allowed to grow in the vicinity of the plants.
- A small coating of manure or compost used as a winter mulch can help the rhubarb. The crowns should not be covered.
- Before new growth begins, divide every eight to ten years in the spring. The formation of inferior, narrow stems at the start of the season may suggest that the plant needs to be divided, even if it has been nourished regularly and is growing healthily. Divide and transplant the rest of the plant. It is feasible to divide in the late fall, but be sure to provide a winter mulch.

Harvesting Rhubarb
- Harvesting should not be done in the year of planting or the following year. In the third year, a four-week harvest is conceivable, and harvesting might extend for eight to ten weeks after the plant has established. After the harvest, the leaves that sprout will become the plant's summer leaves, replenishing the root and crown.
- When the stalks are 10 to 15 inches long, harvest them (usually beginning in late April or May). Pull the stalk to one side by grabbing it at the base. It should be simple to separate. It's best not to cut the stalk since budding buds are easily damaged. You should remove more than two-thirds of the emerging stalks on a single plant at no point. Stop picking if all leaf stems have shrunk in size and thickness.
- Depending on the variety, rhubarb stalks can be green, red, or green mottled with pink. When the weather is chilly, the color is normally brighter, but as the temperature rises, the color fades.

Potential Challenges to Growing Rhubarb

Rhubarb is relatively trouble-free. Some potential diseases include:

- In damp locations, slugs and crown rot might be a concern.
- Leaf spot infections can appear but seldom affect production.
- Two insect pests found in grass and weeds are stalk borer and rhubarb curculio. Controlling weeds near rhubarb (particularly curly dock, which belongs to the same plant family as rhubarb) is an effective approach to keep these pests at bay.
- Rhubarb can blossom (bolt) in infertile soil, intense heat or cold, drought, or lengthy days, creating a tall flower stem. Older plants are more likely to bolt. As soon as the flower stem begins to develop, cut it off.

Rutabaga (*Brassica napus var. napobrassica*)

Family	Season	Sun	Soil	Hardiness	pH
BRASSICACEAE	Cool	Full Sun Min. Shade	Well-drained composted, moist	2 to 11	6.0 to 7.5
Height	**Spread**	**Tolerance**	**Ease-of-Care**	**Germination**	**Emergence**
2–3'	2–3'	Slight Alkalinity, Frost	Moderately Challenging	45°F–85°F	4–7 days

The **Brassica family** – also known as the mustards, the crucifers, or the cabbage family includes broccoli, Brussels sprouts, cabbage, cauliflower, collards, kale, kohlrabi, mustard, radishes, rutabaga, and turnip.

Rutabagas are best cultivated in the fall since they take four weeks longer to develop than turnips. The roots are rounder, bigger, and tougher than turnips, and the leaves are smoother. Rutabaga is most typically cultivated in the northern states and Canada, although it should thrive wherever there is a long cold season in the fall or early winter.

Smooth, bigger than turnips, somewhat oblong, white or pale yellow with or without purple at the top, the edible roots are white or pale yellow with or without purple at the top. The leaves resemble collards, and the seeds have a cabbage-like flavor. Rutabagas are a gardener's dream. They began as a hybrid between cabbages and turnips in the Middle Ages and have evolved into high-yielding, nutritious, and easy-to-grow crops. Rutabagas, like turnips and radishes, are members of the cabbage family. Rutabagas resemble turnips in appearance and may be cultivated for both their greens and roots.

Rutabagas are known by various names, including Swedish turnip, table turnip, mangel-wurzel, Macomber, and turnip-rooted cabbage. Rutabagas take a little longer to mature than turnips, but they grow similarly. Growing rutabagas benefit from not becoming pithy if left in the ground past their maturity period; they are also often sweeter than turnips. They also last longer in the refrigerator, have harder root meat, and contain more vitamin A than turnips.

Planting Rutabaga

Planting Type	Depth	Initial Spacing	Row Spacing	Thinned
Seed	½ inch	2 inches	12–18 inches	6 inches

- Early to mid-summer, around three months before projected harvest soon after the first frost, plant seed 2 inches apart and ½ inch deep in rows 18 to 24 inches apart.
- Frost boosts the quality and flavor of Rutabaga. Sow seed as soon as you can till the soil in the spring for early crops.

Growing and Caring for Rutabaga

- Rutabaga is extremely similar to turnip, but it is bigger, reaching a height of 2 feet, and matures in 85 to 95 days. Even though seed can be put directly into the garden six weeks before the typical last frost date, spring planting is risky. After the seedlings sprout, prolonged cold weather (50°F–55°F) might cause the plant to bolt. The roots develop and become highly woody in hot weather if the temperature rises fast.
- The greens of the rutabaga plant are edible. Rutabaga should be planted in a broad row (4 to 6 inches).
- When the plants are 4 to 6 inches tall, side-dress with 2 ounces nitrogen per 100 square feet.
- Plants reach around 2 feet – harvest when the swollen roots have reached 3 to 5 inches.

- Planting rutabagas or other brassica crops in the same bed more than once every three years will assist in minimizing illness.
- To protect your crop from early pests, use floating row coverings.
- Temperatures exceeding 80°F for an extended period might induce extremely rapid growth and root breaking.
- The yield per 10-foot row is estimated to be 35 pounds – a handsome return on effort.

Harvesting Rutabaga

Plant 90 days before the first frost for maximum flavor – check your region's last and first frost dates table in **Chapter 4 – Weather Conditions**. Rutabaga takes 85 to 95 days to mature and benefits from exposure to light frost. Summer plantings for a fall harvest are almost always successful, and your last planting's maturation should be just after the first frost date. Note that larger seeds generally germinate faster and may be ready for harvest five to six weeks sooner than smaller seeds.

Potential Challenges to Growing Rutabaga
- Like most plants in the brassica family, rutabaga may be challenged by cutworms, cabbage loopers, cabbage worms, flea beetles, cabbage root maggots, cabbage aphids, slugs, snails, and nematodes. An early coving with a floating cover will aid your fight against these pests.
- The diseases common to the brassica family (except collards, kale, and the radishes) are clubroot, black rot, black leg, Alternaria, and cabbage yellows.

Scallions / Green Onions (*Allium fistulosum*)

Family	Season	Sun	Soil	Hardiness	pH
LILIACEAE	Cool	Full Sun Part Shade	Well-drained, fertile, composted, moist	5 to 9	6.2 to 6.8
Height	**Spread**	**Tolerance**	**Ease-of-Care**	**Germination**	**Emergence**
1–3 '	0.5–1'	Frost	Moderately Challenging	45°F–95°F	4–5 days

The **Lily family** includes asparagus, chives, garlic, leeks, onions, scallions, and shallots.

Scallions are not bulbous and are also called green onions or bunching onions. Raw and cooked, their blanched below-ground sections and green tips are eaten. They might be juvenile bulbing onion varieties or other species that never produce bulbs. Evergreen White Bunching is a non-bulbing scallion cultivar that may be planted in the early spring for summer harvest or late summer or early fall for overwintering; cover with mulch in northern regions.

This species produces long, thin plants with a little bulge towards the end. It's a perennial that grows anywhere from Siberia to the tropics. Bunching (a cluster of numerous small bulbs) and non-bunching bulbs are the two types of bulbs. In Asian cuisine, they're a common element. Japanese bunching onions are the name given to several cultivars. The onion species known as Welsh is shown here. The name is derived from the German term '*Welche*,' which means 'foreign,' and has no link to the Welsh language. Zones 6 and maybe 5 are hardy for *Allium fistulosum*. In the garden, grow like you would an ordinary onion. If you want a longer white portion, mound earth loosely around the plant as it grows, 5 to 6 inches or more. Before replanting, dig up the cluster and remove a portion of the stems. Single stems can also be separated and transplanted in another location to create new plants.

Growing Scallions

Planting Type	Depth	Initial Spacing	Row Spacing	Thinned
Seed Trays	Sow and cover with perlite	Touching	6–8 inches	Size Wanted
Set Bulbs	1.5 inches	-	6–8 inches	Size Wanted

- Scallions can be produced from seed, transplants starting from seed, or sets.
- Pick a weed-free, well-drained spot. Raised beds are the best option – intercropping scallions with other garden plants, particularly early-maturing spring greens. Planting should not be done in areas where other onion family crops have been cultivated in the previous three years.
- Scallions are best planted directly in the garden.
- Direct-seed in the spring when the soil temperature reaches 50°F. Plant seed ¼ inch deep in rows 12 to 18 inches apart, ½ inch apart, and scallions should be spaced about 1 inch apart.
- Transplants should be started indoors eight to ten weeks before the final frost date – plant four or five seeds in each cell, or ¼ inch deep and ½ inch apart in flats. Trim tops back to around 3 inches tall with scissors if they become too tall and droop – transplant two to four weeks before the latest frost date after hardening off. Scallions should be spaced 1 inch apart.

Growing and Caring For Scallions

Scallions require continuous hydration and weed control because of their shallow root systems. Water regularly and mulch to keep moisture in and weeds out if the weather is dry.

Potential Challenges to Growing Scallions

Avoid soaking the leaves if you have purple blotch (*Alternaria porri*) or Botrytis leaf blight. To guarantee that above-ground plant parts dry quickly, water early in the day. Plants should not be crammed together. Check to see if there is adequate space for air to circulate. Remove weeds from surrounding plants and the garden space to improve air circulation. While the plants are not damp, plant sanitation carefully removes or discards damaged plant portions. In the autumn, rake and dispose of all fallen or damaged leaves and bulbs.

Shallots (*Allium cepa var. aggregatum*)

Family	Season	Sun	Soil	Hardiness	pH
LILIACEAE	Cool	Full Sun Part Shade	Well-drained, fertile, composted, moist	5 to 9	6.2 to 6.8
Height	**Spread**	**Tolerance**	**Ease-of-Care**	**Germination**	**Emergence**
1–3'	0.5–1'	Frost	Moderately Challenging	Moderately Challenging	4–5 days

The **Lily family** includes asparagus, chives, garlic, leeks, onions, scallions, and shallots.

Planting Shallots

Planting Type	Depth	Initial Spacing	Row Spacing	Thinned
Seed Trays	Sow and cover with perlite	1 inch	6–8 inches	Wanted size
Set Bulbs	1.5 inches	1 to 2 inches	6–8 inches	Wanted size

- Shallots can be grown from seed, transplants starting from seed, or sets.
- Pick a weed-free, well-drained spot. Raised beds are the best option – intercropping shallots with other garden plants, particularly early-maturing spring greens. Planting should not be done in areas where other onion family crops have been cultivated in the previous three years.
- Two to four weeks before the typical last frost, direct sow ½ inch deep, halt to 1 inch apart, in rows 10 to 18 inches apart. Each plant will normally produce one bulb at this rate. Sow five seeds and space them 6 to 8 inches apart to form bulb clusters.
- Shallots require rich, loose soil, so amend the bed with compost, decomposed manure, or other organic matter before planting. Before planting shallots in clumps, split them into individual sets (bulbs).
- In the spring, plant as soon as the soil is workable. Plant with the pointed tip up below or peeking through the dirt. Mulch or cultivate to keep weeds from competing for moisture. Because the shallot's roots are shallow, they must be carefully cultivated. On the surface of the earth, shallot bulbs grow.
- Only cover with soil if required. Shallots, used in the green onion stage or as bulbs, have a subtle flavor that gourmet cooks love.

Growing and Caring for Shallots
- Shallots require continuous hydration and weed control because of their shallow root systems.
- Be cautious not to mix up your shallots with grass when weeding; they're extremely similar.
- If the weather is dry, water weekly (1 inch) and mulch to preserve moisture and reduce weeds; avoid soaking the shoots overnight; water in the morning.

Harvesting Shallots
- Pull green shallots out when they are about a ¼ inch in diameter and store them in a cool, wet place for a few days.
- Mature, dry bulbs are dug when the tips die back in mid to late summer.
- Allow a week for curing in a warm, dry environment. Mesh bags should be used to keep items in cool, dry conditions.
- Use smaller bulbs as soon as possible because they don't keep well.

Potential Challenges to Growing Shallots
Typically, shallot gardeners are seldom challenged by pests or diseases. Onion thrips and maggots challenge shallots crops (rarely). Potential diseases include bacterial soft rot, downy mildew, and neck rot. Guard against bruising or planting too deeply, which can cause bulb rot.

Soybean (*Glycine max*)

Family	Season	Sun	Soil	Hardiness	pH
FABACEAE	Warm	Full Sun	Consistently moist	6 to 13	6.0 to 6.8
Height	**Spread**	**Tolerance**	**Ease-of-Care**	**Germination**	**Emergence**
1–3'	1–2'	Average Ferility	Easy	70°F–80°F	8–10 days

The **Pea family** consists of all the legumes – beans, peas, lentils, chickpeas, fava beans, lima beans, and soybeans.

Vegetable soybeans, sometimes known as *edamame*, are kinds of fresh-shelled beans. Plants grow to be 3 feet tall, yet they are strong and erect and do not require any support. Rhizobium inoculation may aid plant growth and yield. Because rabbits and woodchucks eat soybean plants, you may need to put up fences to prevent damage by these visitors.

Pick the pods after they have swelled due to the plump seeds, but they are still green. The hairy pods should not be eaten, and the beans should be cooked in boiling water while still in the pod and shelled afterward.

Soybeans should not be eaten uncooked.

Soybeans are not only delicious but also nutritious. They are abundant in vitamins A and B, calcium, iron, and fiber and contain over 40% protein (11 grams per half a cup cooked beans). According to recent studies, soybeans are high in essential fatty acids and low in saturated fat. A greater intake of soybean products may lower cholesterol and minimize the risk of heart disease, breast cancer, and osteoporosis.

Planting Soybean

Planting Type	Depth (inches)	Initial Spacing	Row Spacing	Comments
Seed in situ	1 to 1.5	2 to 3 inches	>18 inches	Repeat planting

- Propagate by seed, remembering that beans do not like to be transplanted.
- Plant seeds directly in the soil after it has warmed to 60°F, usually a week or fortnight after the last frost date. If soil is too cold, germination will be slow, and the seed may rot. Seeds can be purchased pre-treated with a fungicide to minimize the risk of this happening.
- Plant 1 inch deep in heavy soils or 1½ inches in sandy soils. Mulching lightly with compost or sand will help seedlings emerge in heavier soils.

Growing and Caring for Soybean
- Beans planted on more moisture-retentive soils may only require watering during periods of extreme drought, but those produced in sandy soils will need to be watered often.
- A weekly rainfall of 1 inch is ideal.
- Sandy soil will be wet to a depth of 10 inches with 1 inch of water, whereas heavy clay soil will be wet to 6 inches.
- To determine how deep down the soil is damp, use a trowel. Keep the water going if it's only an inch or two.
- Weeds will be killed by frequent, shallow cultivation before they become an issue.
- Bean plants have a deep taproot, but they also have lateral roots that grow closer to the soil's surface, so it's crucial not to cultivate them too deeply. When cultivating, take care not to harm the plants.
- Weeds will be discouraged by a dense stand of bush beans in the row.
- Mulching to a depth of 3 to 4 inches with herbicide-free grass clippings, weed-free straw, or other organic material will help prevent weed development and reduce frequent maintenance.

Harvesting Soybean
Vegetable soybeans, or edamame, are farmed the same way as ordinary pasture crop soybeans, but the pods are picked when they are green or 'shell' stage. Soya beans are abundant in protein and have a sweet, buttery flavor and a nutty texture.

It's crucial to harvest edamame at the correct moment. A month after blossoming, beans reach their sweetest point. When the beans fill 85% of the pod, which should be brilliant green and look like snow peas, the quality is excellent. A 2-foot-tall plant can produce up to 30 pods. Individual beans can be picked from the plants, or the entire plant can be pulled out of the ground after most of the beans are grown and picked later.

Potential Challenges to Growing Soybean
Edamame is resistant to pests and illnesses. Bean leaf rollers can stifle development in the South, and powdery mildew can destroy the beans on the plant before harvest. However, these issues are rarely serious enough to need yield reductions or limits.

Spinach (*Spinacia oleracea*)

Family	Season	Sun	Soil	Hardiness	pH
AMARANTHACEAE	Cool	Full Sun Part Shade	Well-drained, fertile, composted	2 to 11	6.5 to 7.5
Height	**Spread**	**Tolerance**	**Ease-of-Care**	**Germination**	**Emergence**
0.5–1'	0.5–1'	Frost	Moderately Challenging	40°F–75°F	6–10 days

The **Amaranth family** includes beets, chard, spinach, sugar beets – and quinoa.

The sight of spinach sprouting in the garden heralds the arrival of spring. Vitamin A, iron, calcium, and protein are all abundant. Spinach may be cultivated both in the spring and in the fall. During rainstorms, crinkled-leafed species tend to collect soil. To avoid 'gritty' spinach, choose a kind with simple leaves.

As the days grow longer and the temperatures increase, this cool-season crop is prone to bolting. Plant spring spinach as soon as possible for a yield in the early summer. For an autumn crop, plant again from late July to September. Beet green, New Zealand spinach, and chard are heat-tolerant spinach replacements that are also simpler to cultivate.

This healthy, easy-to-grow cool-season crop is among the earliest to be harvested. Plant it early, though, since as the weather warms and the days longer, it will quickly turn bitter and go to seed (bolt). Savoyed cultivars' dark green color and attractive texture make them ideal for edible landscaping.

Planting Spinach

Planting Type	Depth	Initial Spacing	Row Spacing	Thinning
Seeds in situ	0.5	1 inch	12 to 18 inches	3 to 4 inches

- Sow seed ½ inch deep, 1 inch apart in rows 12 to 18 inches apart as soon as the soil can be worked in the spring (or broadcast seed across a wider area). Spacing should be between 2 and 6 inches in a square-foot garden. Plants that are spaced closer together are more likely to be stressed and go to seed (bolt) sooner.
- Bolting is encouraged by dry soil, heat, and the lengthening of days; thus, it's vital to plant early. Other crops provide some mild shade for later plantings, and warm-season crops such as tomatoes or beans should be planted after the early plantings.
- Plantings should be made every week or two until the average last frost date. Later plantings should be made using bolt-resistant cultivars. For an autumn crop, sow again in the middle to late summer. To compensate for the fact that seeds do not germinate properly in warm soil, increase the sowing pace. Alternatively, pre-germinate seeds by putting them in a plastic bag between sheets of damp paper towel and refrigerating until they sprout.
- Transplanting spinach seedlings is difficult. Start spring crops inside only if your garden is too moist to enable direct sowing in the spring. Three to six weeks before the final frost, start transplanting inside.
- Spinach is a shallow-rooted plant that must be kept wet to avoid bolting. Keep the soil moist. Mulch once the plants have established themselves to keep moisture in the soil and prevent weeds. To avoid pest damage, use floating row coverings.
- Don't use too much nitrogen in your fertilizer. Supplemental fertilizer should only be used if the leaves are light green. Make sure the pH is at least 6.0 by adding lime. If germination is sluggish and leaf tips and edges are yellow or brown, your soil may be excessively acidic.
- For an early spring yield, plant in the autumn and firmly mulch.

Harvesting

The plants may be picked when the leaves are large enough to utilize (a rosette of at least five or six leaves). Late thinnings can be collected and consumed as entire plants. Plants should be cut at or just below the soil's surface. If you chop spinach when it's still young, it'll be of the highest quality. Two or three separate short-row seedings might produce harvest over a long period. Some gardeners prefer to take the outer leaves when they reach 3 inches long and let the younger leaves mature for harvest later. Because leaves swiftly decay as blooming begins, harvest the whole remaining crop as seed stalk development begins.

Potential Challenges to Growing Spinach

- Watch out for leaf miners – cover plants with fine netting or cheesecloth or floating row cover to protect plants from adult flies. Handpick and destroy infested (mined) leaves. Control weeds.
- The cucumber mosaic virus causes a condition in spinach called blight. Downy mildew and other fungal leaf diseases are a problem, especially in wet, humid, or both seasons. Some resistance is available through variety selection. Raised beds create excellent air and water drainage in the spinach bed, which also helps prevent infections.

Squash – Summer (*Cucurbita pepo*)

Family	Season	Sun	Soil	Hardiness	pH
CUCURBITACEAE	Warm	Full Sun	Well-drained composted, fertile	4 to 11	6.8 to 7.2
Height	**Spread**	**Tolerance**	**Ease-of-Care**	**Germination**	**Emergence**
1-6'	1-6'		Easy	65°F–105°F	7-21 days

The **Cucurbits family** includes cucumbers, melons, squashes, pumpkins, and gourds.

Also known as zucchini, pattypan squash, yellow squash, scalloped squash (or flying saucers, as my son would say).

Straight green fruit (zucchini, cocozelle, Caserta), yellow fruit (crookneck or straight neck), and scalloped fruit (scallopini or patty pan), which are typically white, are all common kinds.

The majority of summer squash cultivars are bushy plants rather than vines.

Planting Summer Squash

Planting Type	Depth	Initial Spacing	Row Spacing	Thinning
Seeds in situ	1 inch	-	>30 inches	24 to 36 inches

Plant seeds four directly ½ to 1 inch deep, 24 to 36 inches apart in rows at least 30 inches apart. In a square foot garden, separate plants 24 to 36 inches apart. Plant three plants 4 feet apart in hills if you're using that system.

Alternatively, start inside in 2 to 3-inch pots placed on a heating mat three to four weeks before transplanting outside for additional early harvests. Sow three or four seeds per pot, then trim to one or two plants by snipping out the weaker ones to prevent injuring the roots of the ones that remain. Reduce the amount of water and the temperature before transplanting to harden the plant. After all risk of frost has gone, plant transplants 2 to 3 feet apart in the garden.

Germinates at soil temperature between 65°F and 105°F; does not germinate in cold soil. Plant only when the soil temperature reaches at least 65°F, ideally above 70°F. At 95°F, it germinates optimally.

Days to emergence: five to ten. With a soil temperature of 70°F and proper moisture, seeds should germinate within a week.

Growing and Caring for Summer Squash
- Squash prefers warm soil and is quite susceptible to frost. So don't hurry into planting in the spring. Wait until the threat of frost has gone and the soil temperature has reached around 70°F or approximately two weeks after the last frost date.
- Use black plastic mulch to warm the soil before direct sowing or transplanting to speed up the first harvest by up to two weeks. Poor pollination causes early fruits to wrinkle, turn black, or rot.
- To prevent mildew, remove or till in vines at the end of the season. Early in the season, use row covers to protect plants and avoid pest infestations. Remove the cover before blossoming to enable insect pollination or when the weather warms up.
- Mulching plants keeps moisture in the soil and keeps weeds at bay. Squash borers are discouraged from depositing eggs by mounding dirt at the base of the plants.

Harvesting Summer Squash
- When the elongated types (zucchini, crookneck) are less than 2 inches in diameter and 6–8 inches long, harvest them. Scalloped kinds should have a diameter of 3–4 inches. It's too ripe for the table if the rind is too rough to be marked with a thumbnail. After 40–50 days, the first fruit is ready to pick. The yield per 10-foot row is estimated to be 60 fruits (about 15 lb).
- Summer squash is collected when the fruit is still young, and the skin and flesh are soft. If squash is collected regularly, the plants will continue to produce fresh flowers and fruit, producing squash throughout the summer.
- Summer squash is ready to pick in four to eight days after pollination. The squash will rapidly grow too huge if you don't monitor the plants every day or two. Flowering time may be reduced. Pick and discard any overripe fruit you come across.

Potential Challenges to Growing Summer Squash
- Pests attracted to the cucurbit family are striped and spotted cucumber beetles, aphids, and vine borers. Diseases may include bacterial wilt caused by striped or spotted cucumber beetles, powdery mildew, scabs, cucumber mosaic virus, anthracnose, leaf spot, and downy.
- Cover young plants with thin netting or cheesecloth tents, or use floating row covers. Place at the time of planting and remove at the time of flowering. Beetle control may have a role in avoiding bacteria wilt.

Squash – Winter (*Cucurbita maxima, C. pepo, C. moschata*)

Family	Season	Sun	Soil	Hardiness	pH
CUCURBITACEAE	Warm	Full Sun	Well-drained composted, fertile	4 to 11	6.8 to 7.2
Height	Spread	Tolerance	Ease-of-Care	Germination	Emergence
1–6'	1–6'		Easy	60°F–105°F	7–21 days

The **Cucurbits family** includes cucumbers, melons, squashes, pumpkins, and gourds.

Winter squash needs to mature before harvesting. It's called winter squash because it stores well over winter. Butternut makes a fabulous soup, and the other varieties are commonly used in pies (think Mother Hubbard). There are bush, semi-bush, and vining cultivars available. Winter squashes include acorn, butternut, Hubbard, Turk's turban, and cushaw.

Planting Winter Squash

Planting Type	Depth	Initial Spacing	Row Spacing	Thinning
Seeds in situ	1 inch	Plant 4 seeds	>6 feet	24 to 36 inches

- Seeds are used to propagate.
- 60°F to 105°F germination temperature; does not germinate in cold soil. Plant only when the soil temperature reaches at least 65°F, ideally 70°F or higher. It germinates best around 95°F.

- Five to ten days till emergence. With a soil temperature of 70°F and enough moisture, seeds should germinate in less than a week.
- Seeds should be planted 1 inch deep. Plant shrub variety in rows 6 feet apart, spacing 24 to 36 inches apart. Each hill of vining winter squash requires 50 to 100 square feet. Allow 5 to 6 feet between hills with three plants and at least 7 feet between rows for vining kinds. Thin to two plants per hill, 4 feet between hills, and 8 feet between rows for semi-vining kinds.

Growing and Caring for Squash
- Squash prefers warm soil and is quite susceptible to frost. So don't hurry into planting in the spring. Wait until the threat of frost has gone and the soil temperature has reached around 70°F or approximately two weeks after the last frost date.
- There's no need to start winter squash inside unless you're growing a long-season variety in a location that experiences early frosts.
- Plant inside in 3-inch pots, if you prefer, three to four weeks before transplanting outside if you need to start seedlings early. Sow three or four seeds per pot, then trim to one or two plants by snipping out the weaker ones to prevent injuring the roots of the ones that remain. Reduce the amount of water and the temperature before transplanting to harden the plant. After all risk of frost has gone, plant transplants in the garden at the same final spacings as above.
- Black plastic mulch can help plants grow faster, particularly in chilly, short-season climates. To prevent mildew, remove or till in vines at the end of the season. Early in the season, use row covers to protect plants and avoid pest infestations. Remove before flowering to allow insect pollination or when the weather warms up.
- Mulching plants keeps moisture in the soil and keeps weeds at bay. Squash borers are discouraged from depositing eggs by mounding dirt at the base of the plants.

Harvesting Squash
- Harvest when the color is rich, and the rind is firm, just like pumpkins. Harvest before a heavy frost to avoid a mild freeze (cold weather boosts taste). Leave a 2-inch stem on the picked fruit. Fruit that has been chopped, bruised, or frozen is no longer edible. Keep dry at 50°F to 55°F. Limit stacking to two fruits deep. Each plant should yield several fruits.
- From seed to maturity, winter squash takes 85–100 days. The fruit matures approximately 60–90 days after pollination depending on the type.
- Expect a yield of up to 10 pounds per 10-foot row.

Potential Challenges to Growing Winter Squash
- Squash bug insects are a major pest and can be picked by hand. Plant leftovers should be buried or composted after harvesting.
- Remove the squash vine borer by hand. Butternut squash is a hardy vegetable.
- Striped cucumber bugs – make tents out of thin netting or cheesecloth, or cover immature plants with floating row cover. Place at the time of planting and remove before blossoming. Beetle control may have a role in avoiding bacterial wilt.
- Pests attracted to the cucurbit family are striped and spotted cucumber beetles, aphids, and vine borers. Diseases may include bacterial wilt caused by striped or spotted cucumber beetles, powdery mildew, scabs, cucumber mosaic virus, anthracnose, leaf spot, and downy.

Swiss Chard (*Beta vulgaris var. cicla*)

Family	Season	Sun	Soil	Hardiness	pH
AMARANTHACEAE	Cool	Full Sun Part Shade	Well-drained sandy loam	2 to 11	6.5 to 7.0
Height	**Spread**	**Tolerance**	**Ease-of-Care**	**Germination**	**Emergence**
1'	0.5'	Low Fertility	Easy	50°F–85°F	5–8 days

The **Amaranth family** includes beets, chard, spinach, sugar beets – and quinoa.

Chard is a beet that has been selected for leaf production over storage root development. Fresh white, yellow, or red leaf stalks are produced by chard, and it's a lovely decorative that brightens up the veggie garden.

The first year of harvesting chard is a cool-season biennial. It's a beet grown for its leaves rather than its bloated roots. It can withstand hot temperatures. A spring planting will flourish throughout the summer and last until the first harsh winter. Chard comes in two varieties: green-white stalks and red stalks. The stalks of the Bright Lights cultivar come in various colors, including vivid reds, orange, peach, yellow, pink, cream, gold, and purple – all are edible and can withstand some shade.

Planting Swiss Chard

Planting Type	Depth	Initial Spacing	Row Spacing	Thinning
Seeds	0.5 to 0.75 inch	1 to 1.5 inches	18 to 24 inches	6 to 10 inches

- Early to mid-spring is the best time to direct sow chard into the garden.
- Plant seeds at a depth of ½ to ¾ inch, spacing them about 1½ inches apart – to be thinned to a 4-inch spacing
- Seedlings should be spaced 4 to 6 inches apart or even 2 to 3 inches apart, then harvest the surplus plants whole when they are mature enough for greens – when they reach a height of 6 to 8 inches – leaving a final spacing of 9 to 12 inches between plants.
- Maintain adequate soil moisture to ensure healthy plant growth.
- Suitable for 3-gallon (or bigger) containers.

Growing and Caring for Swiss Chard

- Make succession plantings until late summer if you wish to harvest full plants.
- After the last frost date, plant Ruby Red or Rhubarb chard, some types may go to seed (bolt) if seeds are exposed to cold conditions.
- Start seeds inside for early yields or to arrange different colored plants of the Bright Lights type.
- Mulch plants to keep moisture in and weeds out.
- When the leaves have reached a viable size, you may begin harvesting. Cut plants an inch or two above the earth for cut-and-come-again harvest, or remove a leaf or two from each plant. Harvest the plant without injuring the growth point in the middle.
- Older leaves get tougher as plants age. To foster a flush of new, sensitive growth, cut plants down to around 3 to 5 inches tall.
- Maintain adequate soil moisture to ensure healthy plant growth.

Harvesting Swiss Chard

Chard can be harvested in two ways:

- When the sizable outer leaves reach 8 to 12 inches long, cut them off at about 1 inch above the soil. Chard will continue to generate new leaves until frost if you don't hurt the plant's growth point in the middle.
- Alternatively, you can harvest the entire plant by cutting it off at the soil line around 60 days after planting.
- Expect a yield of about 10 to 12 pounds per 10-foot row.

Potential Challenges to Growing Chard

Swiss chard crops may have aphid and leaf miner pest challenges. Diseases are leaf spot and downy mildew, which can be avoided with proper care.

Tomatoes (*Solanum Lycopersicum*)

Family	Season	Sun	Soil	Hardiness	pH
SOLANACEAE	Warm	Full Sun	Well-drained composted, fertile	11 to 13	6.0 to 6.8
Height	**Spread**	**Tolerance**	**Ease-of-Care**	**Germination**	**Emergence**
2-6'	2-6'		Moderately Challenging	60°F-95°F	6-12 days

The **Solanaceae family** (nightshades) consists of eggplant, pepper, potato, and tomato.

The most popular garden veggie, tomatoes, come in various sizes, shapes, and colors. For early harvest or chilly weather, choose determinate varieties. Compact cultivars are also suitable for use in pots and flower gardens. The following are the main types of varieties:

- Cherry
- Grape
- Extra Early
- Early
- Main Season
- Paste (or Jam)
- Heirloom

Planting Tomatoes

There is such a wide variety of tomato cultivars that some knowledge of the basic categories is important before considering adding tomatoes to your first vegetable garden. Two main categories are important – determinate and indeterminate tomatoes.

Determinate Varieties

Determined tomatoes have a genetically programmed growth restriction, reaching a specific height before flowering and producing fruit all at once. They are great for container plants or in garden settings with limited space since they are compact with bushier growth rather than vining.

- Containers are ideal for growing determinate varieties.
- Plant is smaller and grows at a slower rate.
- Fruit ripens early in the season, producing a large quantity of fruit at once, perfect for processing and storage.
- Little staking or caging is required.
- It's possible to include it in flower gardens.

Indeterminate Varieties

Throughout the growing season, indeterminate tomatoes continue to develop and produce. Indeterminate tomatoes may become fairly substantial bushes if allowed to grow. Throughout the season, they will also require extra staking or caging. The growth pattern on certain indeterminate kinds is so strong that regular wire cages are frequently insufficient.

- Ideal for big, devoted vegetable gardens.
- Plants having a wide spread of growth.
- The fruit matures from early to late in the season, and production continues until frost.
- Large pots may work, but in-ground planting is preferable.
- Ideal for big, devoted vegetable gardens.

Planting Type	Depth	Spacing	Row
Determinate	Sow and lightly cover	12 to 24 inches	5 feet
Indeterminate (Staked)	Sow and lightly cover	14 to 20 inches	5 feet
Indeterminate (Unstaked)	Sow and lightly cover	24 to 36 inches	12 feet

- Tomatoes may be grown from seeds sown indoors or purchased as transplants. Tomato seeds are seldom directly sown in the garden.
- Start seeds inside, four to six weeks before the usual last frost date, by planting them 1/8 to ¼ inch deep in a sterile mix. The final chance to plant is a 100 days before the first frost. Seedlings emerge in about six days at ideal germination conditions of 75°F to 80 °F and grow them around 60°F to 75°F.
- As the seedlings grow, transplant them into larger pots and provide ample light to keep the plants short and stocky.
- When buying transplants, search for strong, short, and dark green plants. Plants that are tall, leggy, yellowish, or begun to flower should be avoided. Plants that are too old are more likely to stall after transplantation, whereas younger, smaller plants yield more fruit earlier.
- When you start your plants from seed, you have more options on which varieties to cultivate. If you're starting your plants, be sure you have an area where they'll get adequate light. Even a bright, south-facing window is insufficient. To complement sunlight, consider utilizing a grow light.
- Plants should not be started too early. Six to eight weeks before transplanting outside, sow seedlings inside. Plant them 1/8 inch deep in sterile seed, starting mix in flats or cells. Seeds germinate best between 75°F and 90°F. Then, at around 70°F, cultivate the grafts.
- Also, don't transplant too soon. Plants can be stressed by cold soil and air temperatures. After the last frost, wait at least a week or two. Temperatures

should remain continuously above 45°F at night. To keep plants warm early in the season, use black plastic mulch to warm the soil or row covers, hot caps, or other protection. When the temperature rises over 85°F, remove the covers.
- Plants should be hardened off before transplanting by lowering water and fertilizer rather than exposing them to cold conditions, which can stress them and hinder their growth. Transplants exposed to chilly temperatures (60°F to 65°F during the day and 50°F to 60°F at night) are more prone to catfacing.
- Plant determinate varieties 12 to 24 inches apart, staked indeterminate kinds 14 to 20 inches apart, and unstaked indeterminate types 24 to 36 inches apart.
- Tomatoes, unlike other plants, thrive better when planted slightly deeper than when cultivated in pots. Plant them so that the soil level is slightly below the lowest leaves. Roots will grow along the buried stem, forming a more powerful root system.
- To limit the danger of root disease, don't plant for at least two years on soils that have recently grown tomatoes, potatoes, peppers, or eggplant.

Growing and Caring
- Mulch plants once the earth has warmed up to keep the soil wet and weeds at bay. Tomatoes require a steady supply of moisture. If there isn't enough rain in a week, water to make up the deficit – 1 inch to 1½ inches is needed.
- Total output, initial harvest, and fruit quality are affected by several factors (in addition to the variety you choose). Raised beds, black plastic mulch, and watering or drip irrigation to provide continuous hydration are ideal strategies to boost all three.
- Plant performance can also be influenced by how you support them. Staking is not required for determinate varieties. On the other hand, sticking and pruning indeterminate kinds can speed up the first harvest by a week or more, increase fruit quality, keep the fruit cleaner, and make harvesting simpler. Staking and trimming diminish total production, although the fruits are generally bigger. Plants that have been staked and clipped are more prone to blossom end rot and sunscald. Allowing indeterminate types to sprawl saves time and money, but it also takes up more room and makes the plants more susceptible to disease.
- Although equivalent materials can be used, wooden tomato stakes are normally 6 feet long and 12 inches square. To avoid root injury, stakes should be driven at least 8 to 10 inches deep at or soon after transplanting.
- Snap off 'suckers' (stems sprouting from where leaf stems meet the main stem) when they are 2 to 4 inches long to reduce tomatoes to one or two robust stems. Form a figure-8 with the stem in one loop and the stake in the other using soft

string, twine, or fabric tied to the stake. This allows the stem to stretch without feeling suffocated. Begin tying around 8 to 12 inches above the ground and keep tying at the same intervals as the plant grows. Grow multiple plants in a row between heavy-duty stakes or posts spaced approximately 4 feet apart instead of individual stakes, then weave twine in and out of posts and plants.

- Tomatoes grown in cages effectively balance time-consuming staking and letting them spread. Tomato cages may be purchased at your local garden shop, or you can make your own by bending a 6-foot-long piece of 4- to 6-inch wire mesh into a 22-inch-diameter cylinder. (This can be done using cattle fence or concrete reinforcing wire mesh.) Soon after transplanting, build a cage around the plants and secure it with stakes.
- Excessive nitrogen treatment might result in excessive foliage and a poor fruit set. Also, avoid applying fresh manure or fertilizers with a high nitrogen content (those with three or more times nitrogen than phosphorus or potassium). Heavy rain or temperatures that are either too warm (above 90°F) or too low (below 40°F) can also induce a poor fruit set (below 55°F).
- When the fruits are approximately 1 inch in diameter and harvest begins, side-dress about half a cup of 5-10-5 per plant worked shallowly into the top inch of soil.

Potential Challenges to Growing Tomatoes

A typical tomato challenge to avoid is blossom end rot – keep the soil equally wet. This can also help avoid cracking when fruit absorbs too much water after a hard rain after a period of drought. Leaves that shade the fruit and prevent sunscald should not be removed. Due to cold weather, incomplete pollination causes catfacing (misshaped, malformed fruit). Wait until the weather has settled and the soil is warm before transplanting.

Aphids, whiteflies, Colorado potato beetles, cutworms, and flea beetles are pests that might cause problems with tomatoes (and can be avoided by using floating covers).

Blossom end rot, catface, early blight, Fusarium, and Verticillium wilt are diseases that can make your crop fail.

Turnip (*Brassica rapa*)

Family	Season	Sun	Soil	Hardiness	pH
BRASSICACEAE	Cool	Full Sun Min. Shade	Well-drained composted, moist	2 to 11	6.0 to 7.5
Height	**Spread**	**Tolerance**	**Ease-of-Care**	**Germination**	**Emergence**
2–3'	2–3'	Slight Alkalinity, Frost	Easy	45°F–85°F	4–7 days

The **Brassica family** – also known as the mustards, the crucifers, or the cabbage family includes broccoli, Brussels sprouts, cabbage, cauliflower, collards, kale, kohlrabi, mustard, radishes, rutabaga, and turnip.

Turnip and rutabaga are biennials that are harvested after their first growing season. Both belong to the mustard family (Brassicaceae) and, like broccoli, cabbage, and cauliflower, do best when grown in cooler temperatures. Turnip leaves are used as greens. Turnips and rutabagas are also cultivated for their swollen roots, which may be used in soups and stews. The tops of turnip roots are generally purple with a white base, and rutabagas are typically brown with yellow flesh.

When both types of roots are taken before they get huge, they are more sensitive and have a greater flavor. Because each plant's root may only be picked once, many plantings will assure a continuous harvest. Turnips and rutabaga are both frost resilient. Plantings ready to harvest around the usual first frost date can simply be left in the ground and picked as required until the first frost. A thick layer of straw mulch will prevent the soil from cooling too soon, making harvesting simpler. Root maggots attack turnips and rutabagas, as well as radishes. Crop rotation will be beneficial.

Planting Turnips

Planting Type	Depth	Initial Spacing	Row Spacing	Thinned
Seed	¼ to ½ inch	1 inch	12–18 inches	2 to 4 inches

- Turnips reach a height of 18 inches, may be planted in the spring or fall, and tolerate light shade. There are several types to choose from, some for greens and others for turnip roots.
- Plant seeds straight into the garden six weeks before the typical final frost in the spring. When the soil temperature is 40°F or warmer, seeds germinate in five days or less. For the following four to six weeks, repeat the planting process every ten days.
- Turnips are typically planted thickly and trimmed to 2 to 4 inches after the leaves reach around 4 inches. This will be your first turnip greens harvest. Within a broad row, the spacing is 2 to 4 inches.
- If growing for greens, side-dress with 2 ounces of nitrogen per 100 square feet when the greens are roughly a third mature. Side-dressing is typically unnecessary when growing for roots.

Growing and Caring for Turnips

- Plant every two weeks to ensure a steady supply of produce. When the weather is chilly, the quality and flavor of the fruit are at their peak.
- To protect your crop from early pests, use a floating row cover.
- Planting turnips or other cole crops in the same site more than once every three or four years will assist in minimizing illness.

Harvesting Turnips

- The optimal time to harvest spring turnip crops is while the weather is still chilly. Light frost improves the taste of fall crops. Don't overlook the greens, which are delicious, both raw and cooked.
- When the leaves are 4 to 6 inches long, harvest them as needed. Greens take around 30 days to mature, and turnip roots take about 60 days.
- Remove the entire plant from the ground when the roots are 2 to 3 inches in diameter. Planting during the fall season can begin as early as July and plan for the final planting to be ready around the time of the usual first frost.

- With shelter, fall turnips may withstand temperatures as low as the low 20s.
- Expect yields of 8 pounds per 10-foot row (roots or greens).

Potential Challenges to Growing Turnips
- Like most plants in the brassica family, kohlrabi may be challenged by cutworm, cabbage loopers, cabbage worms, flea beetles, cabbage root maggots, cabbage aphids, slugs, snails, and nematodes. An early coving with a floating cover will aid your fight against these pests.
- The diseases common to the brassica family (except collards, kale, and the radishes) are clubroot, black rot, black leg, Alternaria, and cabbage yellows.

Watermelon (*Citrullus lanatus*)

Family	Season	Sun	Soil	Hardiness	pH
CUCURBITACEAE	Warm	Full Sun	Well-drained composted, moist	4 to 11	6.5 to 7.5
Height	Spread	Tolerance	Ease-of-Care	Germination	Emergence
1–2'	3–20'		Moderately Challenging	70°F–95°F	3–5 days

The **Cucurbits family** includes cucumbers, melons, squashes, pumpkins, and gourds.

- In cooler climates, choose short-season kinds, start them inside, warm the soil with black plastic or IRT mulch, and shelter young plants with fabric row covers to boost your chances of success.
- Watermelons as little as 6 pounds and as large as 22 pounds may be grown by combining several hybrids.
- Seedless watermelons can also be grown. These melons' seeds are created by crossing a cultivar with four sets of chromosomes with one with two sets of chromosomes (two is the normal number). The resultant seed (with three sets of chromosomes) will germinate, grow, and blossom, but only a few soft seeds will form in the fruit's developing fruit following pollination. Because the seedless type produces no viable pollen, a seeded variety must be planted nearby. You'll be able to recognize the fruits distinct once harvested if you grow a seeded variety with a different color or form. A few seeds of a seeded type are included in most seedless watermelon seed packs. Before planting, you can distinguish the seeds by their size; the seedless type contains bigger seeds.
- Watermelons are tropical species that can withstand greater heat and drought than other cucurbits.

- Large watermelons take longer to grow than smaller ones, taking 120 days for the larger ones against 70 to 80 days for the smaller ones. The fruit develops around 42 to 45 days after pollination.

Planting Watermelon

Planting Type	Depth	Initial Spacing	Row Spacing	Thinned
Seed	½ inch	1 foot	6 feet	3 feet

- Direct-seed into the garden if you have lengthy, hot growth seasons. Choose fast-maturing, small-fruited varieties, start plants inside, and use black or IRT plastic mulch and fabric row covers to warm soil and protect plants in places with shorter growing seasons and cooler weather.
- When the soil temperature is 70°F or higher, direct sow one to two weeks after the typical last frost. For bush variations, plant ½ inch deep, six seeds per hill with hills spaced 3 feet apart from each direction, or 3 feet apart in rows 8 feet apart for vining forms. Two to three plants per hill should be thinned.
- Seeds should be planted ½ inch deep, and watermelons should be planted 24 to 48 inches apart in 6-foot rows. Hills should be 6 feet apart, in rows at least 7 feet apart, with three plants per hill if growing in hills.
- Sow seeds indoors ¼ inch deep in peat pots (2-inch square or larger) two to four weeks before transplanting. Set out three plants per hill, 3 feet apart from each direction for bush kinds, or 3 feet apart in rows 8 feet apart for vining types, two weeks after the average last frost. Transplants are a sensitive procedure. When transplanting, keep the soil intact.

Growing and Caring for Watermelon
- Mulch plants once the soil has warmed up to help keep moisture constant and weeds at bay.
- Remove cloth row coverings after flowering to facilitate bee pollination. Fruit set is dependent on good pollination.
- Until pollination, plants require constant hydration. Only water when the fruit is approximately the size of a tennis ball and the soil is dry, and the leaves are withering.
- Place watermelons atop pots or pieces of wood to keep insects away from maturing fruits.
- Support fruit with slings fashioned from netting, cloth, or pantyhose if growing melons on a trellis. Trellising enhances air circulation around plants and can aid in preventing foliar disease. Reduce plant spacing and choose small-fruited kinds.
- Planting cucumber family crops (melons, squash, and pumpkins) in the same location for two years in a row is not recommended.

Harvesting Watermelon
- When watermelons are fully ripe, harvest them.
- To identify whether watermelons are ripe, use a combination of the four signs listed below:
  - Near the site of fruit attachment, the light green, curled tendrils on the stem turn brown and dry. This can happen five to ten days before the fruit is completely ripe in certain kinds.
  - The fruit's glossy surface color fades, and the hue becomes drab.
  - The skin gets tough, and your thumbnail may easily pierce it.
  - Generally, dark green cultivars will become a buttery yellow on the ground side. Lighter melons will turn yellow, although not to the same extent as darker melons.
- Watermelons should be kept cool but not cold and then placed in the refrigerator to chill down immediately before eating.
- You can expect a yield of four to ten watermelons per 10-foot row.

Potential Challenges to Growing Watermelon
- To protect immature watermelon plants against striped or spotted cucumber beetles, make tents of thin netting, cheesecloth, or floating row cover. Place at the time of planting and remove at the time of flowering. To avoid bacterial wilt, keep bugs at bay.

- Aphids may be removed from plants with a hard stream of water. Early in the day, if necessary, wash off with water. Natural enemies such as gray-brown or bloated parasitized aphids and alligator-like larvae of lady beetles and lacewings should be looked for.
- Squash vine borer – cut up vines with a knife and pull them out by hand.
- Squash bugs should be handpicked. Plant leftovers should be buried or composted after harvesting.
- Flea bugs – protect plants from early insect damage using row crop coverings. Place at the time of planting and remove at the time of flowering. Weeds must be controlled.

Diseases Common to Watermelon

- Powdery mildew – if at all possible, avoid watering plants. Water early in the day to ensure that aboveground plant parts dry rapidly. Plants should not be crowded and allow air circulation by spacing them apart. To increase air circulation, remove weeds from surrounding plants and the garden space.
- Cucumber mosaic virus-affected plants should be removed and destroyed. Cucumber beetles and aphids should be dealt with as soon as they arise.
- Scab – if at all possible, avoid soaking the leaves. Water early in the day to ensure that aboveground plant parts dry rapidly. Plants should not be crowded, and there should be enough room for air to circulate.
- Fusarium wilt – plant fresh plants in alternative garden regions each year. Tolerance varieties should be planted.
- Other illnesses include: Phytophthora, Anthracnose.

CHAPTER 8
GROWING HERBS

Herbs are plant leaves, whereas spices are non-leafy portions such as seeds, berries, roots, and bark. Some plants are classified as both herbs and spices. Cilantro and dill leaves, for example, are herbs, whereas their seeds are spices (e.g. coriander and dill seed).

Basil (*Ocimum spp.*)

Basil is a fragrant, spicy-tasting warm-season plant. Basil comes in a variety of sizes, colors, and flavors. While sweet basil is the most prevalent, there are also Thai, purple, cinnamon, lemon, and other types. African blue basil has a lot of blossoms that attract pollinators, but the flavor isn't very good. From early spring through late fall, plant basil transplants or seeds and pinch off and utilize the delicious stem tips as they develop. This  will promote branching and leaf growth. Remove any flower spikes that appear, or the leaves will lose their taste. The fragile leaves can be utilized fresh or dried at any time. Basil loves damp (but not soggy) soil and modest fertilizer treatments periodically. Cuttings are simple to root. In the South, Basil Downy Mildew is a severe fungal disease. Choose disease-resistant cultivars like Amazel Basil, Pesto Besto, and others.

Fresh basil should be stored in a cool but not cold environment since the leaves brown below 40°F. Basil keeps best in vinegar or other liquids since it neither freezes nor dries well. Purple basil will color white wine vinegar maroon. In salsa and pesto, use vinegar instead of fresh basil. Drying basil between layers of coarse salt produces flavorful salt (after the basil is dried and brown, remove it).

Bay Leaf (*Laurus nobilis*)

The bay leaf is a huge evergreen shrub/small tree native to the Mediterranean that grows slowly to about 30' but may be maintained smaller by trimming. Fresh or dried leaves can be used to season soups, stews, and other foods, but they should be removed before serving. In the South, several trees are referred to as 'bay,' so check the scientific name before propagating. Bay leaf may be cultivated in Hardiness Zones 8–10, although it is sensitive to cold and should be sheltered during a hard frost. Its thick growth habit makes it a visually appealing addition to the environment.

Borage (*Borago officinalis*)

Borage is a cool-season annual with a cucumber-like odor and flavor. The leaves and stunning blue, star-shaped blossoms are used in salads and drinks, and the plant looks lovely in a flower garden. Bees are drawn to the blossoms. Plant in full to partial light and anticipate plants to reach a height and width of around 2 feet. Borage will self-sow from seeds for years after it has been established. This Mediterranean plant also has anti-deer and anti-drought properties.

Cardamom (*Elettaria cardamomum*)

Cardamom is a tropical, perennial spice in the ginger family that grows in 12-foot-tall clusters with bold-textured leaves. Coffee, sweets, cakes, and other delicacies are flavored and scented with the seeds. Cardamom requires part shade, continuous moisture, and somewhat acidic soil. Cardamom grows best in Zones 10 and 11, where it is not affected by the cold. At 50°F, the plant dies and will not blossom or set seed the next year. Small yellowish blooms appear near the ground, followed by rectangular ribbed seed capsules. These are collected while green and then sun-dried until they become brown and break open.

Chervil (*Anthriscus cerefolium*)

Chervil, often known as French parsley, is a cool-season annual planted for its fragrant, fern-like leaves, which have an anise-like flavor. Pick leaves as required and use them immediately to decorate salads, soups, egg dishes, sauces, and other cuisines. Some varieties have thick roots that are eaten like carrots. Chervil thrives in full to partial sun and in rich, wet soil. Chervil can endure frigid temperatures, but it bolts (goes to seed) in hot weather and becomes bitter when it blossoms.

Cilantro/Coriander (*Coriandrum sativum*)

Coriander is a cool-season annual used for its fragrant seeds (coriander) and aromatic leaves (cilantro). Its feathery texture and lovely blossoms make it an appealing addition to a flower garden or landscape. You can ensure a continual harvest by sowing seeds every two or three weeks in well-drained, rich soil in the autumn, winter, or spring. Warm conditions cause it to bolt, set seed, and die soon. Cilantro grows best when sowed directly rather than transplanted. Seeds should be covered ¼ inch deep, and plants should be spaced 2 to 4 feet apart. Tiny fruits emerge after blooming and become brown when ripe, ready to harvest and be screen-dried. After drying, remove the seeds from the seed heads and store them in a dry, airtight container.

Culantro (*Eryngium foetidum*)

Culantro is a biennial plant native to Latin America, commonly grown in Zones 7 to 11 as a summer annual. It is a common ingredient in salsa, sofrito, ceviche, and soups and grows best in well-watered, shaded areas, whether planted in the ground or in a container. It is a member of the same plant family as cilantro, but it has a distinct appearance. The tall, stiff leaves are comparable to cilantro but have a stronger flavor, making it a good summer alternative for cilantro, which prefers cooler temperatures. To harvest, remove the oldest leaves from the plant's base, letting the newer leaves grow. To preserve the taste of the leaves, cut them and utilize them fresh or frozen. Small plants can be purchased in nurseries or cultivated from seed. Seeds require light to sprout. Thus, they must be distributed openly on soil, maintained moist, and left undisturbed for two to three weeks until they germinate. Culantro is a delicate tropical plant that would perish if exposed to frost or cold conditions. When the bloom stalk develops, cut it off to postpone flowering and encourage ongoing foliage development.

Cumin (*Cuminum cyminum*)

Cumin is a warm-season annual with delicate, thin leaves and large, umbel-shaped flower heads. Cumin should be grown in full light and watered regularly, but the soil should be allowed to dry between waterings. Cumin is not picky about soil type. Although some people pick and consume the leaves, the pungent flavor of the ground seeds is more popular. Allow the pods (which form after flowering) to completely dry and become brown before harvesting the seed. Rub the pods or hang the stalks upside down to release the seed.

Dill (*Anethum graveolens*)

Dill pickles get their name from the young leaves and seeds of dill. It is an annual plant that grows to 4 feet and has a strong odor. The yellow blossoms produce fruits that can be eaten fresh or dried. Plant dill in early fall and spring when pleasant temperatures are not too hot or cold. Make sure you have a sunny spot with healthy, well-drained soil. Fruiting tips, as well as young leaves and stem segments, can be utilized fresh or dried. Keep in mind that the caterpillars of the black swallowtail butterfly eat on dill, fennel, and parsley, so plant some extra.

Fennel (*Foeniculum vulgare dulce*)

Because there are two types of fennel, the common word 'fennel' is misleading. Common fennel (*Foeniculum vulgare*) is grown for its tasty shoots, leaves, and seeds. Florence fennel (*Foeniculum vulgare var. azoricum*), also known as sweet fennel, bulbing fennel, and finocchio, is produced primarily for its thicker, bulbous leaf base, which is consumed raw or cooked. Except for the broader, aboveground base of the Florence fennel leaves, the two are remarkably similar in look and flavor (licorice-like). The plant resembles dill with slender, finely feathered leaves, brilliant yellowish-green hollow stems, and umbrella-like seed formations. Fennel grows best as a cool-season annual and may be picked three to four months after planting. Bronze fennel is not only tasty but also quite decorative.

Ginger (*Zingiber officinale*)

Many decorative gingers thrive in the South, but *Zingiber officinale* is the culinary species. It's a hardy perennial that yields a lot of fruit. The underground rhizomes are thick, white, tuberous, and utilized in food and drinks, medications, and personal care goods. Buy fresh ginger from your local grocer and cut the rhizomes into 2- to 3-inch chunks with many developing buds ('eyes'). Plant them 2 inches deep in good, wet soil in a shaded spot that receives some early sun. When the stalks drop down in winter, the rhizomes are ready to harvest nine to twelve months after sowing. Outer rhizomes can be collected as the rest of the plant grows and clumps over the next few years.

Lavender (*Lavandula spp.*)

Lavender has long been prized for the calming aroma it imparts to soaps, lotions, oils, sachets, and fresh or dried flowers. Lavender is becoming popular for the mild taste it imparts to pastries, sorbets, main courses, jams, and various drinks. Lavender is indigenous to the western Mediterranean, where the weather is moderate and dry. Several varieties are available at garden shops, but plant it in well-drained soil in full sun with enough air circulation no matter which one you pick. Water lightly during establishment; after that, just a little water and fertilizer are required.

Lemon Balm (*Melissa officinalis*)

Lemon balm is a mint-scented perennial plant with a lemony smell and grows into 2-foot-tall clusters with vivid green leaves. Plants are propagated through the use of seeds or cuttings. In early spring, sow seeds shallowly in wet, healthy soil in a sunny position, spacing plants 18 inches apart. It might take up to two years for the plant to establish a good-sized cluster. Fresh or dried, the leaves and fragile stems are medicinal and used to flavor beverages, salads, and other meals.

Lemon Grass (*Cymbopogon citratus*)

Lemongrass is a delicate clumping perennial grass. It has a lovely lemony scent and is used in cooking, drinks, herbal medications, household goods, and personal-care items. The thick stalks at the plant's base and the leaves are picked for use. Lemongrass is also popular as a fragrant garden plant. It may reach 6 feet in height and turns crimson in the fall. It prefers full sun and good soil, with frequent watering because it dislikes drying out. Propagation is by division.

Lemon Verbena (*Aloysia triphylla*)

Lemon verbena resembles lemon oil, and hence the most intensely flavored, of all the plants with the word 'lemon' in their names. Long, slightly sticky, and deciduous leaves. This woody shrub thrives in full sun and well-drained soil, and it is only hardy in Zones 10 and 11. Grow it in a planter and bring it inside for the winter (treat it beforehand with insecticidal soap, as it is susceptible to whiteflies and spider mites).

Lovage (*Levisticum officinale*)

Lovage is a perennial herb that loves full sun to partial shade with a hardiness index of Zone 3. Lovage can grow to about 8-foot tall and is a fragrant deciduous plant with dark green, glossy, upright compound leaves. It is used to flavor dishes and as a medicinal plant. It germinates by seed in darkness and can be sown in the winter.

Marjoram (*Origanum majorana*)

Marjoram has a subtle flavor and is used in cooking, herbal remedies, and as a dry decoration. Sweet marjoram (*Origanum marjorana*), pot marjoram (*Origanum onites*), and wild marjoram (*O. vulgare*) are the three types of marjoram that are typically used as herbs. Herb gardens are commonly used to cultivate sweet and pot marjoram. They are quite similar, except that sweet marjoram grows erect while pot marjoram grows along the ground. Pot marjoram should be spaced about 12 inches apart, while sweet marjoram should be spaced 6 inches apart. Plants can be started from seeds, cuttings, or clump divisions in the early spring. Marjoram thrives in full sun and well-drained soil, and the leaves can be eaten fresh or dried. Marjoram is visually appealing enough to make a superb border planting for a flower garden. Pot marjoram (*O. onites*) is not hardy.

Mustard (*Brassica juncea*)

These spicy greens are high in vitamins and antioxidants, making them one of the healthiest crops you can cultivate. Mustard is a fast-growing plant that thrives in mild conditions but can withstand considerable heat but benefit from some shade in hot weather. Make many sowings to provide a steady supply of delicate leaves. Germinate between 45°F and 85°F and emerge within a week. Use floating covers to protect against pests (flea beetles, whiteflies, and aphids).

Oregano (*Origanum vulgare*)

Oregano comes in Mexican (*Lippia graveolens*) and European (*Origanum spp.*). Mexican oregano has a strong, earthy taste with citrus undertones, whereas European oregano is softer. Plant in full sun in sandy, loamy soil; once established, it is drought resistant. It can develop to be a 5-foot-tall woody shrub in a few years if cultivated in frost-free areas. The taste of European oreganos varies depending on whether they are Italian, Greek, or Golden oregano. Frost kills oregano because it is a delicate perennial. It may be cultivated from seed sown in the spring or by cutting propagation. Harvesting the leaf tips on a regular basis creates a fuller and more compact habit.

Parsley (*Petroselinum hortense, P. crispum*)

Parsley is technically a biennial, yet it thrives as a cool-season annual in Florida. When planted in the fall, parsley thrives in chilly temperatures before flowering, producing seeds, and dying in late spring/early summer. Growing it in light shade will extend its life, but it will ultimately blossom and die. Flat-leafed (Italian) parsley is used for seasoning, but curly-leaf parsley is more commonly used as a garnish. The white roots of root parsley (*Petroselinum crispum var. tuberosum*) resemble immature parsnips and are eaten as a cooked vegetable, notably in soups. Parsley needs rich, wet soil and grows best in full sun or light shade.

Pepper (*Capsicum spp*)

Hot peppers belong to several plant species. Members of the species *Capsicum annuum* include Anaheim, cayenne, serrano, and jalapeno peppers. *Capsicum chinense* peppers include habanero, Scotch bonnet, and Bhut Jolokia. Tabasco peppers belong to the species *Capsicum frutescens*.

Pepper plants thrive in well-drained, full-sun soils. The planting location should get at least 6 hours of direct sunlight each day. Peppers are a warm-season crop that requires a long growing season for the best yield. Temperatures between 70°F and 85°F are ideal for plant development throughout the day. Plants of peppers may be purchased at garden centers, or seeds can be sown inside six to eight weeks before the anticipated outdoor planting date. After the threat of frost has passed, plant peppers in the garden. After transplanting, properly water the plants.

Plant pepper plants about 24 inches apart, allowing enough sun for each plant. If a soil test has not been performed, it is typically advised that 2–3 pounds of 5-10-5 per 100 square feet be applied and incorporated shortly before planting. Conduct a soil test in the autumn or early spring to get precise suggestions. Fertilize pepper plants after transplanting using a starting fertilizer solution. Water about 1 inch a week.

Peppermint (*Mentha spp.*)

Mints are low-maintenance perennial herbs that thrive in Florida gardens. Hundreds of types and cultivars provide a diverse spectrum of tastes. Spearmint (*Mentha spicata*) and peppermint (*Mentha piperita*) and apple, chocolate, and orange mints are two of the most popular. Mint is used as an insect repellent in drinks, meals, and personal care items. The leaves vary in color but are typically dark green, tiny, and pointed, slightly notched edges. Small blooms are white, blue, or violet. Mint may be grown from seed, rooted runners, divisions, or tiny potted plants. Both fresh and dried leaves and blooming tops are utilized. Mint is a prolific spreader and should be cultivated in areas where it can be kept under control.

Rosemary (*Rosmarinus officinalis*)

Rosemary is a 2 to 3-foot evergreen perennial with an aromatic scent. The tiny, thin green leaves are utilized fresh or dried in various cuisines. In the second or third year, little lavender blooms appear. Rosemary is difficult to grow from seed, so start with cuttings or a bought plant. Once planted, rosemary is drought and salt  resistant, and it thrives in sunny, dry conditions. It will be harmed by overwatering and shade. Rosemary is a lovely low-maintenance shrub that may be used in a water-wise or coastal setting.

Sage (*Salvia officinalis*)

 Sage is a short-lived perennial with grayish-green leaves that grows to around 2 feet tall. The fragrant purple blooms develop in the second year and are particularly appealing to bees and butterflies. If using sage as a culinary herb, cut the tops of the branches to avoid blooming, which will keep the leaves' taste ideal. Fresh or dried leaves are utilized. Sage is a beautiful, low-growing border plant in the landscape and should be grown in full sun on well-drained soil.

Savory (*Satureja hortensis, S. montana*)

The two types of savory are summer savory (*Satureja hortensis*) and winter savory (*Satureja montana*). The leaves of both savory species have a strong peppery taste. However, winter savory is more intense. Winter savory is a perennial shrub, whereas summer savory is a warm-season annual. Plants may be difficult to locate in  nurseries, but they may be grown from seed; for best results, plant in full sun in rich, well-drained soil. Because the leaves become brown after blooming, save the savory-trimmed stem tips to avoid flowering. Fresh or dried, the zesty, peppery-tasting leaves are employed.

Tarragon (*Artemisia dracunculus var. sativa*)

French tarragon is a tough plant to cultivate in the South since it dies out in the heat and humidity of the summer. Because the rare blooms are sterile and do not generate seed, cuttings are the only way to reproduce them. Tarragon seed is frequently sold as Russian tarragon (*Artemisia dracunculoides*), with a similar flavor. Mexican tarragon (*Tagetes lucida*) has an anise-like taste and may be used in place of French tarragon. Mexican tarragon is native to the southwest United States and Mexico, and it can withstand the hot, humid summers.

Thyme (*Thymus spp.*)

Thyme (*Thymus vulgaris*) is a shrubby perennial herb with tiny gray-green leaves (Figure 16). Purplish flowers are formed at the ends of the stems. Some varieties are creeping while others grow upright to 18 inches. Lemon thyme is a variety that adds lemon flavor and aroma. Plant in full sun and well-drained soil. Thyme is drought  tolerant. Replant thyme every three to four years for best growth because it tends to get woody. Thyme leaves and flowers can be used fresh or dried.

There are almost 300 different types of thyme! The most prevalent are classified into two categories: culinary and decorative. *Thymus vulgaris* (common, English, and French thyme), often known as Mother of Thyme, has little green leaves and an erect habit. Lemon thyme (*T. citriodorus*) also comes in erect, creeping, and variegated varieties (*T. citriodorus vars.*). Silver thyme (*T. x argenteus*) is largely an ornamental plant with lovely pink blossoms. Thymes can also be used as a grass replacement or slope retainer. Woolly thyme (*T. praecox*), Miniature thyme (*T. praecox minimus*),

Mother of Thyme (*T. pulegioides*), and caraway thyme (*T. herba-barona*) are examples of low-growing thymes. Thyme flowers range in color from deep rosy pink and red to lavender and white. *T. serpyllum var. coccineus* has a really lovely red flower. Although garden thyme (*T. vulgaris*) may be produced from seed, many varieties can only be propagated by cuttings, division, or layering. If you give thyme a sunny spot with proper drainage, it will live for many years without insect or disease issues.

Turmeric (*Curcuma longa*)

Turmeric, a member of the ginger family, thrives in warm, damp environments. Its spice is obtained from the rhizomatous roots, which may be used fresh or dried and powdered into a yellow-orange powder. Turmeric has a taste that is characterized as warm, earthy, and black pepper-like. It is widely used in many Asian recipes and as a dye. Turmeric develops as a gorgeous 3-foot-tall tropical perennial with lovely white blooms. The foliage dies to the ground in the winter and resurfaces in the spring. Plants may be bought at garden centers or grown from rhizomes available in the produce department of some supermarkets. Cut or break up rhizomes into 1 to 2-inch pieces with budding buds ('eyes') and plant them 1 inch deep in pots or straight into a shaded garden. Homegrown rhizomes are collected after the foliage fades back in the late fall or winter. Allow the 'hands' to dry for a day or two after breaking them apart. They may be frozen or stored at room temperature in a pail of dry playground sand to be used as required over the winter. Keep a few for replanting in the ground or big pots the following spring.

CHAPTER 9
MANAGING PESTS AND DISEASES

Managing Home Vegetable Garden Pests

A variety of mechanical and cultural approaches may aid in the reduction of insect pests in home vegetable gardens. Some are more practical than others, and your ability to work at them will determine your success. An integrated strategy to pest management (combining many treatments) is frequently the most effective.

Learning which insects are pests, their habitat, their life cycle, what they will feed on, and a little about their behavior is one of the most significant tactics in dealing with insects. This knowledge will assist you in deciding what to do. Many insects in the garden are not pests, and some are even useful.

1. Maintain strong, healthy plants — there is evidence that plants growing in stressed environments are more prone to be attacked and suffer major harm. Plants can be harmed by fertilization, liming, too little or too much water, and planting too close together. Check the fertility and pH of the soil regularly and make any necessary adjustments – thin plants to the prescribed spacing.
2. Planting the same crop in the same location year after year may lead to insect infestation. Crop rotation is especially important in areas where soil insects (such as grubs, wireworms, and maggots) are a problem. Plant crops sensitive to grubs or wireworms in areas where grass grew the previous year.
3. Choose suggested types for your location and resistant cultivars to pests known to exist in your area, if available. As an example, butternut squash is resistant to the squash vine borer.
4. Sanitation in and around the garden is critical. Many vegetable pests spend the winter in or near the garden, hiding in weeds or plant debris. Remove weeds and organic mulch, which provide great habitat for insects, slugs, and snails. Collect and kill pests before planting transplants or sowing seed in areas where mulch cannot be removed.
5. Consider planting timing – may the pest be avoided by planting sooner or later?
6. Handpicking entails removing pests from plants and killing them. Most insects are killed by immersing them in soapy water (or water laced with dish detergent).

7. Some insects can be controlled by placing physical barriers around plants, such as 4-inch-high cardboard collars (or roofing paper) around young transplants to prevent cutworms from cutting the stems, and squares of tar paper or carpeting securely around the stems of young cabbage family crops to prevent the cabbage maggot fly from depositing eggs at the base of the plants.
8. Row covers are placed over plants until the pest has been eradicated or the plants have grown. As temperatures rise in the mid-summer, all coverings should be removed four to six weeks into the season. Cucumbers, melons, and squash, for example, require insect pollination to produce a harvest. Covers made of polypropylene, polyester, and polyvinyl alcohol are available commercially, although cheesecloth or screening can also be used. These let light and water in, allowing the plant to develop. Many pests are kept at bay by using vented plastic row coverings.
9. Certain mulching materials, such as aluminum foil, have been demonstrated to repel aphids, thrips, and other insects. Although this material is costly, it may be used on a small scale.
10. Traps like yellow sticky boards can assist monitor insect populations, but they are rarely effective in controlling them. They do, however, serve to keep whitefly numbers in check as long as sticky material is replenished when insects cover the boards.
11. Biological control by introducing predators, parasites, or illnesses is becoming more practicable as we understand more about pest management. When introducing or maintaining predators or parasites, keep in mind that if there aren't enough hosts for them to feed on, the beneficial insects will migrate elsewhere.
12. Pesticides may also be employed as part of a pest management program. Use no more than you need and treat only the crops that require it. Spot treatments are effective and may be appropriate for household gardening. Check the label before using any pesticide – both the crop and the pest must be specified on the label. If not, do not use the insecticide.
    a. It is crucial to note that just because a pesticide is botanical does not mean it is non-toxic. Some botanical pesticides are more harmful than manufactured ones. Biological pesticides, such as *Bacillus thuringiensis* (B.t.), a bacterium that attacks caterpillars, are alternatives to some chemical pesticides.
    b. Insecticidal soaps are an alternative to some chemical pesticides and may be effective in the home garden for some pests, particularly aphids.
    c. Desiccant diatomaceous earth (silicon dioxide) is occasionally used to manage insects, slugs, and snails. However, once wet and compacted, it loses its potency.

Whatever tactics you choose, attempt to maintain a record of what you did and whether or not it was successful. Such a record will be extremely useful in the future when faced with similar pest management issues.

Common Pests In Vegetable Gardens

Aphids

Aphids, often known as plant lice, are microscopic, soft-bodied insects that eat by sucking plant juice. They are distinguished by their pear-shaped bodies and rather lengthy antennae. Aphids come in various colors, including white, gray, green, brown, red, yellow, and black. They are frequently found in big colonies on the undersides of leaves or stems. Most aphid species have both winged and wingless aphids. While feeding, aphids release honeydew, a pleasant sticky, glossy material found on plants. Honeydew is mostly made up of surplus sap consumed by the insect and transported through its body.

Monitoring

Inspect plants carefully for the beginnings of an aphid population development. Mummies, gray-brown bloated parasitized aphids showing wasp parasites at action, and alligator-like larvae of lady beetles and lacewings are examples of natural enemies in action. Yellow sticky boards are also used to monitor aphid numbers, and aphids are drawn to the yellow hue and are frequently visible on the cards before being found on the plant.

Management

Additional treatments may not be necessary if there are many mummies or big populations of ladybird beetles or lacewings in addition to the aphids. In general, controlling numbers early in the season eliminates the need for spraying. Wash aphids off with water as required early in the day. A forceful jet of water will kill many of them. Aphids on the following vegetable plants should be controlled with insecticides:

- *Beans:* use insecticidal soap, horticultural oil, pyrethrins, or malathion on beans.
- *Cabbage, cauliflower, broccoli, Brussels sprouts, and other cole crops*: spray with insecticidal soap, oil (horticultural), pyrethrins, or malathion when infestations are severe and as needed weekly. Wait seven days before harvesting if using malathion.
- *Cucumber, pumpkin*: insecticidal soap, oil (horticultural), or malathion; spray when vines are dry as needed. Wait one day before harvesting while using malathion.
- *Eggplant*: insecticidal soap or malathion can be used to treat eggplant as needed.
- *Peas*: spray one to three applications weekly with insecticidal soap or malathion. Wait three days before harvesting after using malathion.
- *Pepper*: spray as required with insecticidal soap, oil (horticultural), or malathion. If malathion is used, wait three days before harvesting; if insecticidal soap is used, wait one day.
- *Potato*: spray with malathion as needed once a week.
- *Tomatoes*: spray as needed with insecticidal soap, oil (horticultural), or malathion. Wait at least one day before harvesting.

Asparagus Beetles

The common asparagus beetle's larvae and adults cause harm to asparagus plants. Adults that have overwintered emerge and begin feeding on the fragile developing tips of newly emerged asparagus. They chew holes in the tissue, causing a brownish hue. The grubs will eat the sensitive young tips as well as the leaves. Plant growth is severely hampered, and appropriate root formation is hampered, reducing crop quantity and quality.

Management

Over the winter, remove any dead asparagus stems. Pick insects by hand in tiny plants. During the cutting season, cutting the shoots very cleanly and just below ground level every day or two can help to eliminate the eggs of the common asparagus beetle before the larvae may establish themselves in a home garden patch. Gathering and removing asparagus berries in small plots will aid in the management of the spotted asparagus beetle.

Bean Leaf Beetles

The bean leaf beetle is a pest of snap beans (also called string beans or green beans). Adult beetles feed on the undersides of leaves, leaving circular, 1/8-inch-diameter holes, and they can even feed directly on the pod. Adults are active from mid-May to early June and from mid-July to September. Bean leaf beetles are more abundant in the South than in the north. Adult bean leaf beetles like to feed on fragile young plant tissue. Adults in large numbers can defoliate the first genuine leaves and destroy new seedlings. Excessive feeding can dehydrate the plant and lower output – it also causes black patches on beans. Bean leaf beetle eating causes black patches on beans. Adults will feed on the exterior surface of pods when they mature later in the season, and this feeding does not affect the pods' appearance.

Management
- Plant in early to mid-June to minimize damage.
- Check your plants regularly between midday and 4 pm.
- Remove the beetles off plants.

Brown Marmorated Stink Bug

The brown marmorated stink bug (BMSB) is an invasive species. They eat over 200 different plant species, including many fruits, vegetables, and row crops, and spend the winter in structures, including residences in cities. BMSB nymphs and adults feed by puncturing and sucking fluids from plant tissue with their straw-like mouthpart. They can induce seed abortion, discoloration, and distortion when feeding on growing fruit. BMSB has caused substantial damage to apples, beans, eggplants, grapes, peppers, sweetcorn, Swiss chard, and tomatoes in other states.

Management

Remove the bugs and place them in a bucket of soapy water. Exterior pesticide sprays may provide some relief from pests where entirely sealing the exterior is impractical or impossible. Applications should include a synthetic pyrethroid and should be sprayed by a qualified pest control operator in the autumn, right before insect gathering. Unfortunately, because sunshine breaks down pesticides, their residual action is reduced and may not kill insects for several days or a week.

Cabbage Loopers

Imported cabbageworm, cabbage looper, and diamondback moth are the most prevalent caterpillar pests of cole crops. The most frequent caterpillar in gardens is the imported cabbageworm. All caterpillars eat on the cole crop's big veins and midribs. Older, bigger caterpillars cause the biggest feeding harm. Caterpillars should be treated when they are still little and before they cause too much feeding harm.

Management

- Use a lightweight row cover to keep egg-laying moths at bay in early April. When caterpillars are little, spray with *Bacillus thuringiensis* (Bt), which is most effective. Spray the undersides of leaves, where juvenile caterpillars love to eat.
- On cole crops, look for caterpillars and their feeding damage on both sides of the leaves. Check at least once a week for the first week after planting and more frequently as the season advances.
- Immediately destroy crop debris to eliminate sheltered locations that imported cabbageworm may exploit to survive the winter.
- To destroy the caterpillars, take them up and dump them into a basin of soapy water.
- Adult moths are prevented from depositing eggs on plants by floating row coverings made of lightweight all-purpose garden cloth.
- Natural enemies of the cabbage looper, imported cabbageworm, and diamondback moth include predators such as parasitic flies and wasps such as *Cotesia glomerata*.

Cabbage Maggots

The cabbage maggot has the potential to badly harm cabbage, cauliflower, turnip, radish, and other crucifer crops. Early-planted crucifers, as well as seedbeds of late-planted crucifers, are more prone to be attacked. The baby grub feeds on the delicate rootlets before rasping a channel in the plant's main root. The sign of the cabbage plant withering excessively during the day's heat is an early indicator of an assault. The plants may have a blue hue. The plant either dies within a few days or remains weak. When a plant dies fast, there are frequently many maggots that riddle the root, allowing decay organisms to get in and swiftly take control. If such a plant is pulled up, the whitish maggots, which may resemble a grain of rice at first, should be seen in the soil surrounding the roots of the wounded plants. Brown tunnels can also be seen in the stems or roots of older plants.

Management

Crop rotation will aid in the control of cabbage root maggot populations. Crucifer crop trash should be disposed of immediately after harvest. The early brood is critical because plants (transplants and direct-seeded) are tiny and vulnerable to assault, and older plants are more resistant to harm. Radishes may be cultivated in home gardens in repeated weekly plantings; some will avoid injury. Infested radishes serve as a trap crop and should be plucked and killed (rather than composted) as soon as they are discovered.

The most effective control is to keep the flies from depositing eggs in the first place. Row coverings made of spun-bonded yarn can be utilized. Row coverings work nicely but be careful to bury the edges, or flies will escape and destroy the crop. Allow adequate space for plants to grow under the cover.

They can be successful if:

- there are no holes or tears in the material
- the material is spread over the crop before or soon after crop emergence or transplanting
- crops are cycled, with no hosts of the pests produced on that location the previous year. Shields made from tarpaper or old carpets can also be employed.

Adult flies will be unable to lay eggs because of the shield. The shields are cut into 6-inch squares or 10-inch circles with a tiny hole in the center and a slit cut across the middle. These are inserted around the transplant's base and pressed against the dirt to prevent adult flies from crawling below.

There are no insecticides recommended for use in the home garden, but entomopathogenic nematodes can be employed as directed on the box. Often, the plants are too damaged to recover when the injury is discovered, and abandoning the plants is the best alternative.

Carrot Rust Fly / Carrot Root Fly

Carrots, parsnips, celery, parsley, celeriac, fennel, dill, caraway, and coriander are host plants attacked by the carrot rust fly. Larvae mine in the roots, leaving holes that secondary organisms can decay. Adult flies are thin, measuring little less than ¼ inch in length, and have a metallic blue-black body color. The larvae or maggots are whitish, legless, and frequently found in the host plant's root.

Management
Row coverings can aid in the prevention of early-season damage. Once diseased plants have been destroyed, rotate crops and safeguard fresh plantings.

Click Beetle Wireworm

The click beetle does not cause harm; it is the wireworm that feeds on crops and is a nuisance. Corn, tiny grains, grasses, potato tubers, flowers, beans, peas, tomatoes, and cucurbits are all hosts for wireworm. The larvae mostly feed on the plant's tiny roots, but they will also devour the insides of seeds, limiting germination. They will also dig into bigger roots and underground stem portions, cutting off the plant's supply of nutrients and water. As a result, the plants become stunted or wilted. Wireworm infestations are not always evenly dispersed over a field, resulting in patches of damaged regions.

Management

Baits are the most efficient technique of pest control in a home garden. Baits can be buried 2 to 4 feet deep and 3 to 10 feet apart. Cover the holes with a board or tile and a mixture of sprouting peas, beans, or corn. Uncover the baits and kill the wireworms gathered in one week. Pour syrup on an exposed surface near the garden area, such as a fence post, to catch and kill click beetles. Some adult species are drawn to the sweet syrup and glued to it, allowing for simple removal.

Colorado Potato Beetle

The Colorado potato beetle is a significant potato pest in North America. Adults develop in the spring when potato plants sprout from the ground. Larvae and adults eat on leaves and can defoliate plants. Many insecticides are ineffective due to the Colorado potato beetle's chemical resistance. A mixture of pest management strategies can minimize the amount of Colorado potato beetles.

Old larvae (the fourth or last larval instar) are responsible for up to 75% of feeding damage. In the vegetative stage, potatoes can normally withstand up to 30% defoliation and are substantially more sensitive when tubers begin to bulk and can only withstand around 10% defoliation. Tuber bulking occurs shortly after blooming, making this period crucial for insect control.

Management
- Keep the garden clean.
- Plant early maturing varieties.
- Pick beetles off plants.
- Encourage lady beetles and stink bugs – they feed on the beetle eggs.

Cucumber Beetles

Cucumber beetles come in two varieties, one striped and the other with a dozen black dots. Cucumber beetles are significantly more plant pests than their name suggests. Aside from cucumbers and their relatives (squashes, gourds, and melons), these beetles have been observed feeding on beans, peas, maize, and the blooms of various wild and cultivated plants. The spotted cucumber beetle consumes an even broader range of cultivated plants, including potatoes, beets, tomatoes, eggplants, and cabbage. The spotted cucumber beetle larva is also known as the southern corn rootworm, and it infests peanuts, tiny grains, and various wild grasses and corn roots. Cucumber beetles are more damaging to cucumber-family hosts than many other pests because they spread lethal illnesses, mosaic and bacterial wilts.

Adults spend the winter amid weeds and plant detritus, appear in the spring after the final frost, and invade gardens as the growing season begins. They may initially be noticed inside squash blooms. They deposit orange eggs at the base of host plants, and white larva with brown heads emerge to munch on the roots. Short northern seasons allow for only one generation each year, but two or more generations are common in the South and warmer portions of the West.

Management

Look for cucumber and squash types that are resistant to these pests. Floating row coverings can be used to protect young plants. To limit the number of overwintering adults, knock, shake, or handpick beetles off plants and out of flowers in the fall, and tidy up garden trash. Insecticides containing pyrethrum should be applied to plants and flowers.

Cutworms

Cutworms are night-flying moth larvae (caterpillars). Adult moths either feed on nectar or do not eat at all, and the harm is only done during the larval stage. Cutworms come in various kinds, each with its distinct look. Many more common species have thick, soft-bodied, smooth, and cylindrical larvae. The color spectrum runs from brown to gray to black. Cutworms can be spotted or striped, or they might have no markings. Adult moths are muscular, dull-colored moths known as millers that fly only at night.

Management

Cutworms can be deterred from eating on garden plants by wrapping a cardboard collar around the stem and extending it above and below ground level. Cutworm moths deposit their eggs on weeds and grasses, so remove them from your garden. Insect traps and barriers are common and have been on the market for a long time.

Diamondback Moths

These nocturnal moths are slender and light brown. The folded wings have a three-white-diamond design. Eggs are creamy-white and small and are placed near leaf veins on the leaf. The hatching caterpillars are light green, tapered at both ends, and grow about 1/3 inch long, considerably smaller than imported cabbageworm and loopers, and respond when touched.

Management

See cabbage loopers.

Flea Beetle

Flea beetles are prevalent pests that cause significant damage to vegetable crops. Flea beetle feeding damage can stress and harm young plants. Feeding may scar leaves or fruit on growing crops, resulting in aesthetic harm and lower crop value at harvest. Some species are major crop disease vectors. When warm spring weather arrives, flea beetles penetrate crops, and major damage can occur soon. Corn, potato, crucifer, eggplant, striped, horseradish, pale striped, and tobacco flea beetles are found in the northeastern United States. Some are persistent pests, while others do major harm only on rare occasions.

Management
Frequent cultivation has been reported to 'drive' flea beetles off plants. Large numbers of flea beetles can be captured by placing a box with the inner walls coated with insect-trapping stickers that can be passed over infested plants to capture flea beetles as they jump off plants.

Imported Cabbage Worm

Imported cabbageworm, cabbage looper, and diamondback moth are the most prevalent caterpillar pests of cole crops. The most frequent caterpillar in gardens is the imported cabbageworm that eats on the cole crop's big veins and midribs. Caterpillars should be treated when they are still little and before they cause too much feeding harm.

During the day, adult butterflies may be observed fluttering about plants. Adults are white with black markings on their forewings. The eggs are golden and oblong, and they may be found on both the top and bottom sides of the leaves. Caterpillars can grow to be 1 inch long and are velvety green with faint yellow stripes going down the back and sides. When prodded, they move slowly.

Management
See Cabbage Loopers.

Japanese Beetle

Japanese beetles are a major pest of roses, grapes, raspberries, and various ornamental plants and shrubs. They consume the leaves, flowers, and fruit of over 250 different plants. They are roughly ½ inch long and have a bright metallic copper tint, often known as greenish-brown. Adults are seen in July and August when they cause the most havoc.

Management

As irritating as it may appear, handpicking and squashing or drowning these pests is the most effective remedy accessible to the amateur grower. Fill a receptacle with soapy water, such as a coffee can, and flick the beetles into it. Later, cover it and throw it away. The technique is simple since the beetles travel slowly and do not conceal, and early attempts result in a greatly diminished population. The effectiveness of other Japanese beetle management strategies varies.

Many beetles are caught with Japanese beetle traps, which utilize a pheromone, or sex-attractant, to draw them in. However, if you place them far enough away from your yard, you will attract even more bugs in the direction of your plants. Before falling into the trap, the beetles may pause to munch! Another method is to use strong-smelling plants such as chives, garlic, or white geraniums as companion plants to discourage the insect. This method has not been properly or scientifically proven. Nonetheless, some gardeners claim success with this approach.

A variety of natural predators eats Japanese beetles. Among birds, only starlings consume beetles, while numerous species consume larvae in the spring. Assassin bugs and Tiphia wasps are two helpful insects that destroy Japanese beetle larvae.

Leafhoppers

Leafhoppers (LH) have sucking mouthparts that pierce plant tissues. They extract plant sap (similar to a mosquito taking blood). This results in a stippled or speckled pattern of color loss in the areas where the LH was supplied. Stunting, whitening, overall yellowing, leaf curling, crinkling, browning, tipburn, and a general reduction in vigor are all possible symptoms. The leaf edges are frequently curled upwards as well. When certain LH feed, they induce a burnt browning disease of the leaves known as 'hopperburn.' This might be due to a poison administered during feeding or due to the plant's response to the feeding activity. LH are also major virus and disease vectors, such as Aster yellows, curly top of sugar beets and other crops, yellow dwarf potatoes, etc.

Management

To date, LH predators and parasites seldom give satisfactory control, especially where the LH is a disease carrier. Cultural control measures may relieve LH damage depending upon LH species, crop and companion crops, etc.

Leafminers

Leafminers feed on dead tissue within leaves, causing huge patches or meandering tunnels of dead tissue to form. The spinach leafminer and the vegetable (serpentine) leafminer are the most prevalent leafminer species in Minnesota vegetable gardens. Leafminers have little effect on plant development but can harm edible vegetable leaves. Plants can be protected using a mix of nonchemical and pesticide approaches.

The spinach leafminer (*Pegomya hyoscyamine*) is a blotch leafminer that produces irregular round-shaped mines. The mines are initially long and thin but later form an unevenly shaped area. The larvae are pale and carrot-shaped, with no visible legs or head. The mature fly is hairy, approximately ¼ inch long, and grey to brownish.

Vegetable leafminer larvae (*Liromyza sativae*) thread themselves snake-like across the leaves, creating meandering tunnels. The larvae have a cylindrical yellowish-green body, and they lack legs and a visible head. Vegetable leafminer flies are yellow and black and are smaller than spinach leafminer flies (1/15 inch long).

Management
- Check young seedlings for leaf mines regularly, especially if leafminers have already invaded your garden. The majority of mines appear on the first genuine leaves.
- Vegetable leafminers are generally kept under control by their natural enemies, and no management is required.
- When spinach leafminers attack the leaves of a root crop, such as beets, it is not required to cure them. However, treatment may be required if it occurs on spinach or another leafy green.
- To protect the plants from insects, use fine-mesh netting row coverings.
- Use a material that will not block sunshine and rain from reaching the plants (e.g. cheesecloth).
- Apply in locations where there hasn't been a leafminer problem in at least a year.
- If leafminer problems have been noted in the previous year, this netting will not assist since pupae that survived the winter are still inside the row cover and can infest plants.

Mexican Bean Beetle

The Mexican bean beetle, formerly known as the bean ladybird, is one of the most damaging insect pests of beans. The beetle feeds on the leaves of nearly all bean varieties, including snap, lima, pinto, navy, kidney, and soybeans. Bush snap bean types appear to be more susceptible to assault than pole kinds.

The Mexican bean beetle does the most damage in July and August. The adult and larval stages eat on the foliage, biting holes in the leaves. They mainly feed on the undersides of the leaves and will occasionally attack immature pods and stems. Only the veins remain because of the feeding, giving the leaves a lacy look.

Management
Handpicking and smashing the beetles and eggs will only give you limited control. Because beetle populations are at their peak in the mid to late summer, planting the heaviest crop of beans for preserving and freezing early in the season may also help minimize some of the beetle damage. Good management may be gained if the first Mexican bean beetles or their damage are detected. Home gardeners can apply carbaryl, malathion, neem (repels beetles), or rotenone. Harvest with carbaryl, malathion, or rotenone after one day.

Onion Maggot

One of the most damaging insect pests of onions and allied plants is the onion maggot. The first sign of onion maggot damage is withering foliage, and the plant gradually turns floppy and falls. When the plants are seedlings, this form of damage is quite visible. Light infestations will not destroy onions, making them more vulnerable to rot. Onions of all sizes can be attacked, especially in the fall when the temperature is colder, and the maggots are more active. Damaged onions are unmarketable and will decay in storage, contaminating other onions. Once onion maggots have infested a region, they remain an issue annually. White onions are more vulnerable to assault than other types.

Management
Ground beetles, birds, parasitic wasps, nematodes, and a parasitic fungus that is particularly effective in chilly, rainy conditions are among maggots' natural enemies. There appear to be no resistant cultivars at present, except a Japanese bunching onion, which exhibits resistance or tolerance at times. The home gardener may not always be able to use rotation as a technique of maggot control, but removing wild onions should assist. Volunteer onions and chives may cause infestations. The onions should be removed, and the trash should be burnt rather than plowed into the soil. Flies may be attracted to soil that is rich in organic matter.

Sap Beetles

Beetles emerge during harvest and feed on damaged, overripe, or rotting fruits and vegetables. They are most prevalent on overripe maize, tomatoes, raspberries, strawberries, and muskmelons being the most prevalent. Effective sanitation regimens are the most effective way to manage them, and pesticides are ineffective and are discouraged from being used. Sap beetles are little, oval-shaped insects measuring between 1/8 and ¼ inches in length. On occasion, they are normally black, with orange or yellow patches. Sap beetle antennae feature a club (knob) at the end. This trait is present in all sap beetles and is a valuable aid for recognizing sap beetles.

Management
- Watch for sap beetles in gardens beginning in early July, when adults emerge. Check overripe strawberries in particular; however, they can also be detected in ripening produce.

- Remove any damaged, diseased, or overripe fruits and vegetables from the garden at regular intervals.
- To reduce beetle food supplies, collect apples, peaches, melons, tomatoes, and other rotting fruits and vegetables and bury them deep in the soil or destroy them.

Scale

Scale insects of diverse species damage numerous fruits and ornamental plants around the country. They adhere as little bumps on branches, twigs, and the undersides of leaves. Cottony cushion scale is thick, white, and coated with a waxy or fuzzy material, but some are flattened and brown.

The leaves of affected plants become yellow, and the plant's general vitality suffers. Plants that are severely affected may perish within a few seasons. Under their protective shells, mature females eat, lay eggs, and rear families. Crawlers eat by sucking plant secretions from eggs. Crawlers develop a shell-like coat and lose their legs as they age. Each year, there may be numerous generations.

Management
Spray horticultural oil as suggested on the package.

Slugs and Snails

These mollusks may be found across North America, although they are most common in damp, temperate areas. Snails require calcium for their shells and are thus less prevalent in locations where this element is deficient. Slugs are soft-bodied and gray to black or brown, with a soft hump in the center; snails have a hard calcium shell. Snails and slugs will eat almost any plant, although they prefer fragile young transplants, green vegetables, and succulent components. Large irregularly shaped holes in plant leaves and glistening slime trails indicate their existence. They are primarily active at night and in damp conditions. Slugs and snails are extremely prolific; some species can lay up to 500 eggs each year.

Management
Reduce the number of daytime hiding spots in the garden to make plants less accessible. Slugs and snails should be picked up and destroyed when you come across them; you can catch more by 'hunting' at night. To catch slugs and snails, fill shallow containers with beer and place them in the soil. Surround plants with copper barrier strips, which give slugs a little shock when they come into touch with them. Poisonous iron phosphate baits are an environmentally friendly alternative to other insecticides. Decollate snails, like toads, feed on other types of snails and slugs.

Spider mites

There are many different mites, often known as spider mites, and many of them feed on plants. They cluster in thick colonies on the undersides of leaves in webs. Silvering or a stippled look on the leaf top are symptoms of their eating. However, the exact symptom varies according to the plant. Turning over injured leaves may reveal spider mite webbing; rubbing the leaf will feel gritty. Mites graze on various edible and decorative plants, and houseplants are a popular prey item.

Management

Mites thrive in hot, dry, dusty environments. Plants should be carefully watered and washed regularly. If you find an infestation, spray the plants with a strong stream of water to knock the mites off the leaves. If the infestation persists, spray the plants with insecticidal soap or horticultural oil. Alternatively, you can buy and release predatory mites in orchards and promote any already present by avoiding spraying pesticides.

Spittlebugs

Spittlebugs are named from the frothy spittle mass they make when feeding on plants such as clover, strawberries, herbs, and various other garden plants. Spittlebug nymphs feed on plant fluids by piercing plant stems. Spittlebug feeding is often not harmful to plants, especially on annuals and perennials. Feeding can cause leaves to lose their form if too many spittlebugs are present.

Management

Check for spittlebug foam and nymphs at the base of the plants every two weeks in late April or early May. Look for them on the undersides of young leaves as the plants mature. Remove weeds around your gardens to eliminate a food source for them. Handpick them and shower them with a vigorous blast of water to dislodge the nymphs from the plants. Pesticides are ineffective against spittlebugs because the nymphs are shielded from pesticide sprays within their spittle masses.

Squash Bugs

The squash bug is a common squash and pumpkin pest, feeding on young seedlings and blossoming plants. They have the potential to cause young plants to wilt and perish, but squash bugs do little to no damage to plants in the late summer and fall. Squash bugs typically affect squash and pumpkins, but they can also attack other cucurbit-family plants such as cucumbers. They extract sap from plants using their piercing-sucking mouthparts, and their eating causes yellow dots to develop into brown spots. The feeding also impacts the movement of water and nutrients, and when severe enough, it can induce withering. Squash bugs, unlike cucumber beetles, do not transmit illness. Larger, sturdier plants are more resistant to feeding harm, whereas immature plants may perish due to feeding.

Management

- To help prevent squash bug damage, maintain healthy, robust plants with adequate fertilizer and watering.
- Adult squash bugs are tough to destroy, so remove them from the plant as soon as possible.
- Drop nymphs and adults into a bucket of soapy water to destroy them. This is only feasible if only a few plants are impacted.
- Squash bugs may be difficult to remove because they hide under leaves and move swiftly when disturbed.
- Crush any eggs that have been adhered to the undersides or stems of leaves.
- Lay down boards or pieces of newspaper to trap squash bugs. Squash bugs will congregate under the boards at night, which you may gather and eliminate in the morning.

Squash Vine Borers

The squash vine borer is a common clearwing moth with larvae that eat inside the vines and crowns of summer squash, winter squash, and pumpkins and is most active from mid-June to July. Whole crops may be lost in a year with high borer numbers in household gardens and small farms. Larvae feeding produces yellowing and withering of the leaves.

Adult moths are distinct in that they fly during the day and resemble wasps. Moths have an orange abdomen with black spots and are roughly ½ inch long. The first set of wings is metallic green, while the second pair is transparent. When at repose, the rear wings are folded and may be difficult to spot.

Management

Beginning in the last week of June, check your squash for the presence of adult borers. Adult squash vine borers can be detected using one of two ways.

- Keep an eye out for their behavior in the garden. These moths are easily identified due to their distinctive black/orange color and a pretty loud buzzing noise while they fly.
- For trapping, use a yellow-colored container (pan, bucket, bowl) filled with water and a drop of dish soap (break surface tension). Adult squash vine borers are drawn to yellow, and they'll fly to the container and become stuck when they fall into the water. Set traps by late June, monitoring them at least once a day.
- Make a meticulous strategy for your planting timetable – plant squash vine borers-resistant vine crops such as butternut squash, cucumbers, melons, and watermelons.
- In early July, sow a second crop of summer squash. These plants will grow after the adult borers have laid eggs and will be unharmed.
- Pull and remove any plants that have been destroyed by squash vine borers as soon as possible.
- Place floating row covers over your vine crops as plants begin to vine (or, for non-vining types, in late June or early July) or when squash vine borer adults are first detected.
- Maintain the barriers for about two weeks after the first adult borer is spotted.
- Secure the row coverings so that adults cannot move beneath them.

- Row coverings should not be used if cucurbits were planted in the same region the previous year because squash vine borers spend the winter in the soil near their host plants. When the adults emerge the following summer, they may become trapped behind the row cover rather than kept out.

Threelined Potato Beetles

A threelined potato bug is similar to a striped cucumber, except they eat on different plants. The threelined potato beetle is about ¼ inch long and has cream to reddish-yellow wing coverings and three black bands along its back.

Even if you observe a lot of threelined potato bugs in one region, they are typically not a concern. If you encounter these beetles in your garden and wish to get rid of them, handpick them and place them in a bucket of soapy water.

Thrips

Thrips are drawn to flower pollen, although both immatures and adults mostly feed on plant tissue. Thrips eat by extracting plant juices with their rasping/sucking mouthparts. Feeding damage shows on the leaf surface as coarse stippling. Thrips populations in large numbers inflict considerable plant damage, resulting in a silvery or scratchy look on leaf surfaces. Thrips also eat on floral tissue, causing marginal necrosis and petal browning.

Fava beans should be planted in greenhouses where thrips infestations are feared. Blue adhesive cards are more effective than yellow sticky cards at attracting thrips and should be put right near to fava beans, and this will draw thrips to the fava beans, increasing the likelihood of thrips eating on them. Remove the blooms from fava beans to encourage thrips to feed on the leaves rather than the flowers. Plants should be kept in the greenhouse for at least three weeks.

Management

Thrips control is critical because they can act as disease vectors. Total eradication is typically not attainable, especially given the possibility of pesticide resistance in thrips populations. To manage thrips numbers, growers should employ a combination of cultural, chemical, and biological management measures. To avoid resistance, pesticides should be alternated. Plants infected with TOSPO viruses should be removed to limit the risk of viral transmission.

Tomato Hornworms

Tomato hornworms are massive caterpillars with horn-like tails. Their preferred plant is tomato, which they can fully defoliate, although they have also been detected on potatoes, eggplant, and pepper. Many plants, such as horsenettle, jimsonweed, and nightshade, act as alternative hosts. Caterpillars in large numbers may defoliate plants fast in home gardens. Tomato hornworm caterpillars begin munching on the top leaves of the plants. The caterpillars blend in with the foliage and may go unnoticed until most of the damage has been done. They produce dark green or black droppings that are easily visible while feeding. Older tomato hornworms may wreak havoc on several leaves and the fruit. The final caterpillar stage eats almost as much as all the younger stages combined.

Management

- During the summer, inspect plants for tomato hornworms at least twice a week.
- Weeds should be removed to minimize the number of places where worms can lay eggs.
- After harvest, till the soil to kill burrowing caterpillars and pupae.
- Picking hornworms off plants is the most efficient control method, and their enormous size makes them easier to discover. To kill them, immerse them in soapy water.
- The tomato hornworm has several natural predators, including general predatory insects such as lady beetles and green lacewings, prey on the eggs, and juvenile caterpillars.
- When caterpillars are little, use *Bacillus thuringiensis* (Bt).
- If you come across a caterpillar with what seems to be white rice grains stuck to its body, do not remove it. The "grains" are the larvae of a parasitic wasp that feeds on hornworms. Allow the parasitized caterpillar to remain in the garden so that the pupae it carries can develop into new wasps to help manage other hornworms.

Whitefly

This pest may be found all across the United States. The small insects eat in enormous numbers by sucking plant fluids off the leaves and stems of various plants such as tomatoes, cucumbers, lettuce, flowers, trees, and shrubs. Whiteflies exude honeydew, a sticky, sugary material that can trigger the formation of a sooty black fungus on foliage. Eggs placed on the undersides of leaves develop into small larvae resembling flat, round, semitransparent scales. The larvae attain maturity approximately a month after hatching.

Management

Before using insecticidal soap or another authorized solution, spray plants with a stream of water from a garden hose to remove the bulk of the bugs. Follow the recommendations on the product package for an appropriate spray schedule for optimal control.

Whiteflies are unable to survive in subzero conditions. They are brought to northern regions by wind and infected plants each year. Before purchasing plants, thoroughly inspect them for whiteflies.

Plants that Attract Beneficial Insects

Plants that attract beneficial insects such as lady beetles, lacewings, parasitic wasps, and minute pirate bugs are anise, aster, basil, black locust, bee balm, canola, caraway, common knotweed, coneflower, coriander, cosmos, cowpea, crimson clover, daisy, dill, fennel, flowering buckwheat, hairy vetch, lovage, marigold, mint, nasturtium, oregano, parsley, poppy, Queen Anne's lace, sage, salvia, spearmint, sweet alyssum, sweet fennel, subterranean clover, tansy, wallflower, white sweet clove, wild buckwheat, wild mustard, yarrow, and zinnia.

Animal Garden Pests

Birds

Many birds are beneficial to gardeners because they eat dangerous insects and weed seeds. However, we label them as pests when they prey on our crops. Blackbirds, starlings, and even robins have been observed pulling up delicious corn seedlings, munching on blossoming cherries, peaches, and blueberries, and digging holes in lawns in search of insects. The extent of the damage will vary based on the year's weather and local food supplies. Birds will attack many different fruits and vegetables, such as tomatoes and melons, seeking food and moisture in dry years.

Management

Any fear device will work for a few days, but birds are intelligent and adapt quickly. Hanging metal pie tins, reflecting Mylar tape, and giant fear eye balloons (that mimic the scary eyes of predator birds) are all good visual scare tactics. Radios and intermittent cannon exploders are also handy noisemakers. Commercial bird repellents, as well as homemade hot pepper spray sprayed to preferred fruits, are effective. On the other hand, exclusion is the most effective method of controlling bird damage. When erected two to three weeks before the fruit matures, bird netting protects the tree fruit and berries. To deter birds, wrap ripening corn ears with paper bags and place floating row covers over growing seedlings.

Chipmunks and Squirrels

These fuzzy rodents are frequent visitors to many backyard birdfeeders and will attack various garden items, including young seedlings, berries, fruits, and vegetables. They've also been known to decapitate flowers like tulips, ostensibly for fun. Chipmunks are particularly adept at digging up bulbs, devouring newly planted seeds, and nibbling on mature root crops.

Management

These rodents are quite intelligent, and they'll find a means to get to their chosen destination given enough time. As with birds, it's essential to alter your technique from time to time to keep the rodents on their toes. An effective exclusion technique is to place a baffle on fruit tree trunks or birdfeeder poles. New "squirrel-proof" feeders arrive in catalogs regularly; they may include counter-weighted or electric perches that surprise the rodents when they approach the feeder. Some gardeners have successfully sprayed animal repellents on or around plants, such as cayenne pepper mix, predator urine, and commercial concoctions. Trapping is the most effective method of removing troublesome rats, and live traps are extremely efficient for catching obnoxious squirrels or chipmunks.

Mice, Voles, and Rats

These rodents, which range in size from the tiniest house mouse to the biggest Norway rat, dwell everywhere people do. Rats and mice are only active at night, but voles can be observed scurrying around at any time of day or night. These critters like digging and burrowing, making them important pests of subterranean garden plants. Mice and vole activity is indicated by partially consumed potatoes or carrots. They eat newly sowed seeds and most flower bulbs (except daffodils). Spring melting frequently shows chewed bark from the base of young tree trunks.

Management

The first line of defense is to make the environment hostile to mice by eliminating food, water, and shelter. Seal any entrances to buildings, clean up pet food bowls, and store rubbish in locked containers. The old-fashioned trap is the most effective family control. Place a snap or live trap on mouse pathways, baited with peanut butter or bacon. Delay adding fluffy mulches like straw in the garden until late in the season. Mice enjoy wintering in this material because it allows them free access to your plants under the snow. When used as intended, ammonium-based repellents can be effective against rodents.

Raccoons

Raccoons are nocturnal animals that prosper due to greater human contact, as anybody with an open dumpster or garbage can will confirm. Wild populations prefer regions with adjacent trees and water. However, they are increasingly observed roaming city streets at night due to man's generosity in giving fresh food, drink, and shelter supplies. Aside from garbage cans, raccoons are well-known for their fondness for sweetcorn. These omnivores will also consume strawberries, tree fruits, peas, potatoes, melons, and grass grubs. They will eat mature tree fruit and burrow holes in growing melons. They dig holes in lawns and mulch piles in search of insects to consume. They, like squirrels, have been observed cleaning out birdfeeders.

Management

To deter raccoons from entering your yard at night, keep water and food items, such as pet bowls and birdfeeders, out of reach. Raccoons can also be deterred with repellents, scare tactics, and a strong fence. A sprinkle of baby powder, cayenne pepper, or blood meal on vegetables and corn ears is a successful DIY repellant. Cover individual corn ears or melons with taped-closed bags in a small garden. To keep raccoons from climbing fruit trees, install baffles on their trunks. Remove any overhanging limbs that raccoons could use to jump into the fruit tree; control grubs and other insects to prevent lawn damage.

Rabbits

These lovely, fuzzy critters can do a lot of damage to your garden and landscape. Rabbit and hare species abound across the country, and as the saying goes, they breed like… well, you know. They dwell in tunnel networks known as warrens and do not go far to feed. Peter Rabbit's cuisine includes young shoots of peas, beans, lettuce, flowers, tulips, clover, and deciduous tree bark. Fortunately, after plants have grown past the seedling stage or trees have developed strong bark, they are typically protected from bunny assaults. Look for cleanly cut leaves and stems to identify rabbit damage from a bug or other animal damage.

Management

Rabbits can be deterred, trapped, and fenced out. Install an area of alfalfa or clover apart from the garden to keep rabbits away from cherished crops. In the winter, use tree guards to protect young trees. Remove brush piles and tall grasses from areas where rabbits may hide in your garden. Although some gardeners employ repellents such as human or dog hair, chili powder, blood meal, fish emulsion, and commercial treatments, a fence is the most dependable approach to keep rabbits out of the garden.

Diseases

Alternaria

Alternaria, sometimes known as black spot, is one of the most frequent diseases of broccoli, kale, and other Brassica crops. It wreaks havoc on leaves, frequently causes head rot, and can severely reduce production. While this illness is not new, it has become more prevalent in recent years, especially on broccoli and, to a lesser extent, cauliflower. Leaf symptoms include circular, brown patches with concentric rings and a yellow halo that can fracture through the center. Spots usually appear first on older leaves. As the illness advances, the spots on the leaves might merge to form massive necrotic patches on the leaves. Head rot symptoms might begin as little brown patches on a healthy-looking head.

Management
- If symptoms emerge only on a few plants, remove contaminated plants as soon as they appear. Ensure that the entire plant, not just the leaves, is removed. Remove diseased leaves from all plants if they are afflicted.
- If you come into contact with sick leaves, thoroughly wash your hands before dealing with healthy Brassica plants. After contacting sick plants, wash and sterilize your pruning equipment.
- Purchase clean seed from trusted sources.

- Only preserve seeds from healthy plants if you want to save them.
- Think about heat-treating your seed.
- Remove or bury any leftovers in your garden.
- Allow three years before replanting Brassica plants in the same spot.
- If this disease has been an issue for you, avoid using cover crops in the Brassica family, such as tillage radish.
- Increase airflow by keeping plants at a reasonable distance apart. Broccoli spacing should be 10–18 inches apart in rows 18–36 inches apart.
- Keep an eye out for weeds in the Brassica family, including shepherd's purse, black mustard, and field mustard. Remove them from your garden to avoid serving as a host for black rot.
- Each time you start seeds, clean and sterilize the trays.

Angular Leaf Spot

This bacterial disease may be found everywhere cucurbits are produced, although it is most harmful in humid climates. Cucumbers, muskmelons, and summer squash are particularly vulnerable. The infection first emerges as water-soaked sores on the undersides of leaves. The dots have an angular shape as they develop between veins. Spots become straw-colored or brown, then dry up and fall out, leaving ragged holes on the leaves. Spots may discharge a milky substance that dries on the leaf's surface. The disease survives the winter on seed, and plant remnants and splashing water spreads germs among plants.

Management
Use a two-year rotation at the very least. Plant resistant cultivars and seed stock from arid areas. Drip irrigation is preferable to overhead watering. When the plants are damp, avoid working in the garden. To prevent the spread of infection, destroy sick plants as well as those nearby.

Anthracnose

This fungus may be found globally. It is especially bothersome in the humid eastern section of North America. Beans' pods and stems grow circular, dark, sunken patches. The veins on the undersides of the leaves become black. Cucumber and muskmelon leaves get yellow spots that dry up and fall off; watermelon leaves acquire black dots.

Sunken patches with black edges cover infected apples. Tomatoes acquire sunken patches on ripe fruits, which turn black in the center. The illness spreads more easily in wet conditions. The fungus survives the winter in plant remnants in the soil.

Management
Compost enriches the soil, which helps plants withstand the assault. Get disease-free seed and cultivate resistant cultivars. Working with plants when they are damp is not a good idea. Irrigate using drip rather than overhead sprinklers. Rotate crops at least once a year (a two-to-three-year rotation is better). Keep ripening fruits away from the dirt. When used as stated on the product label, copper fungicides are effective as a preventative. It's better not to rely too much on this form of management since copper may accumulate in the soil to dangerous levels for earthworms and bacteria.

Black Rot

All cabbage family crops are affected by this bacterial disease. It can be found over much of North America, but it is more widespread in the east. Young seedlings infected with the pathogen become yellow and perish. Older plants have yellow, wedge-shaped regions that extend into the leaf's center at the leaf margins. Within this dead tissue, the veins become dark. Older leaves near the plant's base are the first to be damaged. Symptoms may appear first on one side of the plant. The head may begin to rot as the condition spreads. Insects, splashing water, and infected instruments propagate black rot. Warm, humid weather promotes the spread of this illness, which may live for two years on plant remnants in the soil.

Management
Plant disease-free seeds and transplants. Remove diseased plants. Irrigation systems that moisten the tops of plants should be avoided. Give a two-year gap before planting susceptible plants.

Blight (Bacterial)

Bacterial blight affects the majority of the United States. Both snap and a variety of strains can infect lima beans. Common blight (seen) generates huge, water-soaked, light green patches on leaves, which eventually turn brown. In wet conditions, water-soaked patches occur on pods and may generate yellowish slime. Plants affected with

Halo blight have many little dead patches with yellow halos around them on their leaves. When the weather is humid, spots on pods release cream-colored slime. The transmission of this illness is aided by cool, damp weather. More prevalent on limas, brown spot blight generates little reddish-brown patches with definite edges on the leaves and pods.

Management
For beans, use a three-year crop rotation. When the plants are damp, avoid working in the garden. Save no seeds from diseased plants. When used as indicated on the product label, copper fungicides are effective as a preventative but harm the soil biota.

Blight (Corn Leaves)

Northern corn leaf disease creates huge (½ inch to six inch) grayish-green to tan patches on corn leaves. Southern corn leaf blight develops little (½ inch by ¼ inch) tan patches with reddish-brown margins on the leaves. Corn leaf blights are found in the eastern region of North America. The infection normally does not kill the plant but weakens it, making it more susceptible to other illnesses. Young plants are more vulnerable. Warm, rainy weather favors these blights, and the fungus survives the winter on infected plant residues in the soil.

Management
Plant disease-resistant cultivars and only buy certified disease-free seeds. After the season, rotate crops and clear up garden trash.

Blight (Early)

Throughout much of North America, this fungal disease kills tomatoes and potatoes. Plants that are stressed or have a big fruit load are the most vulnerable. Older leaves are the first to develop dark brown markings with concentric rings. Infected leaves become yellow and eventually die. Brown, corky patches cover the potato tubers. Tomato fruits can get infected at any moment; a dark, sunken, leathery patch grows at the stem end. Warm, damp circumstances aid disease development. The fungus survives the winter in plant remnants in the soil.

Management

Plant in well-drained soil with sufficient air circulation. Rotate crops and remove any stray potato or tomato plants. When watering, avoid wetting the leaves. Amend the soil with compost and fertilize plants sparingly to preserve plant vitality. Ensure that your seed potatoes and tomato transplants are disease-free. Tomato plants with early blight gradually lose their leaves, but ripe tomatoes can typically be harvested unless the infection is severe. At the first indication of the illness, use a copper-based fungicide as instructed on the product label.

Blight (Late)

Late blight affects tomatoes and potatoes at any stage of development in North America. On the leaves, irregular gray patches appear on the undersides of these patches, white mold forms. Infected leaves become brown and dry. Gray, water-soaked patches on sick fruits turn dark brown and corky after a while. Infected tubers have brown areas where decay occurs. The transmission of the illness is aided by wet weather with cold nights and warm days. The fungus survives the winter on infected plant detritus.

Management

Fertilize sparingly, as excess nitrogen promotes the illness. Avoid watering from above. To prevent the spread of the disease, use a flame weeder to remove diseased plants. To avoid infecting tubers, wait a week after potato plants die before harvesting at the end of the season. Use a flame weeder to eliminate plant remnants before digging tubers for an early harvest.

Club Root

This fungal disease affects all cabbage family crops and is widespread across North America. Plants wilt during the day and recover at night; older leaves yellow and drop; roots swell and become twisted; plants get stunted and may die. The fungus may survive in soil for up to ten years. The disease thrives in acidic soil and warm, rainy conditions.

Management

There is no treatment for diseased plants. Improve soil drainage, keep soil pH above 7.2 (may be incompatible with other crops), and utilize at least a four-year rotation between sensitive crops.

Leaf Spot (Bacterial)

This disease is most prevalent in eastern North America, affecting tomatoes and peppers. Green fruits have small, black, corky, elevated dots with somewhat depressed centers. Rot organisms may enter through the holes and decompose the fruit. Infected blooms drop; tiny, black spots appear on leaves, which yellow and fall. Plants are weakened due to this defoliation, which exposes growing fruits to sunscald. Warm, damp weather promotes the fungus spread, which survives the winter in soil-plant residue.

Management

Use a three- to four-year crop rotation. Destroy any volunteer tomato and pepper plants and any contaminated fruits. Only buy transplants that have been verified as disease-free. Plants should be watered and fertilized regularly. Allow enough space between plants and support vines to allow proper air circulation. Avoid overhead watering and working around damp plants to keep the illness from spreading. While the weather is conducive to disease spread, spray actively aerated compost tea every seven to ten days.

Leaf Spot (Septoria)

This fungal disease, which can occur at any moment, can affect tomato plants in various regions of North America. Symptoms emerge initially on the oldest, lowest leaves – areas of gray-brown feature gray cores and a darker border. The black border lacks the characteristic rings of early blight. Many minute, black spores may be seen in the cores of the discolored patches, and a yellowish area may surround the darker spots. It normally defoliates plants gradually, although harvesting is still viable.

Management

Spray actively aerated compost tea every seven to ten days. Grow resistant tomato types such as "potato-leaved" (leaves with no indentations on the borders) and rugose-leaved (leaves with a puckered leaf surface).

Mildew (Downy)

Downy mildew fungus causes illness in various crops across North America. Irregular brown or yellow dots appear on the top leaf surface; during humid conditions, the bottom leaf surface underneath these spots is coated with a hairy white or purple mold. Leaves that are severely affected perish. The fungus that infects cucumbers and muskmelons (and, less commonly, squash and pumpkins) is mostly found in the East. Infected plant fruits are tiny and bitter. Cabbage family members are frequently affected as seedlings, which become yellow and die quickly. Sunken black patches on mature plants' heads are common. Wet conditions aid the propagation of this fungus.

Management

Employ resistant cultivars. Plant in well-drained soil in locations with good air circulation. Weeds that can host the illness must be controlled. Use disease-free transplants or treated seeds. Crop leftovers should be tilled into the soil to decrease spore generation. When watering, avoid soaking the tops of the plants. To limit disease transmission, organic gardeners might use actively aerated compost tea.

Mildew (Powdery)

This fungal disease affects many plants in North America, including beans, cucurbits, lettuce, and peas. The upper surface of the leaves is covered in a powdery white growth, which gradually becomes yellow and dries. In most cases, older leaves are affected first. The fungus competes with the plant for nutrients, lowering production and even weakening or killing the plant if the infection is

severe. Mildew can also be seen on fruits and pods. This disease appears late in the season on established plants and thrives in dry and humid conditions, and it spreads quickly.

Management
Where resistant cultivars are available, plant them. Potassium bicarbonate fungicides are effective when used as directed on the label.

Wilt (Bacterial)

This sickness affects the majority of the United States. Cucumbers and muskmelons are usually affected, as are pumpkins and squash. Individual leaves wilt in the heat of the day but rebound overnight. Part or all of the vine wilts and dies as the illness advances. Cut a wilted stem at the plant's base to check for the illness. Remove the sap from the stem by squeezing it. Bacterial wilt is most likely present if it is sticky and white and forms a thread when the tip of a knife is pressed to it and dragged away. (Cucumbers work well for this test.) The illness survives the winter in the guts of cucumber beetles and spreads to plants while the bugs eat.

Management
Cucumber beetle control is essential for prevention. Look for cucumber and squash cultivars that are resistant to cucumber bugs. Floating row coverings can be used to protect young plants. To limit the number of overwintering adults, knock, shake, or handpick beetles off plants and out of blooms, and clear up plant debris. Plants and flowers should be dusted with pyrethrum pesticides as instructed on the product label.

Wilt (Verticillium and Fusarium)

The fungus Verticillium and Fusarium can cause contagious tomato wilt illnesses. These soilborne fungi infiltrate the plant's root system and eventually clog the vascular tissue causing yellowing and withering of the plant's leaves from the bottom upwards. Infected plants die young, bearing little or no fruit.

Aside from the wilt symptoms, infected plants have brownish-red staining of the vascular tissue in the lower stem. This may be seen by cutting a knife through the lower stem and crown tissue, and the discoloration may spread some way up the stem.

Management
Rotate away from tomato family crops (tomato, pepper, potato, and eggplant) over several years and obtain VF-resistant varieties. This will aid in the reduction of fungus colonies in the soil. Plant tomatoes in well-drained soil rich in compost that contains beneficial microorganisms.

Mold (Gray)

Botrytis spp., a fungus with over 200 hosts, causes gray mold. Plants that serve as hosts include fruits (such as strawberries, brambles, and grapes), vegetables (such as lettuce, onion, and beans), and ornamentals (ex. peony, geranium, petunia). Gray mold can cause significant losses in prospective flowers (blossom blight) and mature fruits. The illness is most severe during seasons of prolonged dampness and rainfall (or overwatering) and chilly temperatures.

Bean symptoms begin as water-soaked patches on blooms, stems, leaves, and pods that rapidly expand and become coated in a cottony white mold. Infected leaves wilt, become yellow, and eventually die. Mycelia (vegetative propagules) and spores of the fungus can be detected as signs of the fungus by a fuzzy white to gray mold. As it develops, the fungus can create sclerotia (minor, hard, black, irregularly shaped survival structures) for overwintering. Stone fruit brown rot should not be confused with it.

Management
Maintaining enough air circulation for plants, which includes correct plant spacing when planting or transplanting, and trimming to minimize overcrowding in raspberries, is one of the best strategies to prevent the development of this disease. This will assist in reducing the amount of moisture held in plant canopies, hence lowering the potential of spores to germinate and infect. When there is moisture or dew on the plants, minimize wounding since injuries might be an advantageous region for the fungus to begin colonization. Use a three- to four-year crop rotation with non-susceptible plants such as corn, beets, or spinach.

Scab (Potato)

This disease, produced by a bacterial-like organism, damages potatoes throughout North America. The outside of the tubers is covered with brown, corky regions or pits. Neutral and alkaline soils aid scab growth. Beets, turnips, carrots, rutabagas, and parsnips are also vulnerable, though scab is normally not a severe problem on these.

Management
Plant potato cultivars that are resistant. Maintain a pH of less than 5.2 in the soil. Use a three-year rotation of sensitive crops. In the potato patch, use well-composted manure; new manure may include scab-causing organisms.

Viruses

Viruses may infect a wide range of plants in North America, including beans, celery, maize, cucurbits, peas, peppers, spinach, and tomatoes. Symptoms vary depending on the virus, but may include mottling, streaking, puckering, or curling leaves. Cucumber mosaic virus, for example, infects cucurbits, tomatoes, and peppers, causing green and yellow mottling of foliage, curled leaves, stunted plants, and fruits with light splotches warty pimples. Many viruses are transmitted from plant to plant by sucking insects like aphids and leafhoppers as they eat.

Management

Control disease-carrying insects. Infected plants should be removed and burned. When available, select resistant kinds. Purchase virus-free seed potatoes. Weeds that carry viruses must be controlled.

Plant Problems and Possible Causes

Rapid leaf drop:

- Extreme temperature or light changes
- Root loss from transplanting
- Overwatering
- Underwatering

Gradual leaf drop:

- Insufficient light
- Insufficient fertilizer
- Overwatering
- Underwatering

Wilting of the entire plant:

- Exposure to cold
- Excess fertilizer
- Overwatering
- Underwatering

Loss of leaf color:

- Excess light
- Insufficient light
- Insufficient fertilizer
- Overwatering

- Underwatering
- Spider mite damage

Spotted leaves:

- Leaf scorch
- Sunburn
- Cold water on leaves (particularly African violets)
- Bacterial or fungal disease
- Air pollution
- Overwatering
- Spider mite damage

Leaf tips turning brown:

- Low humidity
- Incorrect potting mix pH
- Air pollution
- Poor water quality (fluoride, sodium)
- Excess fertilizer
- Overwatering
- Underwatering

Stunted plants:

- Excess fertilizer
- Overwatering
- Underwatering
- Root-bound
- Insufficient light intensity
- Insufficient fertilizer

Leaf droop or curl:

- Air pollution
- Underwatering
- Aphids

Pale and spindly new growth:

- Insufficient fertilizer
- Insufficient light
- Underwatering

Wilted or blackened new growth:

- Cold or hot drafts
- Sunburn
- Temperature too warm
- Temperature too cold
- Excess fertilizer
- Underwatering

White spots on leaves:

- Spider mites

Cottony masses on stems:

- Mealybugs and some scale species

Dark bumps on leaves or stems:

- Armored scales

Sticky spots under the leaves:

- Honeydew excreted by aphids, mealy bugs, scale, or white flies

CHAPTER 10
MONTHLY TASKS

January

- Send for seed catalogs for the garden.
- If you have not already done so, take soil samples to your County Extension office for analysis.
- Sketch your garden plans on paper, including what to grow, spacing, arrangement and number of plants needed.
- Consider planting a few new varieties along with the old favorites.
- Order seeds and plants as early as possible for best selection. Buy enough quality seed for two or three plantings to lengthen the production season.
- Wood ashes from the fireplace can be spread in the garden, but don't overdo it. Wood ashes increase soil pH, and excess application can make some nutrients unavailable for plant uptake. Have the soil tested to be certain of the pH before adding wood ash.
- Apply compost and plow it under if you did not do so in the fall.
- Apply lime, sulfur, and fertilizer according to the soil-test results and vegetable requirements.
- Get plant beds or seedboxes ready for growing plants such as tomato, pepper, and eggplant. Have beds ready for planting in early February.
- Check on your compost pile and make sure it is ready for use in the spring.

February

- Order seeds before it's too late for this year's planting.
- If you have not yet done so, sketch your garden plans. Remember to include plants to replace or replant crops that you will harvest in spring or early summer.
- Prepare or repair lawn and garden tools for the upcoming season.
- Start seeds indoors for cool-season vegetables to be ready to transplant to the garden early in the season. It would help if you started broccoli, cauliflower, and cabbage seeds five to seven weeks before transplanting.

- Make early plantings of your choice from the following: carrots, collards, lettuce, mustard, English peas, Irish potatoes, radishes, spinach, and turnips.
- Test leftover garden seeds for germination. Place ten seeds between moist paper toweling or cover with a thin layer of soil. Keep seeds warm and moist. If fewer than six seeds germinate, then purchase fresh seed.
- Plant seedboxes. Peppers and eggplants will take eight weeks to grow from seed to transplant size, while tomatoes will take six weeks. When the seedlings form their third set of true leaves, transplant them to individual containers.
- Prepare land for planting – winter and early spring plantings belong on a ridge (raised bed) for better drainage and earlier soil warm-up.
- If nematodes were a problem last year, plan to plant another crop less susceptible to nematodes in the infected area.
- Use 'starter' fertilizer solution around transplanted crops such as cabbage.
- Replenish the mulch on strawberries.
- Seed herbs for April planting. Make a list of the best ones to buy rather than seed – such as French tarragon and rosemary.

March

- Plant cool-season vegetables and flowers as soon as the ground has dried enough to work. Do not work the soil while it is wet; wait until it crumbles in your hand. If the soil forms a solid ball when you squeeze it, it's still too wet.
- Gradually harden-off transplants by setting them outdoors during the daytime for about a week before planting.
- Follow last fall's soil test recommendations for fertilizer and pH adjustment. It's not too late to test soil if you missed it last year.
- Start the seeds of warm-season vegetables and flowers indoors.
- Remove old foliage from ornamental grasses and perennial flowers.
- Watch for blooms of early spring bulbs, such as daffodils, squill, crocus, dwarf iris, and snowdrops.
- Remove old asparagus and rhubarb tops, and side-dress the plants with nitrogen or manure: plant or transplant asparagus, rhubarb, and small-fruit plants.
- Remove winter mulch from strawberry beds as soon as new growth begins but keep the mulch nearby to protect against frost and freezes.
- Remove weak, diseased, or damaged canes from raspberry plants before new growth begins. Remove old fruiting canes if you did not remove them last year, and shorten the remaining canes if necessary.

- Prune grapevines after you can assess winter injury.
- Make second plantings of quickly maturing crops like turnips, mustard, radishes, and 'spring onions.'
- Thin plants when they are 2 to 3 inches tall to give the plants room to grow.
- Carry out any February jobs not completed.
- Treat seed before planting or buy treated seed for protection against seed-borne diseases, seed decay, seedling 'damping off,' and soil insects such as seed-corn maggots.
- Early-planted crops may need a nitrogen side-dressing, particularly if the soil is cool. Place the fertilizer several inches to the side of the plants and water it in. A little fertilizer throughout the growing period is better than too much at one time.
- Before settling them in the garden, harden-off transplants – place them in their containers outdoors in a sheltered place a few days ahead of planting them.
- Get rows ready for 'warm-season' vegetables to be planted during the last week of March or the first week or two of April as weather permits.
- You might want to risk planting out a few more tender crops and keeping them covered during bad weather.
- Watch out for insects, especially cutworms, plant lice (aphids), and red spider mites.
- Put down mulch between rows to control weeds.

April

- Plant seeds of cool-season crops directly in the garden as soon as the soil dries enough to be worked. When squeezed, the soil should crumble instead of forming a ball. Cool-season crops that can be direct-seeded include peas, lettuce, spinach, carrots, beets, turnips, parsnips, and Swiss chard.
- Plant transplants of cool-season crops, such as broccoli, cauliflower, cabbage, Brussels sprouts, kohlrabi, and onions.
- Plant or transplant asparagus and rhubarb crowns. For best plant establishment, do not harvest until the third year after planting.
- Plant sections of certified, disease-free potato 'seed' tubers.
- Allow the foliage of spring-flowering bulbs to remain in place after blooms fade. Leaves manufacture the food reserves, which are then stored in the bulb for a repeat showing next year.
- Plant hardy perennials, such as daylilies and delphiniums.

- Start tuberous begonias and caladiums indoors for transplanting to garden later.
- Remove winter mulch from strawberries, but keep mulch handy in case late frosts are predicted and to help keep weeds under control.
- Plant or transplant strawberries, raspberries, and other small fruit.
- Prune grape vines to remove dead or weakened limbs and to thin as needed.
- Repair support trellises as needed.
- Plant your choices of the following 'warm-season' or 'frost-tender' crops: beans (snap, pole and lima), cantaloupe, corn (sweet), cucumbers, eggplant, okra, field peas, peppers, squash, tomatoes and watermelon.
- Plant tall-growing crops such as okra, pole beans and corn on the north side of other vegetables to avoid shading. Plant two or more rows of corn for better pollination.
- Make a second planting within two to three weeks of the first planting of snap beans, corn and squash.
- Within three to four weeks of the first planting, plant more lima beans and corn. Remember: for better pollination, plant at least two or more rows.
- Be sure to plant enough vegetables for canning and freezing.
- Cultivate to control weeds and grass, to break crusty soil and to provide aeration.
- Maintain mulch between rows.
- For the crops planted earlier, side-dress as described above.
- Plant tender herbs.
- **Remember:** Do not work in your garden when the foliage is wet to avoid spreading diseases from one plant to another.

May

- Plant frost-tender plants after the danger of frost has passed for your area. This includes warm-season vegetables (such as tomatoes, peppers, eggplant, and vine crops) as well as most annual flowers and tender perennials (such as cannas, gladiolus, dahlias, tuberous begonias, and caladiums).
- Pinch chrysanthemums and annual flower plants to keep them compact and well-branched.
- Make successive plantings of beans and sweetcorn to extend the harvest season.
- Thin seedlings of early-planted crops such as carrots, lettuce, spinach, and beets to their proper spacing.
- Harvest early plantings of radishes, spinach, and lettuce.

- Both asparagus and rhubarb season may be delayed this year due to the slow progression of spring.
- Harvest asparagus by cutting or snapping spears at or just below soil level.
- Harvest rhubarb by cutting or grasping the stalk and pulling it up and slightly to one side.
- Control cucumber beetles (which are carriers of bacterial wilt) as soon as cucumber plants germinate or are transplanted to prevent disease.
- Remove blossoms from newly set strawberry plants to allow better runner formation.
- Remove unwanted sucker growth in raspberries when new shoots are about a foot tall.
- Make third plantings of vegetables mentioned for April (snap beans, corn, squash, lima beans).
- Control grass and weeds; they compete for moisture and fertilizer.
- Locate mulching materials for such crops as tomatoes, peppers, eggplant, Irish potatoes, okra and lima beans. Apply before dry spells occur but after plants are well established (usually by blooming time).
- Pole beans cling to the trellis or sticks more readily if attached by the time they start running.
- Try a few tomato plants on stakes or trellises this year. Now is the time to start removing suckers and tying the plants up.
- Watch out for the '10 most wanted culprits': Mexican bean beetle, Colorado potato beetle, bean leaf beetle, Harlequin cabbage bug, blister beetle, cabbage worm, tomato hornworm, tomato fruit worm (and corn earworm), cucumber beetle and squash bug. Early discovery makes possible early control.
- Begin disease control measures as needed. Check with your County Extension office for more information.
- Water as needed.
- Mulch as needed.
- Keep a logbook of problems and failures that occur so you can avoid or prevent them in the next planting season. Note successful techniques and varieties for consideration next season.
- Make plans now for putting up some of your garden produce. Check with your County Extension office for more information.

June

- Discontinue harvesting asparagus and rhubarb around mid-June to allow foliage to develop and store carbohydrate reserves for next year's harvest. Fertilize after last harvest and water as needed to promote healthy growth.
- Mulch to control weeds and conserve soil moisture after soil has warmed. You can use many materials, including straw, chopped corncobs, bark chips, shredded paper, and grass clippings.
- Blanch (exclude light from) cauliflower when heads are just 2 inches in diameter. Tie leaves up and over the developing head.
- Control weeds. They're easier to pull when they are still young.
- Start seeds of cabbage, Brussels sprouts, broccoli, and cauliflower for fall garden transplants.
- Plan now for your Halloween pumpkin. Determine the days to harvest for the particular cultivar you want to plant (usually on the seed packet) and count backward to determine the proper planting date.
- Harvest spring plantings of broccoli, cabbage, and peas.
- Remove cool-season plants, such as radish, spinach, and lettuce, because they will bolt (that is, form seed stalks) and become bitter during hot summer weather.
- Continue planting carrots, beans, and sweetcorn for successive harvests.
- For staked tomatoes, remove suckers (branches that form where the leaf joins the stem) while they are 1 to 1½ inches long to allow easier training. No need to remove suckers on caged plants.
- Remove the spent blooms of peony, iris, delphiniums after they fade.
- Pinch the shoot tips of chrysanthemums, impatiens, petunias, and coleus to promote bushier growth.
- Remove the tops of spring-flowering bulbs only after they have yellowed and withered.
- Continue planting gladiolus for a succession of bloom.
- Pick strawberries from the garden or a U-pick operation (check with the farm for COVID-19 U-pick protocols).
- Protect ripening strawberries from birds by covering with netting.
- Supplement natural rainfall (as needed) to supply a total of 1 to 1½ inches of water per week to the garden.
- Harvest vegetables such as beans, peas, squash, cucumbers and okra regularly to prolong production and enjoy peak freshness.

- Eat 'high on the hog' this month and in July and preserve enough to last during the winter months ahead.
- For best results, harvest onions and Irish potatoes when two-thirds of the tops have died down. Store potatoes in a cool, dark place and onions in a dry, airy place.
- Clean off rows of early crops as soon as they are through bearing and use rows for replanting or keep them fallow for fall crops.
- Water as needed.
- Plant sweet potatoes and a second planting of Southern peas.

July

- Supplement natural rainfall, if any, to supply 1 to 1½ inches of water per week in a single application.
- Start seeds of broccoli, cabbage, and Brussels sprouts to transplant later for a fall harvest.
- Harvest crops such as tomatoes, squash, okra, peppers, beans, and cucumbers frequently to encourage further production.
- Complete succession planting of bush beans and sweetcorn.
- Harvest summer squash while small and tender for best quality.
- Standard sweetcorn is at its peak for only a day or so. Super sweetcorn varieties maintain their peak quality for a longer period. Harvest when silks begin to dry and kernels exude a milky, rather than watery or doughy, juice when punctured.
- Broccoli will form edible side shoots after the main head is removed.
- Mulch garden to control weeds and conserve soil moisture.
- Make sure potato tubers, carrot shoulders, and onion bulbs are covered with soil to prevent them from developing a green color and off flavors. Applying a layer of mulch will help keep them covered.
- Allow blossoms on newly planted everbearing strawberry plants to develop for a fall crop.
- July is a good time to fertilize strawberries with ½ pound of actual nitrogen per 100 feet of row.
- Harvest raspberries when fully colored and easily separated from stem. After harvest is complete, prune out the fruiting canes to make room for new growth.
- Remove faded blossoms from annual and perennial flowers to prevent seeds from forming.

- Condition flowers cut from the garden for arranging by removing the lower leaves, placing cut stem ends in warm water, and storing them overnight in a cool location.
- The foliage of spring-flowering bulbs can be removed safely after it fades. This also is a good time to lift the bulbs for transplanting or propagation.
- Start planning the fall garden.
- Keep grass from going to seed. Fallow soil to conserve moisture for germination of fall crops and to help reduce the nematode population in the soil.
- Clean off harvested rows immediately to prevent insect and disease buildup.
- Plant the following vegetables not later than July 20 to allow time to mature before frost: tomatoes, okra, corn, pole beans and lima beans. Also plant cucumbers, squash and snap beans.
- Water deeply and less often – as needed to prevent drought stress.
- Plant that big pumpkin for Halloween.
- Be sure to make arrangements for neighbors to harvest and water your garden while you are on vacation.
- Make sure the garden is well mulched to prevent weeds and conserve moisture.

August

- Keep the garden well-watered during dry weather and free of weeds, insects and disease.
- Complete fall garden planting by direct-seeding carrots, beets, kohlrabi, kale and snap beans early this month. Lettuce, spinach, radishes and green onions can be planted later in August and early September. Don't forget to thin seedlings to appropriate spacing as needed.
- Harvest onions after the tops yellow and fall, then cure them in a warm, dry, well-ventilated area. The necks should be free of moisture when fully cured in about a week's time.
- Harvest potatoes after the tops yellow and die. Potatoes also need to be cured before storage.
- Pick beans, tomatoes, peppers and squash often to encourage further production.
- Harvest watermelon when several factors indicate ripeness: the underside ground spot turns from whitish to creamy yellow; the tendril closest to the melon turns brown and shrivels; the rind loses its gloss and appears dull; and the melon produces a dull thud, rather than a ringing sound when thumped.

- Harvest sweetcorn when kernels are plump and ooze a milky juice when punctured with your fingernail. If the liquid is watery, you're too early; if the kernels are doughy, you're too late.
- Keep faded flowers pinched off bedding plants to promote further flowering and improve plant
- Plant the following no later than the dates indicated below:
  —**August 15**: Snap beans and Irish potatoes (seed can be sprouted two to three weeks before planting).
  —**August 31**: Cucumbers and squash; plant varieties resistant to downy mildew.
- In order to calculate the planting date, determine the frost date and count back the number of days to maturity plus 18 days for harvest of the crop. If snap beans mature in 55 days and your frost date is November 15, you should plant on or before September 3.
- Start plants for broccoli, cabbage, cauliflower, collards, kale and onions in a half-shaded area for setting out in September.
- Prepare soil for September to October plantings of 'cool-season' crops. Apply fertilizer and prepare seeds so rains will settle the rows and make it easier to get seeds to germinate when they are planted.
- If watering is necessary to get a stand, open the furrow for seed, pour in water, plant seed and cover. Use starter solution on the transplanted crops.
- Water the garden as needed to prevent drought stress.

September

- Dig onions and garlic after tops fall over naturally and necks begin to dry.
- Plant radishes, green onion sets, lettuce and spinach for fall harvest.
- Thin fall crops, such as lettuce and carrots, that were planted earlier.
- Harvest crops such as tomatoes, peppers, eggplants, melons and sweet potatoes before frost, or cover plants with blankets, newspaper, etc. (but not plastic) to protect them from light frost.
- Mature green tomatoes can be ripened indoors. Individually wrap fruits in newspaper, or leave them on the vine, pulling the entire plant out of the garden. Store in a cool location – about 55°F–60°F.
- Harvest winter squash when mature (skin is tough) with deep, solid color, but before hard frost. Some cultivars will show an orange blush when mature.
- Plant, transplant or divide peonies, daylilies, iris and phlox only if you can apply irrigation during dry spells.

- Save plants such as coleus, wax begonias, impatiens or fuchsia for indoor growing over winter. Dig plants and cut them back about halfway, or take cuttings of shoot tips, and root them in moist vermiculite, soil mix or perlite.
- Watch for garden chrysanthemums to bloom as days grow shorter. Some may have bloomed earlier this summer, which will decrease the number of fall blooms.
- Plant spring-flowering bulbs beginning in late September. Planting too early can cause bulbs to sprout top growth before winter. However, allow at least four to six weeks before the ground freezes for good root formation.
- Dig tender bulbs, such as cannas, caladiums, tuberous begonias and gladiolus, before frost. Allow to air dry, and store in dry peat moss or vermiculite.
- Choose the mild weather during this period to plant or transplant the following: beets, broccoli, cabbage, carrots, collards, lettuce, mustard, onions, radishes, spinach and turnips. Plant your second planting of fall crops such as collards, turnips, cabbage, mustard and kale.
- Refurbish mulch to control weeds, and start adding leaves and other materials for the compost pile. Store your manure under cover to prevent leaching of nutrients.
- Water deeply and thoroughly to prevent drought stress. Pay special attention to new transplants.
- Harvest mature green peppers and tomatoes before frost gets them – it may not come until November, but be ready.
- Harvest herbs and dry them in a cool, dry place.

October

- Harvest root crops and store in a cold (32°F), humid location. Storing produce in perforated plastic bags is a convenient, easy way to increase humidity.
- Harvest Brussels sprouts as they develop in the axils of the leaves from the bottom of the stem. Brussels sprouts will continue to develop up the stem.
- Harvest pumpkins and winter squash before frost, but when rind is hard and fully colored. Store in a cool location until ready to use.
- Harvest gourds when stems begin to brown and dry. Cure at 70°F–80°F for two to four weeks.
- Harvest mature, green tomatoes before frost and ripen indoors in the dark. Warmer temperatures lead to faster ripening.

- Asparagus top growth should not be removed until foliage yellows. Let foliage stand over winter to collect snow for insulation and moisture.
- Remove plant debris from the garden to protect next year's plantings from insect and disease buildup. Compost plant refuse by alternating layers of soil, plant material, and manure or commercial fertilizer.
- Have garden soil tested for fertilizer needs every three to five years.
- Incorporate organic matter in fall to avoid the rush of garden activities and waterlogged soil in spring. Soils prepared in the fall tend to warm faster and allow earlier planting in spring.
- Dig tender garden flower bulbs for winter storage. Gladiolus corms should be dug when leaves begin turning yellow. Caladiums, geraniums and tuberous begonias should be lifted before killing frost. Dig canna and dahlia roots after a heavy frost. Allow to air dry, then pack in dry peat moss or vermiculite, and store in a cool location.
- Complete planting of spring-flowering bulbs.

November

- If frost hasn't taken your garden yet, continue harvesting.
- Harvest mature green tomatoes before frost, and ripen indoors in the dark. Store at 55°F–70°F. The warmer the temperature, the faster they ripen.
- Harvest root crops and store in a cold (32°F), humid location. Use perforated plastic bags as an easy way to increase humidity.
- Remove crop and weed plant debris from the garden and add to the compost pile. This will help reduce the carryover of diseases, insects and weeds to next year's garden.
- Fall tilling, except in erosion-prone areas, helps improve soil structure and usually leads to soils warming and drying faster in the spring. This allows crops to be planted earlier.
- Apply mulch to strawberries to prevent winter injury or death to their crowns. Wait until temperatures have hit 20°F to be sure plants are dormant. If mulch is applied too soon the plant's crown can rot.
- Dig and store tender flowering bulbs, and keep in a protected location.
- Complete planting of spring-flowering bulbs.
- Why not get started early for next year?

- Spread manure, rotted sawdust and leaves over the garden and plow them under; you'll be surprised at the difference this organic matter will make in the fertility, physical structure and water-holding capacity of the soil.
- Take a soil sample to allow plenty of time to get the report back. Lime applied now will be of more benefit next year than if it is applied in the spring before planting. Always apply Dolomitic limestone in order to get both calcium and magnesium.

- Save those leaves for the compost heap.
- Take an 'inventory.' Maybe you had too much of some vegetables and not enough of others – or maybe there were some unnecessary 'skips' in the supply. Perhaps some insect, disease or nematode problem got the upper hand. Make a note about favorite varieties. Start planning next year's garden now!
- You're wise to order flower and vegetable seeds in December or January, while the supply is plentiful. Review the results of last year's garden and order the more successful varieties.
- You may have seeds left over from last year. Check their viability by placing some in damp paper towels and observing the germination percentage. If the percentage is low, order new ones.
- Before sending your seed order, draw a map of the garden area and decide the direction and length of the rows, how much row spacing is needed for each vegetable, whether or not to plant on raised beds, and other details. That way, you won't order too many seeds. This same advice applied to the flower garden. Try new cultivars, add more color, change the color scheme, layer the colors by having taller and shorter plants – don't do it the same way year after year.
- Look around for tools you do not have and hint for these for Christmas presents.

December

- To protect newly planted or tender perennials and bulbs, mulch with straw, chopped leaves or other organic material after plants become dormant.
- Store leftover garden chemicals where they will stay dry, unfrozen and out of the reach of children, pets and unsuspecting adults.
- Once the plants are completely dormant and temperatures are consistently below freezing, apply winter mulch to protect strawberries and other tender perennials. In most cases, 2 to 4 inches of organic material such as straw, pine needles, hay or bark chips will provide adequate protection.

- Check produce and tender bulbs in storage, and discard any that show signs of decay, such as mold or softening. Shriveling indicates insufficient relative humidity.
- Clean up dead plant materials, synthetic mulch and other debris in the vegetable garden, as well as in the flowerbeds, rose beds and orchards.
- Make notes for next year's garden.

ADDENDUM

Glossary

A	
Abiotic disease	A condition caused by nonliving, nonparasitic, or noninfectious agents.
Abscisic acid (ABA)	Is considered a 'stress hormone.' It is a signaling molecule that induces stomatal closure under drought or extreme temperature stress conditions.
Absorption	The intake of water and other materials through root or leaf cells.
Accumulated heat units	Number of heat units in a growing season. Usually calculated at temperatures above 50°F, but can be calculated at other temperatures, depending on the crop. A day's heat units are calculated as: Max temp (°F) + Min temp (°F) divided by 2 - 50°F.
Acid soil	Soil with pH below 7 on a pH scale of 1 to 14. The lower the pH, the more acid the soil. (See also pH.)
Actinomycete	A group of microorganisms, intermediate between bacteria and true fungi. Generally, produce a characteristic branched mycelium, and these organisms are responsible for the earthy smell of compost (Goemin).
Action or damage threshold	The level of a pest population at which control is initiated.
Active ingredient	The chemical in a pesticide formulation that kills the target pest.
Acute toxicity	An injury that occurs soon after exposure to a pesticide.
Additive	When added to a pesticide, a substance reduces the surface tension between two unlike materials (e.g. spray droplets and a plant surface), thus improving adherence. Also called an adjuvant or surfactant.
Adventitious bud	A bud that develops in locations where buds usually do not occur. An example would be buds found on root pieces used for propagation; roots do not have buds.
Adventitious root	A root that forms at any place on the plant other than the primary root system.
Aerated static pile	Forced aeration method of composting in which a freestanding composting pile is aerated by a blower moving air through perforated pipes located beneath the pile.
Aeration or aerification	The practice involving removal of cores or turf plugs and soil with the purpose of reducing compaction and improving air flow.
Aerobic	An adjective describing an organism or process that requires oxygen (for example, an aerobic organism).

After-ripening	The seed maturation process that must be completed before germination can occur.
Aggregate	Soil aggregates are groups of soil particles that bind to each other more strongly than to adjacent particles. The space between the aggregates provides pore space for retention and exchange of air and water.
Aggregation	The process by which individual particles of sand, silt, and clay cluster and bind together to form soil peds.
Agriculture	The science or practice of farming.
Agronomy	The science of land cultivation, soil management, and crop production.
Air drainage	The downward flow of air through the soil caused by gravity; also, as cold air is heavier than warm air, it flows downhill and often fills hollows which become frost pockets.
Alkaline soil	Soil with pH above 7 on a pH scale of 1 to 14. The higher the reading, the more alkaline the soil.
Alternate leaf arrangement	Leaves are attached at alternating points from one side of the stem to the other.
Ambient air temperature	The temperature of the air near the compost pile or plants.
Amendment	An addition to soil or compost to enhance its characteristics.
Ammonium	A form of nitrogen that is commonly found in the soil. An ion of nitrogen and hydrogen. Ammonium is readily converted to and from ammonia depending on conditions in the compost pile.
Anaerobic	An adjective describing an organism or process that does not require air or free oxygen.
Anatomy	The study of a living organisms' structure.
Angiosperm	Flowering plants. Plants that have a highly evolved reproductive system. Seeds enclosed in an ovary such as a fruit, grain, or pod.
Anion	Negatively charged ion, for example, chloride.
Anion exchange	Anion exchange capacity (AEC). The sum total of exchangeable anions that a soil can absorb expressed in meq/100g (milliequivalents per 100 grams) soil.
Annuals	Plants that reproduce by seed and live for a single year.
Antagonists	Organisms that release toxins or otherwise change conditions so that activity or growth of the pest organism is reduced.
Anther	The pollen-bearing part of a flower's male sexual organ. The filament supports the anther; together they are referred to as the stamen.
Anthracnose	Plant disease characterized by black or brown dead areas on leaves, stems, or fruits.

Addendum

Anvil pruner	A pruning tool that cuts a branch between one sharpened blade and a flat, anvil-shaped piece of metal. Has a tendency to crush rather than make a smooth cut.
Apex	The tip of a stem or root.
Aphids	Small soft-bodied insects with long, slender mouth parts with which they pierce stems and leaves to suck out plant fluids.
Arboretum	An area devoted to specimen plantings of trees and shrubs.
Archaea	Microorganisms that are similar to bacteria in size and simplicity of structure but radically different in their molecular organization.
Asexual propagation	Reproduction of a plant using its own vegetative parts. (See also Vegetative propagation.)
Aspect	Direction of exposure to sunlight.
Aspergillus fumigatus	Species of a fungus with spores that cause allergic reactions in some individuals. It can also cause complications for people with existing respiratory health problems.
Assimilation	Building of cell matter from inorganic (minerals) and organic (carbohydrates and sugars) materials.
ATP (adenosine triphosphate)	A molecule that is used in a number of metabolic reactions in plant cells to carry out cellular work.
Available water supply	Soil water that is available for plant uptake. Excludes water bound tightly to soil particles.
Axil	The upper angle formed by a leaf stalk (petiole) and the internodes above it on a stem.
Axillary bud	An embryonic shoot which lies at the junction of the stem and petiole of a plant. As the apical meristem grows and forms leaves, it leaves behind a region of meristematic cells at the node between the stem and the leaf, an undeveloped shoot or flower at the node. Also called the lateral bud.
Azotobacter	A type of bacteria found in compost piles that can fix atmospheric nitrogen into a form plants can use.
B	
Bacillus thuringiensis.	A bacterium used as a biological control agent for many insects and pests.
Bacterium	A group of microorganisms having single-celled or noncellular bodies. Bacteria generally appear as a spheroid, rod-like, or curved entity but occasionally appear as sheets, chains, or branched filaments.
Balled-and-burlapped	A plant dug with soil. The root ball is enclosed with burlap or a synthetic material.
Bare-root	A plant with little or no soil around its roots; deciduous plants and small evergreens are commonly sold bare-root.
Bed planting	Growing vegetables in closely spaced rows that grow together at crop maturity.

Bedding	Dry absorbent material used to provide a dry lying surface for livestock. Bedding material, such as sawdust and straw, absorb moisture from livestock waste, the soil, and the environment
Beneficial fungi	Fungi used in controlling organisms that attack desirable plants.
Beneficial insect	Insects that are beneficial for crop production because they pollinate plants, attack insect pests or serve other useful purposes.
Berry	The fleshy fruit of cane fruits, bush fruits, and strawberries.
Biennial	A plant that lives for two years. It produces leaves in the first and flowers in the second.
Biennial bearing	Producing fruit in alternate years.
Binomial	A biological species name consisting of two names: the genus name and specific epithet.
Biochar	Charcoal that participates in biological processes and has beneficial properties for both soils and compost.
Biodegradable plastic mulch	Plastic mulch that degrades in the environment.
Biological control	Any activity of one species that reduces the adverse effects of another.
Biosolids	A by-product of wastewater treatment sometimes used as a fertilizer, also known as municipal sewage sludge.
Blanch	To exclude light from plants or parts of plants to render them white or tender. Often done to cauliflower, endive, celery, and leeks. Also used to promote adventitious root formation on stems.
Blend, seed	A combination of two or more cultivars of the same species, for example Rebel and Falcon tall fescue.
Blight	Rapid death of leaves and other plant parts.
Blossom-end rot	A calcium deficiency in tomato and pepper fruit that causes the tip of the fruit to blacken and rot.
Blotch	A blot or spot (usually superficial and irregular in shape) on leaves, shoots, or fruit.
Bolting	The formation of a seed stalk instead of an edible portion of the plant.
Bone meal	Ground-up animal bones that are an excellent source of phosphate, calcium and trace elements.
Botanical insecticide	An insecticide, such as rotenone or pyrethrum, derived from a plant. Most botanicals biodegrade quickly. Most, but not all, have low toxicity to mammals.
Botanical maturity	In fruits, refers to a final stage of development when the fruit is still on the plant and cell enlargement and the accumulation of carbohydrates and other flavor constituents are complete.
Botany	The science that studies all phases of plant life and growth.

Botrytis	A fungal disease promoted by cool, moist weather. Also known as gray mold or fruit rot.
Bramble	A spiny cane bush with berry fruits (e.g. raspberries and blackberries).
Branch	A subsidiary stem arising from a plant's main stem or from another branch.
Broadcast	(1) To sow seed by scattering it over the soil surface. (2) To apply a pesticide or fertilizer uniformly to an entire, specific area by scattering or spraying it.
Broadleaf evergreen	A non-needled evergreen.
Broadleaves	Dicot weeds that have meristems at the terminal end of their branches.
Brown rot	Soft rot of fruit covered by gray to brown mold.
BTU	British thermal unit. Amount of heat required to raise the temperature of 1 pound of water 1°F.
Bud	A small protuberance on a stem or branch, sometimes enclosed in protective scales, containing an undeveloped shoot, leaf, or flower.
Buffer capacity	The maximum amount of either strong acid or strong base that can be added before a change of one pH unit occurs.
Bulb	A below-ground stem (e.g. a tulip) that is surrounded by fleshy scale-like leaves that contain stored food.
Bunchgrass, bunch-type growth	Plant development in the absence of rhizome and stolon production; a non-spreading grass.
C	
C	Chemical symbol for carbon.
Cabbageworms	Caterpillars that attack cole crops.
Calcium carbonate	A compound found in limestone, ashes, bones, and shells; the primary component of lime.
Callus	Tissue that forms over wounds.
Calorie	Amount of heat required to raise the temperature of 1 cubic centimeter of water 1°C.
Cantaloupe	A muskmelon of the round-to-oval, firm fleshed, no sutured, heavy-netted type.
Capillary action	The force by which water molecules bind to the surfaces of soil particles and to each other, thus holding water in fine pores against the force of gravity.
Carbon dioxide (CO_2)	An inorganic gaseous compound of carbon and oxygen. Carbon dioxide is produced by the oxidation of organic carbon compounds during composting.
Carbon-to-nitrogen ratio	The ratio of the weight of organic carbon (C) to that of total nitrogen (N) in (C:N ratio) an organic material.
Casaba	A somewhat rounded melon with a smooth rind and white flesh.

Cation	An atom or molecule with a positive charge (ammonium, NH4+).
Cation exchange capacity (CEC)	The ability of clay and humus to attract and exchange positive ions.
Causal organism	The organism (pathogen) that produces a given disease.
Cellulose	A long chain of tightly bound sugar molecules that constitutes the chief part of the cell walls of plants.
Chelate	A complex organic substance that holds micronutrients, usually iron, in a form available for absorption by plants.
Chemical insect control	The use of chemicals, or insecticide, to control insect populations.
Chemical oxygen demand (COD)	A measure of the oxygen-consuming capacity of inorganic and organic matter present in water or wastewater. It is expressed as the amount of oxygen consumed from a chemical oxidant in a specified test. It does not differentiate between stable and unstable organic matter and thus does not necessarily correlate with biochemical oxygen demand.
Chilling injury	A description of plant damage to tropical and sub-tropical species, caused by temperatures that are cold but not freezing, generally ranging from 33°F to 59°F.
Chlorophyll	The green pigment in plants responsible for trapping light energy for photosynthesis.
Chloroplast	A specialized component of certain cells. Contains chlorophyll and is responsible for photosynthesis.
Clay	The smallest type of soil particle (less than 0.002mm in diameter).
Clear plastic mulches	Plastic mulch that is clear and allows light to penetrate.
Climber	A plant that climbs on its own by twining or using gripping pads, tendrils, or some other method to attach itself to a structure or another plant. Plants that must be trained to a support are properly called trailing plants, not climbers.
Cloche	A netted, plastic, glass, or Plexiglas plant cover is used to warm the growing environment and protect plants from frost.
Clone	A plant group whose members have all been derived from a single individual through constant propagation by vegetative (asexual) means, e.g. by buds, bulbs, grafts, cuttings, or laboratory tissue culture.
C:N ratio	The ratio of carbon to nitrogen in organic materials. Materials with a high C:N ratio (high in carbon) are good bulking agents in compost piles, while those with a low C:N ratio (high in nitrogen) are good energy sources.
Cold composting	A slow composting process that involves simply building a pile and leaving it until it decomposes. This process may take months or longer. Cold composting does not kill weed seeds or pathogens.

Cold frame	A plastic-, glass-, or Plexiglas-covered frame or box that relies on sunlight as a source of heat to warm the growing environment for tender plants.
Cole crops	A group of vegetables belonging to the cabbage family; plants of the genus Brassica, including cauliflower, broccoli, cabbage, turnips, and Brussels sprouts.
Collar	A swollen area at the base of a branch where it connects to a trunk. Contains special tissue that prevents decay from moving downward from the branch into the trunk. The place to make a proper pruning cut. (See also Shoulder ring.)
Compaction	Pressure that squeezes soil into layers that resist root penetration and water movement. Often the result of foot or machine traffic.
Companion planting	The practice of growing two or more types of plants in combination to discourage disease and insect pests.
Compatible	Different varieties or species that set fruit when cross-pollinated or that make a successful graft union when intergrafted.
Complementary	In landscaping, use of opposite colors on the color wheel such as red and green, orange and blue, and yellow and violet.
Complete fertilizer	A fertilizer that contains all three macronutrients (N, P, K).
Complete metamorphosis	A type of insect development in which the insect passes through the stages of egg, larva, pupa, and adult. The larva usually is different in form from the adult. (See also Simple metamorphosis.)
Compost	The product created by the breakdown of organic waste under conditions manipulated by humans. Used to improve both the texture and fertility of garden soil. (See also Humus.)
Composting	Biological degradation of organic matter under aerobic conditions to a relatively stable humus-like material called compost.
Compost amendment	An ingredient in a mixture of composting raw material included to improve the overall characteristics of the mix. Amendments often add carbon, dryness, or porosity to the mix.
Compound bud	More than one bud on the same side of a node. Usually, unless growth is extremely vigorous, only one of the buds develops, and its branch may have a very sharp angle of attachment. If it is removed, a wider angled shoot usually is formed from the second (accessory) bud. Ashes and walnuts are examples of plants that typically have compound buds.
Contact herbicide	A chemical that will harm a plant when it comes into contact with green plant tissue.
Contamination	An introduction into the environment (water, air, or soil) of microorganisms, chemicals, wastes, or wastewater in a concentration that makes the environment unfit for its intended use.
Cool-season Vegetables	Vegetables that have optimum growth at temperatures between 60°F and 75°F.

Corm	A below-ground stem that is solid, swollen, and covered with reduced, scale-like leaves (for example, in crocus).
Cormel	A small, underdeveloped corm, usually attached to a larger corm.
Cornicle	A short, blunt horn or tube (sometimes button like) on the top and near the end of an aphid's abdomen. Emits a waxy liquid that helps protect against enemies.
Corolla	Part of a flower; all of the petals together.
Cover crop	(1) A crop planted to protect the soil from erosion. (2) A crop planted to improve soil structure or organic matter content.
Crawler	An early stage of insect development (nymph) that is mobile.
Creeping growth habit	Plant development at or near the soil surface that results in lateral spreading by rhizomes, stolons, or both.
Crop rotation	The practice of growing different types of crops in succession on the same land chiefly to preserve the productive capacity of the soil by easing insect, disease, and weed problems.
Crop seed	Any seed grown for profit, often including undesirable grassy weeds, such as orchard grass.
Cross-pollination	The fertilization of an ovary on one plant with pollen from another plant, producing an offspring with a genetic makeup distinctly different from that of either parent. (See also Pollinizer.)
Cultipack	To firm and pulverize (a seedbed) with a corrugated roller.
Cultivar	A cultivated variety of a species. Propagation of cultivars results in little or no genetic change in the offspring, which preserves desirable characteristics.
Cultivation	In turf, the working of the soil without the destruction of the turf.
Cultural insect control	Controlling an insect population by maintaining good plant health and by crop rotation and/or companion crops.
Cutting	One of several forms of asexual propagation.
Cyme	A flower stalk on which the florets start blooming from the top of the stem and progress toward the bottom.
Cyst	The swollen, egg-containing female body of certain nematodes. Can sometimes be seen on the outside of infected roots.

D

Damping off	Stem rot near the soil surface leading to either failed seed emergence or to the plant's falling over after emergence.
Day-neutral plant	A cultivar or species capable of flowering without regard to day length. (See also Short-day plant, Long-day plant.)
Deadhead	To remove individual, spent flowers from a plant for the purpose of preventing senescence and prolonging blooming. For effective results, the ovary behind the flower must be removed as well.

Deciduous	A plant that sheds all of its leaves annually.
Decomposers	The microorganisms and invertebrates that accomplish composting.
Decomposition	The breakdown of organic materials by microorganisms.
Defoliation	The unnatural loss of a plant's leaves, generally to the detriment of its health. Can be caused by several factors such as high wind, excessive heat, drought, frost, chemicals, insects, or disease.
Degradability	The term describes the ease and extent that a substance is decomposed by the composting process. Material that breaks down quickly and/or entirely during composting is highly degradable. Material that resists biological decomposition is considered poorly degradable or even nondegradable.
Denitrification	An anaerobic biological process that converts nitrogen compounds to nitrogen gas or nitrous oxide. The conversion of nitrates into atmospheric nitrogen by soil microbes in waterlogged soils.
Density	The weight or mass of a substance per unit of volume.
Depredation	Causing damage or loss.
Dermal exposure	Pesticide or allergens absorbed through the skin.
Desiccation	Excessive dryness or loss of moisture resulting in drying out the plant tissues.
Determinate	A plant growth habit in which stems stop growing at a certain height and produce a flower cluster at the tip. Determinate tomatoes, for example, are short, early fruiting, have concentrated fruit set, and may not require staking. (See also Indeterminate.)
Diatomaceous earth	The fossilized remains of diatoms (a type of tiny algae) used to kill insect pests, snails, and slugs.
Dieback	Progressive death of shoots, branches, or roots, generally starting at the tips.
Differentiation	A change in composition, structure, and function of cells and tissues during growth.
Dioecious	Plants that have male and female flowers occurring on separate plants (e.g. holly).
Direct seeding (direct sowing)	Planting seeds into garden soil rather than using transplants.
Distorted growth	Twisted or misformed growth.
Diurnal	Active during the day.
Division	The breaking or cutting apart of a plant's crown for the purpose of producing additional plants, all genetically identical to the parent plant.
DNA	Deoxyribonucleic acid is the genetic information that dictates all cellular processes. DNA is organized into chromosomes and is responsible for all characteristics of the plant.

Dolomitic limestone	Lime that supplies both calcium and magnesium.
Dormancy	An annual period which causes the resting stage of a plant or ripe seeds during which nearly all manifestations of life come to an almost complete standstill.
Dormant	Resting or not growing. A deciduous tree is dormant in the winter.
Dormant oil	An oil applied during the dormant season to control insect pests and diseases.
Double digging	A process whereby the gardener works the topsoil and also loosens the subsoil.
Double worked	Grafted twice, i.e. grafted to an intermediate stock.
Downy	Leaf textures that are covered with very short, weak, and soft hairs.
Downy mildew	Known best by its common name, downy mildew is caused by the oomycete. It is an obligate parasite of vascular plants, meaning that it cannot survive outside of a living host. It does not produce overwintering oospores, but survives from year to year on living plants. These organisms are distinctly different from the powdery mildews.
Drainage	Movement of water away from the surface of a garden either down into the soil or by flow across the surface.
Dried blood	Blood of animals that is collected from slaughterhouses. It contains high levels of nitrogen.
Drip line	An imaginary line on the ground directly beneath the outermost tips of a plant's foliage. Rain tends to drip from leaves onto this line.
Dwarfed	Restricted plant size without loss of health and vigor. (See also Bonsai.)
E	
E. coli	A bacteria associated with animal wastes that can cause serious health problems.
Ear	The female flower of corn that produces seed after pollination.
Ecology, plant	The study of the complex relationships of plants in biological communities.
Economic threshold	The level at which pest damage justifies the cost of control. In home gardening, the threshold may be aesthetic rather than economic.
Ecosystem services	Provisioning services such as food and water; regulating services such as flood and disease control; cultural services such as spiritual, recreational, and cultural benefits; and supporting services such as nutrient cycling that maintain the conditions for life on earth.
Elytra	Hardened opaque outer wings of a beetle.

Endemic	Belonging exclusively or confined to a particular place.
Endoskeleton	The internal body support found in most animals outside of the insect kingdom.
Endosperm	The tissue surrounding the embryo of flowering plant seeds that provides nutrition to the developing embryo, or the food-storage area in a seed for the growing embryo.
Endotoxin	Metabolic products of gram-negative bacteria are part of the cell wall. They will remain in the bacteria after they have died.
Enzyme	Any of numerous complex proteins produced by living cells to catalyze specific biochemical reactions.
Epidemic	A widespread and severe outbreak of a disease.
Ethylene	Is the only hormone that is a gas. It speeds aging of tissues and enhances fruit ripening.
Evergreen	A plant that never loses all its foliage at the same time.
Excise	To remove or extract, as an embryo from a seed or ovule.
Exfoliating	Peeling off in shreds or thin layers, as in bark from a tree.
Exoskeleton	An insect's outer body support.
Exotic	Of foreign origin or character; not native; introduced from abroad, but not fully naturalized
F	
F1 Hybrids	Cultivars resulting from a cross between two different true breeding (referred to as inbred) parents.
Fallow	To keep land unplanted during one or more growing seasons.
Family	A sub-order in the classification of plants.
Feeder roots	Fine roots and root branches with a large absorbing area (root hairs.) Responsible for taking up the majority of a plant's water and nutrients from the soil.
Fertility (soil)	The presence of minerals necessary for plant life.
Fertilizer	Any substance added to the soil (or sprayed on plants) to supply those elements required in plant nutrition.
Fibrous root	A root system that branches in all directions, often directly from the plant's crown, rather than branching in a hierarchical fashion from a central root. (See also Taproot.)
Field capacity	The amount of soil moisture or water content held in the soil after excess water has drained away and the rate of downward movement has decreased. This usually takes place two to three days after rain or irrigation in pervious soils of uniform structure and texture.
Fish meal	Ground-up fish. Contains nitrogen and phosphorus.

Flag or Flagging	Loss of turgor and drooping of plant parts, usually as a result of water stress. Can be seen as branch loss in a tree.
Floating row covers	Covers, usually of a cloth-like material, placed over growing plants and used to protect the plants growing beneath from undesirable pests and climate.
Flower bud	A type of bud that produces one or more flowers.
Foliar fertilization/feeding	Fertilization of a plant by applying diluted soluble fertilizer, such as fish emulsion or kelp, directly to the leaves.
Force	To bring a plant into early growth, generally by raising the temperature or transplanting it to a warmer situation. Tulips and paper whites are examples of plants that often are forced.
Forced aeration	Can be either negatively (vacuum) or positively forced (blowers) supply of air through a composting pile.
Form	(1) A naturally occurring characteristic different from other plants in the same population. (2) The growth habit (shape) of a plant.
Frass	The excrement of insect larvae.
Friable	A soil that is easy to work with.
Frost pocket	A low-lying area where frost occurs late in the season.
Frost-free date	The average last day of frost for a specific area.
Fruit	The enlarged ovary that develops after fertilization occurs.
Fruiting habit	The location and manner in which fruit is borne on woody plants.
Fumigation	The application of a toxic gas or other volatile substance to disinfect soil or a container, such as a grain bin.
Fungicide	A compound toxic to fungi.
Fungus (Fungi)	A plant organism that lacks chlorophyll, reproduces via spores, and usually has filamentous growth. It is possible for them to form long filaments known as hyphae. Hyaline bodies can be formed by the hyphae growing together.

G

Genetically modified	A plant or animal that has had genetic material introduced to its genome from other organisms through artificial means.
Genus	A subdivision of family in the classification of plants. Plants of the same genus share similarities mostly in flower characteristics and genetics. Plants in one genus usually cannot breed with plants of another genus.
Germination	The processes that begin after planting a seed that lead to the growth of a new plant.
Girdled roots	A root system that has outgrown its pot to the extent that the roots are encircling the inside of the pot, restricting nutrient uptake.

Gourd	A fruit with a hard outer rind that is used for decoration.
Grasses	A category of weed that are monocots, have narrow leaves and a growing point at or just below the soil surface.
Gravitational water	Water in excess of a soil's capacity. Drains downward to groundwater.
Green cone	An enclosed composting unit often used for composting food waste.
Green manure	An herbaceous crop plowed under while green to enrich the soil.
Greensand	A ground rock material that contains potassium and trace elements.
Grinding	Operation that reduces the particle size of material. Grinding implies that particles are broken apart primarily by smashing and crushing rather than tearing or slicing.
Groundcover	Plants used for holding soil, controlling weeds, and providing leaf texture.
Growing season	The period between the beginning of growth in the spring and the cessation of growth in the fall.
Growth regulator	A compound applied to a plant to alter its growth in a specific way. May be a natural or synthetic substance. (See also Hormone.)
H	
Habit	The growth, shape, and form of a plant.
Half-hardy	Plants able to withstand some cold, damp weather but will be damaged by frost.
HAPs	Hazardous Air Pollutants. There are 188 HAPs on EPA's list, including at least 29 HAPs that have been quantified in composting air emissions. The kinds and quantities of HAPs tend to be a function of feedstocks, with biosolids composting having the most carefully and thoroughly studied air emission profiles.
Hardening off	(1) The process of gradually exposing seedlings started indoors to outdoor conditions before transplanting. (2) The process of gradual preparation for winter weather.
Hardpan	An impervious layer of soil or rock that prevents root growth and downward drainage of water.
Hardy	Frost or freeze tolerant. In horticulture, this term does not mean tough or resistant to insect pests or disease.
Head	(1) To cut off part of a shoot or limb rather than remove it completely at a branch point. (2) The part of a tree from which the main scaffold limbs originate.
Heavy Soil	A soil that contains a high proportion of clay and is poorly drained.

Heeling in	The temporary burying of a newly dug plant's roots to prevent their drying until a new planting site is prepared. Nurseries heel in bareroot berries, trees, and shrubs.
Heirloom cultivars	Cultivars that are more than 100 years old and whose seeds are passed down from generation to generation.
Herbicide	A chemical used to kill undesirable plants.
Herbicide, contact	Herbicide that injures only those portions of a plant with which it comes into contact.
Hill planting	Planting multiple seeds together in clumps.
Honeydew	1. A sticky substance excreted by aphids and some other insects. 2. A round melon with smooth rind and green flesh.
Hormone	A naturally occurring compound that alters plant growth in a specific manner. (See also Growth regulator.)
Horticultural oil	An oil made from petroleum products, vegetable oil, or fish oil used to control insect pests and diseases. Oils work by smothering insects and their eggs and by protectively coating buds against pathogen entry.
Horticulture	The science of growing fruits, vegetables, flowers, and other ornamental plants.
Host plant	A plant that is invaded by a parasite.
Hotbed	An enclosed bed for propagating or protecting plants. Has a source of heat to supplement solar energy.
Hot caps	Individual structures placed over a vegetable plant that warm the temperature and protect the plant against frost.
Hot composting	A fast composting process that produces finished compost in four to eight weeks. High temperatures are maintained by mixing balanced volumes of energy materials and bulking agents, by keeping the pile moist, and by turning it frequently to keep it aerated.
Humus	The dark or black carbon-rich, relatively stable residue resulting from the decomposition of organic matter.
Hybrid	The results of a cross between two different species or well-marked varieties within a species. Hybrids grown in a garden situation will not breed true to form from their own seed.
Hydrogen sulfide (H_2S)	A gas with the characteristic odor of rotten eggs produced by anaerobic decomposition.
Hydrolysis	The word literally means unbinding by water. It is when water is involved in breaking chemical bonds. In plant biology the process results in complex compounds reduced to monomers.
Hydrophobic	Having little or no affinity for water.
Hydroponics	A method of growing plants without soil. Plants usually are suspended in water or polymers, and plant nutrients are supplied in dilute solutions.

Hygroscopic	Attracts and retains water.
Hypha (or hyphae)	A single filament of a fungus. A fine threadlike structure of cell formed by fungi affecting a plant.
I	
Imbibition	The portion of the germination process that involves the absorption of water, causing the seed to swell, and that triggers cell enzyme activity, growth, and the bursting of the seed coat.
Immobilization	The process by which soil microorganisms use available nitrogen as they break down materials with a high C:N ratio, thus reducing the amount of nitrogen available to plants.
Immune	A plant that does not become diseased by a specific pathogen. (See also Resistance, Tolerant.)
Incompatible	Kinds or varieties of a species that do not successfully cross-pollinate or intergraft.
Incubation	A period of development during which a pathogen changes to a form that can penetrate or infect a new host plant.
Infection	The condition reached when a pathogen has invaded plant tissue and established a parasitic relationship between itself and its host.
Infiltration	The movement of water into soil.
Inoculation	The introduction of a pathogen to a host plant's tissue.
Inoculum	Any part of the pathogen that can cause infection.
Inorganic	Being or composed of matter other than plant or animal.
Insectary plant	A plant that attracts beneficial insects.
Insecticidal soap	A specially formulated soap that is only minimally damaging to plants, but kills insects. Usually works by causing an insect's outer shell to crack, resulting in its interior organs drying out.
Insecticide	A chemical used to control, repel, suppress, or kill insects.
Insectivore	An animal or plant that feeds mainly on insects. Any of various small, usually nocturnal mammals of the order Insectivora that feed on insects and other invertebrates.
Integrated control	An approach that attempts to use several or all available methods for control of a pest or disease.
Integrated insect control	The use of a variety of insect control methods, beginning with simpler.
Integrated pest management (IPM)	A method of managing pests that combines cultural, biological, mechanical, and chemical controls, while taking into account the impact of control methods on the environment.
Intensive gardening	The practice of maximizing use of garden space, for example, by using trellises, intercropping, succession planting, and raised beds.

Intercropping/Interplanting	The practice of mixing plants to break up pure stands of a single crop.
Interiorscape	An interior planting, usually referring to professional designs installed in commercial buildings.
Internode	The area of the stem that is between the nodes.
Interstem/interstock	The middle piece of a graft combination made up of more than two parts, i.e. the piece between the scion and the rootstock. Often has a dwarfing effect.
Invasive	Growing vigorously and outcompeting other plants in the same area; difficult to control.
Ion	An electrically charged particle. In soils, an ion refers to an electrically charged element or combination of elements resulting from the breaking up of an electrolyte in solution.
IR mulches	Mulches that allow infrared radiation to penetrate through the mulch but reflects photosynthetically active radiation.
Isolation	The separation of a pathogen from its host by culturing on a nutrient medium or on an indicator plant.
J	
Joint	A node; the place on a stem where a bud, leaf, or branch forms.
Juvenile stage	(1) The early or vegetative phase of plant growth characterized by the inability to flower. (2) The first stage of an insect's life cycle after the egg, either a larva or a nymph. (3) The immature stage of an organism.
K	
K	The symbol for Potassium also referred to as Potash
L	
Land application	Application of manure, sewage sludge, municipal wastewater, and industrial waste to land either for ultimate disposal or for reuse of the nutrients and organic matter for their fertilizer value.
Larva	(larvae is plural) The immature form of an insect that undergoes complete metamorphosis. Different from the adult in form, a caterpillar for example. The newly hatched, wingless, often wormlike form of many insects before metamorphosis.
Layering	A method of stimulating adventitious roots to form on a stem. There are two primary methods of layering. In ground layering, a low-growing branch is bent to the ground and covered by soil. In air layering, moist rooting medium is wrapped around a node on an above-ground stem.
Leaching	The downward movement of water and nutrients from the soil surface to the water table due to gravity.
Leaf-axil	The area between the leaf or petiole and the stem.

Lesion	A localized area of discolored or dead tissue.
Life cycle	The successive stages of growth and development of an organism.
Lignen	A substance that forms the woody cell walls of plants and the cementing material between them. Lignin is resistant to decomposition.
Light soil	A soil that contains a high proportion of sand.
Lime	A rock powder consisting primarily of calcium carbonate. Used to raise soil pH (decrease acidity).
Litter, poultry	Dry absorbent bedding material, such as straw, sawdust, and wood shavings, spread on poultry barn floors to absorb waste. The manure-bedding combination from the barn is referred to as litter.
Living mulches	Any plant that is used to cover an area of soil and add nutrients, enhance soil porosity, decrease weeds, and prevent soil erosion.
Loam	A soil with roughly equal proportions of sand, silt, and clay particles.
Long-day plant	A plant requiring more than 12 hours of continuous daylight to stimulate a change in growth, e.g. a shift from the vegetative to reproductive phase. (See also Short-day plant, Day-neutral plant.)
M	
Macroclimate	The overall climate of a particular region.
Macronutrient	Collectively, primary and secondary nutrients.
Macropore	A large soil pore. Macropores include earthworm and root channels and control a soil's permeability and aeration. In a substrate, the larger spaces (or pores) that lies between component particles that hold air.
Mandible	The first pair of jaws on insects: stout and tooth-like in chewing insects, needle or sword-shaped in sucking insects. The lateral (left and right) upper jaws of biting insects.
Manure	The fecal and urinary excretion of livestock and poultry. Sometimes referred to as livestock waste. This material may also contain bedding, spilled feed, water, or soil. It may also include waste not associated with livestock excrete, such as milking center wastewater, contaminated milk, hair, feathers, or other debris.
Maturity	(1) In fruit, ripeness, usually the state of development that results in maximum quality. (2) The flowering phase of plant growth.
Maximum temperature	The warmest temperature that germination occurs for seed of a particular vegetable.
Mechanical insect control	Manual removal of insects and eggs from infested plants

Mesic	Characterized by, relating to, or requiring a moderate amount of moisture
Metamorphosis	The process by which an insect develops. The term is a combination of two Greek words: meta meaning 'change' and morphe meaning 'form.' Metamorphosis is a marked or abrupt change in form or structure, like a caterpillar turning into a butterfly. (See also Complete metamorphosis, Simple metamorphosis.)
Microclimate	Climate affected by landscape, structures, or other unique factors in a particular immediate area. The specific environmental conditions of your garden site.
Micronutrient	A nutrient, usually in the parts per million range, used by plants in small amounts, less than 1 part per million (boron, chlorine, copper, iron, manganese, molybdenum, zinc, and nickel).
Microorganism	An organism that requires magnification to be seen.
Micropore	A fine soil pore, typically a fraction of a millimeter in diameter. Micropores are responsible for a soil's ability to hold water. In a substrate, the smaller spaces (or pores) between component particles that are occupied by water or air.
Microscopic	Organisms so small that they can be seen only with the aid of a microscope.
Minimum Temperature	Coolest temperature that seed germination or growth occurs for a particular vegetable.
Mixed buds	Buds that produce both shoots and flowers.
Mixed fertilizer	A fertilizer that contains at least two of the three macronutrients (N, P, K).
Mixture, seed	A combination of seeds of two or more species, for example Kentucky bluegrass and perennial ryegrass.
Moisture content	The fraction or percentage of a substance made up of water. Moisture content equals the weight of the water part divided by the total weight (water plus dry matter part). Moisture content is sometimes reported on a dry basis. Dry-basis moisture content equals the weight of the water divided by the weight of the dry matter.
Monomers	Natural monomers are amino acid from proteins and monosaccharides from carbohydrates amongst others.
Morphology	The study of the origin and function of plant parts.
Mosaic	Non-uniform foliage coloration with a more or less distinct intermingling of normal green and light green or yellowish patches.
Mottle	An irregular pattern of light and dark areas.
Mulch	Any material placed on the soil surface to conserve soil moisture, moderate soil temperature, and/or control weeds.
Mushroom	The fruiting structure of certain families of fungi characterized by gills.

Muskmelon	A melon that has a musky aroma and salmon- to orange-colored flesh when mature. It has a netted rind with deep sutures.
Mutation	A genetic change within an organism or its parts that changes its characteristics. Also called a bud sport or sport.
Mycelia	Masses of fungal threads (hyphae) that make up the vegetative body of a fungus.
Mycology	The study of fungi.
Mycorrhizae	Beneficial fungi that infect plant roots and increase their ability to take up nutrients from the soil.
N	
N	The symbol for Nitrogen, A primary plant nutrient, especially important for foliage and stem growth.
Native plant	A plant indigenous to a specific habitat or area.
Naturalize	(1) To design a garden with the aim of creating a natural scene. Planting generally is done randomly, and space is left for plants to spread at will. (2) The process whereby plants spread and fill in naturally.
Necrosis or necrotic tissue	Death of cells resulting in necrotic or dead tissue.
Nematicide	A material that kills or protects against nematodes.
Nematode	Microscopic roundworms that live in soil and living tissue, as well as water, and survive as eggs or cysts.
Netted veins	Having branched veins that form a network, as the leaves of most dicotyledonous plants.
Nitrate-nitrogen	A negatively charged ion made up of nitrogen and oxygen (NO_3-). Nitrate is a water-soluble and mobile form of nitrogen. Because of its negative charge, soil particles are not firmly held and leached away.
Nitrification	The biochemical oxidation of ammonia nitrogen to nitrate.
Nitrifier	A microbe that converts ammonium to nitrate.
Nitrogen	A primary plant nutrient, especially important for foliage and stem growth.
Nitrogen cycle	The sequence of biochemical changes undergone by nitrogen as it moves from living organisms, to decomposing organic matter, to inorganic forms, and back to living organisms.
Nitrogen fixation	The conversion of atmospheric nitrogen into plant-available forms by rhizobia bacteria living on the roots of legumes.
Nitrogen, quick release	Readily available sources of nitrogen that exhibit fast turf greening, short residual, and high burn potential, such as ammonium nitrate.

Nitrogen, slow release	Slowly available sources of nitrogen that exhibit slow turf green-up, long residual, and low burn potential, such as IBDU, urea formaldehyde.
Nocturnal	Active at night.
Node	The area of the stem that bears a leaf or a branch. A joint where leaves, roots, branches, or stems arise.
Nomenclature	The assigning of names in the classification of plants.
Nonpoint source	A relatively small, nonspecific source of pollutants that, when added to other sources, may pose a significant threat to the environment. (See also Point source.)
Nonselective pesticide	A pesticide that kills most plants or animals.
Nonviable	Not alive; nonviable seeds may look normal but will not grow.
Noxious weed	Weeds that government agencies want to prevent from establishing in a particular area.
N-P-K	Acronym for the three major plant nutrients contained in manure, compost, and fertilizers. N stand for nitrogen, P for phosphorus, and K for potassium.
Nutrient	Any substance, especially in the soil, that is essential for and promotes plant growth. (See also Macronutrient, Micronutrient.)
Nutrient-holding capacity	The ability to absorb and retain nutrients is available to the roots of plants.
Nymph	The immature form of those insects that do not pass through a pupal stage. Nymphs usually resemble the adults, but are smaller, lack fully developed wings, and are sexually immature but eat the same food, and reside in the same environment.
O	
Offset	A new shoot that forms at the base of a plant or in a leaf axil.
Open-pollinated seed	Seed produced from natural, random pollination so that the resulting plants are varied.
Opposite leaf arrangement	Two leaves are attached at the same point on the stem, but on opposite sides.
Optimum temperature	The temperature at which the greatest or most rapid seed germination occurs for a particular vegetable.
Organic	(1) Relating to, derived from, or involving the use of food produced with the use of feed or fertilizer of plant or animal origin without employment of synthetically formulated fertilizers, growth stimulants, antibiotics, or pesticides. (2) Being or composed of plant or animal matter. (3) A labeling term that refers to an agricultural product produced in accordance with government standards.
Organic fertilizer	A natural fertilizer material that has undergone little or no processing. Can include plant, animal, and/or mineral materials.

Organic matter	Any material originating from a living organism (peat moss, plant residue, compost, ground bark, manure, etc.). Chemical substances of animal or vegetable origin containing hydrocarbons and their derivatives.
Organic pesticide	Pesticides derived from plant or animal sources.
Organic production	The production of food using accepted naturally occurring materials.
Organism	A living being.
Ornamental plant	A plant grown for beautification, screening, accent, specimen, color, or other aesthetic reasons.
Osmosis	Passage of materials through a membrane from an area of high concentration to an area of lower concentration.
Outer seed coat	The protective outer shell for the seed.
Ovary	The part of a flower containing ovules that will develop into seeds upon fertilization. Along with the style and stigma, it makes up the pistil (female sexual organ).
Over mulching	Applying too much mulch.
Ovule	Within the ovary, a tissue/structure that will develop into a seed after fertilization.
Oxidative respiration	The chemical process by which sugars and starches are converted to energy. In plants, known as respiration.
Oxygen starvation	Roots cannot get the oxygen they need.
P	
P	The chemical symbol for phosphorus. A primary plant nutrient, especially important for flower production. In fertilizer, usually expressed as phosphate.
Paper Mulches	Mulches made from newspaper or paper fibers.
Parasite	An organism that lives in or on another organism (host) and derives its food from the latter.
Parasitic seed plant	A plant that lives parasitically on other seed plants. An example is mistletoe.
Parent material	The underlying geological material (generally bedrock or a superficial or drift deposit) in which soil horizons form.
Passive Composting	Air movement through composting windrows and piles occurs by natural forces, including convection, diffusion, wind, and the tendency of warm air to rise (thermal buoyancy).
Pathogen	Any organism capable of producing disease or infection. Often found in waste material, most pathogens are killed by the high temperatures of the composting process.
Pathology	The study of plant diseases.

Peat	Unconsolidated soil material consisting mainly of organic matter accumulated under excessive moisture conditions. The organic matter is not decomposed or is only slightly decomposed.
Peat moss	The partially decayed remains of sphagnum moss.
Ped	A cluster of individual soil particles.
Perennial	A plant that lives more than two years and produces new foliage, flowers, and seeds each growing season.
Perlite	Lightweight volcanic material often used in soil less media.
Permanent wilting point	The point at which a wilted plant can no longer recover.
Permeability	The rate at which water moves through a soil.
Persistent	(1) Adhering to a position instead of falling, whether dead or alive, e.g. flowers or leaves. (2) A pesticide that retains its chemical properties in the soil for a long time.
Pest	Plants, fungi, bacteria, nematodes, insects and animals that occur in a place they are not wanted.
Pesticide	A chemical that kills undesirable plants, plant diseases, insects or other pests.
Petals	Highly colored portions of the flower, inside the sepals, that protect the inner reproductive structures. Often attract insects with their color or may contain osmophores which are scent structures both of which facilitate pollination.
pH	The acidity or alkalinity of a solution on a scale of 0–14, with a value of 7 signifying neutral, values below 7 signifying acidic, and values above 7 signifying alkaline. Relates to the concentrations of hydrogen (H+) ions in the soil. pH values are logarithmic (factors of 10).
Phosphate	The form of phosphorus listed in most fertilizer analyses.
Phosphorus (P)	A primary plant nutrient, especially important for flower production. In fertilizer, usually expressed as phosphate.
Photodegradable mulch	Mulch that contains chemicals that cause the plastic to degrade when exposed to ultraviolet radiation.
Photoperiod	The amount of time a plant is exposed to light.
Photosynthate	A food product (sugar or starch) created through photosynthesis.
Photosynthesis	(1) The process in which green plants convert light energy from the sun into chemical energy in order to produce carbohydrates. (2) Formation of carbohydrates from carbon dioxide and a source of hydrogen (as water) in the chlorophyll-containing tissues of plants exposed to light.
Phototropism	The phenomenon of plants growing toward the direction of a light source.

Physiology	The study dealing with the functioning of plants, their mechanisms of response, and their physical and biochemical processes.
Phytoplasm	Microscopic, single-celled organisms that lack distinct cell walls and that cause destructive diseases in plants.
Phytotoxic	An adjective describing a substance that has a toxic effect on plants. Immature or anaerobic compost may contain phytotoxins (acids or alcohols) harmful to seedlings or sensitive plants.
Pinch	To remove a growing tip from a stem, thus causing axillary shoots or buds to develop. (See also Deadhead, Shear.)
Plant cages	Structures made from cloth or plastic that keeps out migrating insects while allowing sunlight, rain and wind to enter. They generally do not protect against cool temperatures.
Plant classification	The scientific grouping and naming of plants by characteristics.
Plant disease	Any lasting change in a plant's normal structure or function that deviates from its healthy state.
Plant nutrition	A plant's need for and use of basic chemical elements. (See also Macronutrient, Micronutrient.)
Plant pathology	The study of diseases in plants: what causes them, what factors influence their development and spread, and how to prevent or control them.
Plant tissue culture	Plant material grown in vitro under sterile conditions in an artificial medium. A primary means of rapidly increasing the number of plants from a single mother plant.
Plug	2- to 4-inch chunks of sod, either round or square, with soil around their roots.
Pollen	A plant's male sex cells, which are held on the anther for transfer to a stigma by insects, wind, or some other mechanism.
Pollen tube	A slender tube growing from the pollen grain that carries the male gametes and delivers them to the ovary.
Pollination	The first step in fertilization; the transfer of pollen from anther to a stigma.
Pollinator	An agent such as an insect that transfers pollen from a male anther to a female stigma.
Potash	The form of potassium listed in most fertilizer analyses.
Potassium	A primary plant nutrient, especially important for developing strong roots and stems. In fertilizers, usually expressed as potash. It is the K in N-P-K.
Powdery mildew	Fine, white to gray, powdery fungal coating on leaves, stems, and flowers.
Predator	An animal that eats another animal.
Preemergence	A product applied before crops or weeds emerge from the soil.

Preharvest interval	The amount of time that must elapse (legally) after application of a pesticide before harvest takes place.
Preplant	A product applied before a crop is planted.
Primary growth	Growth that occurs via cell division at the tips of stems and roots.
Primary nutrient	A nutrient required by plants in a relatively large amount (nitrogen, phosphorus, and potassium).
Processed fertilizer	A fertilizer that is manufactured or refined from natural ingredients to be more concentrated and more available to plants.
Production	Nursery or greenhouse growing area used before plants are put up for retail sales.
Propagate	To start new plants by seeding, budding, grafting, dividing, etc.
Protozoa	Any of a diverse group of eukaryotes, of the kingdom Protista, that are primarily unicellular, existing singly or aggregating into colonies.
Prune	To remove plant parts to improve a plant's health, appearance, or productivity.
Pupa	The stage between larva and adult in insects that go through complete metamorphosis.
Pupae	An insect in the non-feeding stage between the larva and adult, during which it typically undergoes complete transformation within a protective cocoon or hardened case. Only insects that undergo complete metamorphosis have pupal stages.
Q	
Quarantine	A regulation forbidding sale or shipment of plants or plant parts, usually to prevent disease, insect, nematode, or weed invasion in an area.
Quick-release fertilizer	A fertilizer that contains nutrients in plant-available forms such as ammonium and nitrate. Fertilizer is readily soluble in water.
Quiescent	In a state or period of inactivity or dormancy.
R	
Raised bed	Mound the soil up in the planting area above the surrounding soil level. May have a frame around the edges.
Raking, power	Removal of debris with rapidly rotating vertical tines or brush.
Receptacle	The base of the flower stalk that holds the sexual organs of a flower.
Regulatory insect	Term used to describe insects that have an unknown impact in a new environment to which they may be moved.

Relative humidity	The percentage of moisture saturating the air at a given temperature. The ratio of water vapor in the air to the amount of water the air could hold at the current temperature and pressure.
Repotting (or 'transplanting')	The process of moving previously potted plants into new containers, usually of larger size.
Resistance	The ability of a host plant to prevent or reduce disease development by retarding multiplication of the pathogen within the host.
Respiration	The process of burning sugars to use as energy for plant growth. The process by which carbohydrates are converted into energy. This energy builds new tissues, maintains the chemical processes, and allows growth within the plant.
Rhizobia bacteria	Bacteria that live in association with roots of legumes and convert atmospheric nitrogen to plant-available forms, a process known as nitrogen fixation.
Rhizome	A stem that forms the main axis of the plant. An underground creeping stem that can produce roots and shoots at each node. (adj. rhizomatous)
Rhizosphere	The thin layer of soil immediately surrounding plant roots.
Rogue/Roguing	To uproot and destroy diseased plants.
Rootbound	A condition in which a plant's root system has outgrown its pot resulting in root constriction. Typically, the roots begin to encircle the pot's outer edge. Further growth is prevented until the plant is removed from the container.
Root cutting	An asexual method of propagation that involves removing a section of root from a two- to three-year-old plant during the dormant season and placing it into growing medium.
Root hair	Thin hair-like structure that grows from the epidermis of the region of maturation of the root. This structure absorbs water and nutrients from the soil.
Root knots	Swelling and deformation of roots.
Root pruning	The cutting or removal of some of a plant's roots.
Root/stem rot	Soft and disintegrated roots and lower portions of the stem; sometimes results in death of the plant.
Rootstock	The portion of a plant used to provide the root system and sometimes the lower part of the stem for a grafted plant.
Rot	Decomposition and destruction of tissue.
Rotation (rotate)	The practice of growing different plants in different locations each year to prevent the buildup of soil borne diseases and insect pests.
Row cover	A sheet of synthetic material used to cover plants in order to retain heat and exclude insect pests.

Row planting	Growing vegetables in single or double rows with aisles between each row.
Runner	See Stolon. (Examples of runners are strawberries and spider plants.)
Rust	Fruiting structure of certain family of fungi. Raised pustules on leaves, stems, and fruits; contain yellow-orange or rust-colored spore masses.
S	
Sand	Soil particles ranging in size between 0.2 to 2 mm.
Sanitation	The removal and disposal of infected plant parts; decontamination of tools, equipment, hands, etc. Removing sources of pests so as few pests as possible get into your garden.
Saprophytes	Organisms that live on dead or dying organic matter and obtain their energy by breaking plant and animal material down.
Sapwood	The newly formed lighter outer wood located just inside the vascular cambium of a tree trunk and active in the conduction of water.
Scab	Slightly raised, rough areas on fruits, tubers, leaves, or stems.
Scabrous	Leaf textures that are rough to the touch; texture of sandpaper.
Scale	A type of insect pest.
Scout/Scouting	Assessing pest pressure and plant performance. The first step in any IPM plan. Regularly checking crops for pests and damage symptoms; looking in your garden to determine if pests are a problem.
Secondary growth	Growth that increases the girth of stems or roots without elongating them. Secondary growth is seen in some dicots but not in monocots.
Secondary nutrient	A nutrient needed by plants in a moderate amount: calcium, magnesium, and sulfur. (See also Macronutrient, Primary nutrient.)
Secondary root	A type of root system that forms after the primary root emerges from a seed and branches outward.
Seed	Matured ovule that occurs as, or in, mature fruits.
Seed, certified	A seed lot inspected to meet minimum standards and to ensure trueness to type for a given cultivar.
Seed coat	The protective outer layer of a seed that provides protection for the enclosed embryo.
Seed coat impermeability	Caused by a hard seed coat that is impermeable to water, preventing the seed from germinating.
Seed dormancy	An adaptive feature of some plants to keep the seeds from germinating until conditions exist that favor seedling survival.

Seed scarification	Involves breaking, scratching, or softening the seed coat so that water can enter and begin the germination process.
Selective pesticide	A pesticide that kills only certain kinds of plants or animals; for example, 2,4-D kills broadleaf lawn weeds but leaves grass largely unharmed.
Self-fertile	A plant that produces seed with its own pollen.
Self-fruitful	A plant that bears fruit through self-pollination.
Self-pollination	Pollination that can occur when the anther and stigma are in the same flower or if the anther and stigma are in different flowers on the same plant or in different flowers on different plants of the same species, variety, or cultivar.
Self-sterile	A plant that needs pollen from another species, variety, or cultivar (e.g. cross-pollination).
Self-unfruitful	A plant that requires another variety for pollination. (See also Pollinizer.)
Separation	A term applied to a form of propagation by which plants that produce bulbs or corms multiply.
Sexual propagation	The deliberate, directed reproduction of plants using seeds or spores. (See also Asexual propagation.)
Shear	To cut back a plant (as opposed to selective pruning or deadheading). Often used to regenerate plants with many small stems, where dead-heading would be too time consuming.
Shoot	One season's branch growth. The bud scale scars (ring of small ridges) on a branch mark the start of a season's growth.
Short-day plant	A plant requiring more than 12 hours of continuous darkness to stimulate a change in growth, e.g. a shift from the vegetative to reproductive phase. (See also Long-day plant, Day-neutral plant.)
Shredding	An operation that reduces the particle size of material and increases the surface area.
Side-dress	The process of applying soil amendments or fertilizers next to an emerged vegetable crop.
Sign	The part of a pathogen seen on a host plant; the physical evidence of something that has attacked a plant.
Silt	Soil particles between 0.002 and 0.05 mm in size.
Simple metamorphosis	A type of insect development involving three stages: egg, nymph, and adult. The nymph usually resembles the adult. (See also Complete metamorphosis.)
Slow-release fertilizer	A fertilizer material that must be converted into a plant-available form by soil microorganisms.
Soft pinch	To remove only the succulent tip of a shoot, usually with the fingertips.
Soft rot	The water-soaked appearance of cells that don't get enough oxygen.

Soil	A natural, biologically active mixture of weathered rock fragments and organic matter at the earth's surface.
Soil conditioner	A soil additive that improves the soil's resistance to erosion, increases its permeability to air and water, improves its texture, its resistance to surface compaction, and improves tilth.
Soil horizons	A soil horizon is a layer generally parallel to the soil crust, whose physical characteristics differ from the layers above and beneath. Each soil type usually has three or four horizons. Horizons are defined in most cases by obvious physical features, chiefly color and texture.
Soilless mix or substrate	Components used in potting mixes that are not true soils, such as vermiculite, perlite, peat, bark, sand, gravel, sphagnum moss used in container growing mixes but no real soil.
Soil salinity	A measure of the total soluble salts in a soil.
Soil solution	The solution of water and dissolved minerals found in soil pores.
Soil structure	The combination or arrangement of primary soil particles into secondary particles, units, or peas. Compost helps bind primary soil particles to improve the structure of the soil.
Soil texture	How coarse or fine a soil is. Texture is determined by the proportions of sand, silt, and clay in the soil.
Soluble salt	A mineral (salt) often remaining in soil from irrigation water, fertilizer, compost, or manure applications.
Sonic repeller	A sonic wave-emitting unit said to disrupt the activities of small mammals or insects but not proven to be effective.
Sori	A cluster of sporangia borne on the underside of a fern frond.
Species	A group of individual plants interbreeding freely and having many (or all) characteristics in common.
Species-specific	Limited to effecting one species or a certain group of species.
Specimen	An individual plant with outstanding characteristics (leaves, flowers, or bark), generally used as a focal point in a landscape.
Spines	Are modified leaves, leaflets, petioles or stipules. Blackberries or wintergreen barberry (*Berberis juliane*) have spines.
Spore	(1) The reproductive body of a fungus or other lower plant, containing one or more cells. (2) A bacterial cell modified to survive in an adverse environment. (3) The reproductive unit of ferns.
Sport	See Mutation.
Spot treatment	To apply a pesticide to a small section or area of a crop.
Sprig	A stolon or rhizome used to establish turf.
Spur	Short, stubby stems common on fruit trees such as apples and pears. These spurs produce the flower buds.

Stability of compost	The rate of change or decomposition of compost. Generally, stability refers to the lack of change or resistance to change. A stable compost continues to decompose slowly and has a low oxygen demand. Temperatures are constant.
Starch-based biodegradable mulch	Mulch made from plastic that contains starch, which is degraded by bacteria.
Stem cutting	A section of a stem prepared for vegetative propagation; forms adventitious roots on the stem.
Sterile	(1) Material that is free of disease organisms (pathogens), as in potting medium. (2) A plant that is unable to produce viable seeds.
Stolon	An above-ground creeping stem that can produce roots and shoots at each node. This horizontal stem can be either fleshy or semi-woody.
Stoma, stomate, stomata (plural)	Any pore or opening on the surface of a leaf or stem through which gases (water vapor, carbon dioxide, and oxygen) are exchanged. This pore is an opening into a leaf that is formed by specialized epidermal cells on the underside (and sometimes upper sides) of the leaf.
Strain	A variation within a cultivar or variety.
Stratification	Chilling seed under moist conditions. This method mimics the conditions a seed might endure after it falls to the ground in the autumn and goes through a cold winter on the ground.
Stylet	A nematode's lance like or needlelike mouthpart. Used to puncture and feed from plant cells.
Subspecies	A major division of a species, more general in classification than a cultivar or variety.
Succession	The progression of a plant community to a stable mixture of plants.
Succession planting	(1) The practice of planting new crops in areas vacated by harvested crops. (2) Several smaller plantings made at timed intervals.
Succulent	Leaf textures that are fleshy, soft, and thickened in texture; modified for water storage.
Sucker	A shoot or stem that originates underground from a plant's roots or trunk, or from a root- stock below the graft union. (See also Reversion growth.)
Summer annual	Annual plant in which the seed germinates in the spring, and the plant develops, matures, and produces seed by the end of the growing season.
Summer oil	A light refined horticultural oil used during the growing season to control insect pests and diseases.
Sun scald	Winter or summer injury to the trunk or leaves of plants caused by hot sun and fluctuating temperatures. Typically, sun scalded bark splits and separates from the trunk.

Susceptibility	The condition of a plant in which it is prone to the damaging effects of a pathogen or other factor.
Sustainable gardening	Gardening practices allow plants to thrive with minimal inputs of labor, water, fertilizer, and pesticides.
Symbiotic	Mutually beneficial.
Symptom	A plant's response to an attack by animal or pathogen; a visible reaction of a plant to disease such as wilting, necrosis, abnormal coloration, defoliation, fruit drop, abnormal cellular growth, or stunting.
Synthetic fertilizer	Chemically formulated fertilizers, mainly from inorganic sources.
Synthetic pesticide	Chemically formulated pesticide, mainly from inorganic sources.
Systemic	Spreading internally throughout the plant.
Systemic pesticide	A pesticide that moves throughout a target organism's system to cause its death.
T	
Taproot	A type of root system that grows straight down with few lateral roots.
Tassel	The structure at the tip of the corn plant, which is the male flower.
Taxonomy	Classification or naming of plants or animals.
Tender	Not tolerant of frost and cold temperatures. In horticulture, tender does not mean weak or susceptible to insect pests or diseases.
Tendril	A slender projection used for clinging, usually a modified leaf. Easily seen on vines such as grapes and clematis.
Terminal	The tip (apex), usually of a branch or shoot.
Terminal bud	The bud that is found at the tip of shoots.
Texture of composting mix	Characteristic that describes the available surface area of particles. A fine or raw material texture implies many small particles with a large combined surface area. A course texture implies large particles with less overall surface area.
Thermoperiod	The change in temperature from day to night.
Thermophilic	Heat-loving microorganisms that thrive in and generate temperatures above 105°F.
Thin	(1) To remove an entire shoot or limb where it originates. (2) To selectively remove plants or fruits to allow remaining plants or fruits to develop.
Threshold	The point at which plant aesthetic quality or injury leads a gardener to decide action should be taken.

Tiller	A grass plant shoot arising in the axes of leaves in the unelongated portion of the stem. A shoot that arises from a plant's crown.
Tilth	The state of aggregation of a soil especially in relation to its suitability for crop growth, a measurement of soil workability.
Tissue culture	The process of generating new plants by placing small pieces of plant material onto a sterile medium.
Tolerant	A plant that will produce a normal yield even if faced with challenges like disease, insect pest, shade, or frost. Tolerance is generally specified.
Top-dressing	1) The practice of spreading a thin layer (¼ inch) of soil, compost, humus, or a sand and peat mix over the turf or soil. 2) For turf: a sand or prepared soil mix applied to the turf to help smooth the surface, enhance establishment, and reduce thatch buildup.
Tracheophytes	Any plant that has elaborate tissues with water- and nutrient-conducting tissue termed 'vascular tissue' including roots, stems and leaves. Some tracheophytes reproduce with seeds and some with spores.
Trailing	Cane berries that are not self-supporting and have low yields.
Transpiration	The loss of water through the leaf stomata. The transpired water comes from the photosynthetic process and also from water in the cells.
Trap Crop	A trap crop is a plant that attracts agricultural creatures, usually insects, away from nearby crops. This form of companion planting can save the main crop from decimation by pests without the use of pesticides.
Tuber	(1) A below-ground stem used for food storage (e. g. potato). (2) For turf: an underground stem modified for food storage that is attached to the root system as found in yellow nutsedge.
Tuberous root	An underground storage organ made up of root tissue. Sprouts only from the point at which it was attached to the stem of the parent plant. Dahlias are an example.
Tuberous stem	A below-ground stem consisting of a swollen hypocotyl, lower epicotyl, and upper primary root (e.g. in tuberous begonias).
Tunicate	A tunicate bulb has a paper-like covering or tunic that protects the scales from drying and from mechanical injury. Examples of tunicate bulbs include: tulips, daffodils, hyacinths, grape hyacinths (muscari), and alliums.
Turf	A covering of mowed vegetation, usually a grass.
Turgor or turgor pressure (turgid)	Cellular water pressure; responsible for keeping cells firm.

Twig	A young stem (1 year old or less) that is in the dormant winter stage (has no leaves).
U	
USDA zones	Areas derived by the USDA that indicate average-low winter temperatures. Used as a plant hardiness indicator. Other plant hardiness zones developed by other entities use different numbering systems.
V	
Vaporization	The evaporation of the active ingredient in a pesticide during or after application.
Variegated	Having patches, stripes, or marks of different colors.
Variety	A botanical subdivision within a species.
Vascular pathogen	A disease-causing organism that invades primarily the conductive tissues (xylem or phloem) of the plant.
Vascular system	The internal structure of the stem that transports water, minerals, and sugars throughout the plant.
Vascular tissue	Water, nutrient, and photosynthate-conducting tissue. (See also Xylem, Phloem).
Vector	A living organism that is able to transmit or spread a pathogen.
Vegetative propagation	The increase of plants by asexual means using vegetative parts. Normally results in a population of identical individuals. Can occur by either natural means (e.g. bulblets, cormels, offsets, plantlets, or runners) or artificial means (e.g. cuttings, division, budding, grafting, or layering).
Venation	(1) The pattern of veins in leaves. (2) In insects, the arrangement of veins in wings.
Vermicomposting	Composting with worms. Although there are over 6,000 species of worm, only seven have been found suitable for bin composting. One in particular, *Eisenia fetida* (common name: red wiggler), is the most widely used.
Vermiculite	Lightweight expanded mica often used in soil-less media.
Vermin	Noxious or objectionable animals, insects, or other pests, especially small ones such as rats, mice, and flies.
Vernation	The arrangement of new leaves within an older leaf sheath (e.g. on a grass plant).
Viability	A seed's ability to germinate.
Viable	Alive; seeds must be alive in order to germinate.
Vine crop	Crops that produce vines that grow along the ground including watermelon, muskmelon and pumpkins.

Virulent	Capable of causing severe disease.
Virus	An infectious agent composed of DNA or RNA, too small to see with a compound microscope; multiplies only in living cells.
VOCs	Volatile Organic Compounds. Organic compounds or substances vaporize at relatively low temperatures, including alcohol, methane, and ammonia. Volatile compounds are rapidly lost from the composting pile environment.
W	
Warm-season vegetables	Vegetables that grow optimally at temperatures between 80°F and 95°F.
Water-holding capacity (WHC)	The ability of a soil's micropores to hold water for plant use.
Watering-in	The initial watering after plants have been potted or repotted into new containers.
Water-soaking	Lesions that appear wet and dark and usually are sunken and or translucent. Often a symptom of bacterial disease.
Weed	A plant growing where it is not wanted.
Weed-and-feed	A combination fertilizer and herbicide sometimes used on lawns.
Weediness	Likelihood of seeds germinating into unwanted plants that must be removed.
Wetting agent	A chemical that aids in liquid-to-surface contact.
Wetwood	Another name for slime flux.
Wheel hoe	An oscillating or stationary hoe blade mounted on a wheel with handles.
Wilt	Loss of cell turgor; drooping and drying plant parts due to interference with the plant's ability to take up water and nutrients.
Wilting point	Point at which the water content within plant cells is low enough that cellular turgor is lost and the plant wilts.
Winter annual	Annual plant in which the seed germinates in the fall, producing a plant that overwinters, matures, and produces seed the following growing season.
Winter melon	An oscillating or stationary hoe blade mounted on a wheel with handles.
Winter squash	A squash whose fruit are harvested when uniform in color and rind is hard.
Witches' broom	A plant condition suspected to be caused by genetic mutation or a virus where all adventitious buds in a certain part of the plant start growing, resulting in a lot of tiny stems; abnormal brush-like development of many weak shoots.

X	
Xeric	A plant or landscape that conserves water. Most xeric plants need minimal supplemental water after an establishment period (18 to 24 months after planting) unless there is extreme drought.
Xylem	The principal water conducting tissue of vascular plants.
Y	
Yard Waste	Leaves, grass clippings, yard trimmings, and other organic garden debris.
Yield	Refers to both the measure of the yield of a crop per unit area of land cultivation, and the seed generation of the plant itself.
Z	
Zucchini	A summer squash whose fruit is harvested immature, have a green colored skin and are long cylindrical-shaped with little or no taper.

Conversion Tables

LINEAR MEASUREMENT (LENGTH & DISTANCE)			
IMPERIAL	METRIC	METRIC	IMPERIAL
1 inch	25.4 millimeters (mm)	1 millimeter (mm)	0.0384 inch
1 foot (1 foot = 12 inches)	0.3048 meter (m)	1 centimeter (1 cm = 10 mm)	0.3837 inch
1 yard (3 feet)	0.9144 meter (m)	1 meter (1 m = 100 cm)	1.0936 yards
1 mile (1760 yards)	1.6093 kilometer (km)	1 kilometer (1 km = 1000 m)	0.6214 miles
AREA MEASUREMENT			
IMPERIAL	METRIC	METRIC	IMPERIAL
1 square inch	6.4516 cm^2	1 square centimeter (cm^2)	0.155 square inches
1 square foot (144 square inches)	92.9 cm^2	1 square meter (1 m^2 = 10,000 cm^2)	1.196 square yards
1 square yard (9 square feet)	0.8361 m^2	1 hectare (1 ha = 10,000 m2)	2.47 acres

IMPERIAL	METRIC	METRIC	IMPERIAL
1 acre (4840 square yards)	0.040469 hectare	1 square kilometer (1 km² = 100 ha)	247.105 acres
1 square mile (640 acres)	259 hectares		

CUBIC MEASUREMENT (VOLUME)

IMPERIAL	METRIC	METRIC	IMPERIAL
1 cubic inch	16.4 cc or cm³	1 cubic centimeter (cc or cm³)	0.0610 cubic inches
1 cubic foot (1728 in.3)	0.0283 m³	1 cubic meter (1 million cm³)	1.308 cubic yards
1 cubic yard (27 ft.3)	0.765 m³		

CAPACITY MEASURE (VOLUME)

IMPERIAL	METRIC	METRIC	IMPERIAL
1 (imperial) fl. oz. (1/20 imperial pint)	28.41 ml	0.5 liter (5 cm³)	1.056 US pint
1 (US liquid) fl. oz. (1/16 US pint)	29.57 ml	1 liter (10 cm³)	2.11 US pints
1 (imperial) pint (20 fl. oz.)	568.26 ml		
1 (US liquid) pint (16 fl. oz.)	473.18 ml		
1 (imperial) gallon (4 quarts)	4.546 liter		
1 (US liquid) gallon (4 quarts)	3.785 liter		

MASS (WEIGHT)

IMPERIAL	METRIC	METRIC	IMPERIAL
1 ounce	28.35 gram	1 gram (1,000 mg)	15.43 grain
1 pound (10 ounces)	0.3545 kilogram	1 kilogram (1,000 g)	2.205 pounds
1 ton (2240 lbs)	1.016 tonnes	1 tonne (1,000 kg)	0.984 ton

TEMPERATURE			
FAHRENHEIT	**CELCIUS**	**CELCIUS**	**FAHRENHEIT**
32°F	0.0°C	-20°C	-4°F
40°F	4.4°C	-10°C	14°F
50°F	10.0°C	0°C	32°F
55°F	12.8°C	10°C	50°F
60°F	15.6°C	20°C	68°F
70°F	21.1°C	30°C	86°F
77°F	25.0°C	40°C	104°F
90°F	32.2°C	50°C	122°F
105°F	40.6°C	60°C	140°F
120°F	48.9°C	70°C	158°F
140°F	60.0°C	80°C	176°F
145°F	62.8°C	90°C	194°F
150°F	65.6°C	100°C	212°F
160°F	71.1°C	110°C	230°F

METRIC TO IMPERIAL CONVERSION

Convert	To	Multiply by
Kilometers	Miles	0.62
Kilometers	Feet	3280.8
Meters	Feet	3.28
Centimeters	Inches	0.39
Millimeters	Inches	0.039
Liters	Quarts	1.057
Liters	Gallons	0.264
Milliliters	Cups	0.0042
Milliliters	Ounces	0.0338
Celsius	Fahrenheit	°C x 9/5 + 32 = °F
Kilogram	Tons	0.0011
Kilogram	Pounds	2.2046
Grams	Ounces	0.035
Grams	Pounds	0.002205
Milligrams	Ounces	0.000035

IMPERIAL TO METRIC CONVERSION

Convert	To	Multiply by
Fahrenheit	Celsius	(°F - 32) x 5/9 = °C
Inches	Meters	0.0254
Inches	Centimeters	2.54
Inches	Millimeters	25.4
Feet	Meters	0.3
Yards	Meters	0.91
Yards	Kilometers	0.00091
Miles	Kilometers	1.61
Ounces	Milliliters	29.57
Cups	Milliliters	236.6
Quarts	Liters	0.95
Gallons	Liters	3.785
Ounces	Milligrams	28350
Ounces	Grams	28.35
Pounds	Kilograms	0.454
Tons	Kilograms	907.18

Helpful Weights

I advise that you keep your compost at 50% moisture throughout until used (within six months of making it).

A full cubic-yard-sized bin (the size of a standard composting bin) will produce just over 12 cubic feet of compost weighing about 150 pounds – enough to cover 150 square feet of soil an inch deep.

Compost weighs approximately 12.5 pounds per cubic foot (specific gravity 0.2).

A spread of 0.5-inches thick will cover 300 sq. ft. from a single composted pile of 3 cubic feet (cubic yard).

An application of ½ inch is adequate for annual bed maintenance.

EPILOGUE

After following the expert guidance in Your First Vegetable Garden, you have now successfully grown your own delicious and nutritious vegetables. You have learned the importance of choosing the right location, preparing the soil, and selecting the best vegetables for your climate. You have also gained valuable knowledge on how to combat common pests and diseases, ensuring the health and longevity of your garden.

As you continue to nurture and tend to your garden, you will be rewarded with an abundance of fresh produce. The satisfaction and pride that comes with harvesting your own vegetables is unparalleled. You have discovered the joys of gardening and the benefits of growing your own food.

Thank you for choosing Your First Vegetable Garden as your guide on this gardening journey. We hope that you continue to cultivate your green thumb and that your garden brings you endless enjoyment and nourishment.

If you're looking for more gardening information, we recommend Simplify Gardening (simplifygardening.com and youtube.com/simplifygardening). They offer a range of gardening tips and advice for all levels. Check them out to continue learning and improving your gardening skills.

www.ingramcontent.com/pod-product-compliance
Lightning Source LLC
Chambersburg PA
CBHW081614100526
44590CB00021B/3430